AF342061

INTEGRATED COMPUTER NETWORK SYSTEMS

COMPUTER-AIDED ENGINEERING

Series Editor

Mark E. Coticchia
Carnegie Mellon University
Pittsburgh, Pennsylvania

1. Integrated Computer Network Systems, *Frank Welch*

ADDITIONAL VOLUMES IN PREPARATION

CAD/CAM/CAE Systems: Second Edition, Revised and Expanded, *Mark E. Coticchia, Edward J. Preston, and George W. Crawford*

Developing CAD/CAM Systems, *Jack E. Zecher*

INTEGRATED COMPUTER NETWORK SYSTEMS

FRANK WELCH

INTEL Corporation
Phoenix, Arizona

Marcel Dekker, Inc.   **New York • Basel • Hong Kong**

Library of Congress Cataloging-in-Publication Data

Welch, Frank
    Integrated computer network systems / Frank Welch.
        p.   cm. -- (Computer-aided engineering ; 1)
    Includes bibliographical references and index.
    ISBN 0-8247-8742-0
    1. Computer networks.   I. Title. II. Series: Computer-aided
engineering (New York, N.Y.) ; 1.
    TK5105.5.W45 1992
    004.6--dc20   92-11339
                                                        CIP

IBM is a registered trademark and Systems Network Architecture (SNA)
and NETBIOS are trademarks of International Business Machines
Corporation.

ASCII is a designation of the American Standard Code for Information
Interchange.

IEEE is a designation of the Institute of Electrical and Electronics
Engineers.

This book is printed on acid-free paper.

MARCEL DEKKER, INC.
270 Madison Avenue, New York, New York 10016

Current printing (last digit):
10 9 8 7 6 5 4 3 2 1

PRINTED IN THE UNITED STATES OF AMERICA

This book is for computer-literate readers who desire to become computer-*network* literate. When I decided to write a book about computer networks, I discovered that two categories of network documentation exist: protocol specifications and detailed technical literature. Standards organizations and vendors produce the former, highly-skilled technologists produce the latter. The problem is, if you are a computer technician that wants to understand networks, where do you begin? I am familiar with this problem, because I had to struggle through the process of converting my computer knowledge into computer *network* knowledge.

Integrated Computer Network Systems is a technical overview of the terms and concepts of computer network implementations. As computer networks become more and more important in our daily business lives, network expertise attracts the interest of the computer-competent society. For most people, comprehending protocol specifications is a formidable, tedious task. Protocol experts produce various technical literature that assumes the reader has network experience, and again, this material challenges computer engineers and managers.

Computer specialists have various levels of interest in networks. Some want to become experts in protocols, others desire only to become knowledgeable enough to talk to and work with protocol experts. This book satisfies the second criterion and is an excellent place to start. If your goal is protocol expertise, you are ready for protocol specifications and detailed technical literature after you complete this book.

Although I have written articles for the computer network magazines, this is my first book. I do not think I could have completed it without the technical support of my editor and partner, Judy Lee Aguiar. Judy writes for a living and evidence of her writing quality appears throughout the text.

Judy is a consulting technical writer and editor. Judy studied English as an undergraduate and graduate at Arizona State University and plans to continue her studies to obtain a Ph.D. in English. She has been working as a writer and editor for approximately 15 years and has written major publications for such firms as Intel Corporation, Honeywell, and National Semiconductor. Being fluent in German, Judy also provides technical translation services (English-

German) for the computer and semiconductor industry. Judy is currently completing a punctuation and grammar style guide for mass publication and also is working on a fictional novel. Aside from her talents in writing, Judy also is becoming a specialist in hypertext and multimedia integration with text. During the past two years, Judy has been working as a consultant for Intel Corporation. At Intel Corporation, Judy has been writing documentation, developing training courses and materials, and implementing on-line hypertext for the network products being developed in the Network Instrumentation and Services Group in Phoenix, Arizona.

Thanks also to Chris Thomas and numerous other network experts who reviewed and commented on this work. I would like to thank especially Colleen, Fred, and Meghan for giving up so many weekends that we could have spent at the lake, for your encouragement, and for keeping the house quiet.

Frank Welch

Contents

DATA COMMUNICATIONS

NETWORK FAMILIES

UPPER-LAYER COMPONENTS

MIDDLE-LAYER COMPONENTS

LOWER-LAYER COMPONENTS

CONNECTING DEVICES

NETWORK MANAGEMENT

NETWORK SUPPORT GROUPS

ENTERPRISE NETWORK MIGRATION

FIGURES

FIGURES (Continued)

TABLES

INTEGRATED COMPUTER NETWORK SYSTEMS

Chapter 1

Introduction

1.1   Enterprise Networks

Computing devices affect virtually everyone in an enterprise such as a large business, corporation, or government agency. If you are a member of such an enterprise, you have learned to take every advantage possible using computers in your everyday activities and you know that only when these devices communicate, can you realize their maximum potential. Networks allow computing devices to communicate with each other, which enables distributed processes. Distributed processes provide valuable continuity to otherwise disparate computing activities throughout any enterprise.

In the past, you probably thought of your enterprise computer power as a group of isolated machines, often primarily mainframes with limited connectivity to smaller computers. The mainframes performed most of the large business applications, while desktop computers served private, special applications for individuals. Now you view your enterprise computer resources as mainframes, mini-computers, and desktop computers, all interconnected and interworking with each other via networks. This trend is reflected in the success of desktop computer lines and a relative slowing of mainframe sales.

All networks are not the same: some are effective, others are not. Several factors affect the success of your enterprise network:

- **Applications**—You use your network only if you perceive value in using it. Useful network applications drive you to learn how to access the network.

- **Reliability**—You do not use a network that is always under repair. You do not allow yourself to become dependant on a tool that is available only on occasion.

- **Widespread Connectivity**—After you learn to depend on the enterprise network, you tend to expect to use it with any system on your network. Otherwise, you must maintain two ways of doing business; use the network in some cases and use the old-fashioned way in other cases.

- **Performance**—You want adequate response times and reasonable delays during data exchange. Otherwise, you do not learn the network and you just carry a tape or floppy between computers.

- **Cost Effectiveness**—This is not a so much a concern of the users as it is to management. Costs associated with the enterprise network must be manageable.

1.2   What is a Computer Network?

Networks come in a variety of sizes and provide a choice of functions. Some networks are very simple and limited in functionality. The most basic networks require minimal maintenance. Others are so complex that they require a multitude of professionals for support and maintenance. All networks have something in common: they allow data to move from one computing device to one or more computing devices. In the workplace, you can find several kinds of computing devices:

- Personal Computers
- Intelligent Workstations
- Dumb Terminals
- Host Computers
- File and other kinds of servers

The following example network supports three computing devices.

Example: A simple Local Area Network (LAN) can allow a production manager to send messages from his/her workstation to the workstations of two subordinate supervisors.

In network terminology, you say that this network supports three *nodes*. A *node* is a computing device that can access a network. Let us assume that all three workstations are personal computers, and furthermore, that all three personal computers are of the same make and model. Such a network usually is simple to design, install, and maintain. You can build such a network from off-the-shelf technology (i.e., you can go to your local personal computer retailer and purchase a turnkey network).

A *turnkey* network means that you must not add value to the product before it is useful. Adding value means enhancing a product. It is easier and often more cost-effective to buy a turnkey solution than to add value to an incomplete product. The easiest networks to build are those that connect a small number of nodes of the same make and model.

Example: If one of the three personal computers in a network is an Apple™ computer and the other two are IBM™ computers, you must find a way to bridge the gap between the differences in the way the two brands of computers operate. This process can involve writing software, which usually is expensive and time-consuming.

A network can be complex for many reasons. If a network connects computers of different makes or models, this can cause complications. If a network connects computers of the same make and model, but the network is very large then this too can be complex. A large network may mean that the network supports many nodes or it may mean that there is a large distance between the nodes. The most complex network is one that connects many dissimilar computers over a large distance.

1.3　Network Functionality

Functionality is another aspect of a network. It is not sufficient to connect a cable between two computers and call it a network. A network must allow programs to exchange information.

1.3.1　File Transfer and Real-Time Messaging

Two common functions are file transfer and real-time electronic messaging. One distinction between the two is performance:

- **File transfer**—Usually means that the time lapse between transmission and reception of the data is not critical.

- **Real-time messaging**—Implies that the data must arrive at its destination in a predictable amount of time. This usually means that the data must arrive quickly. Real-time applications must have a deterministic communication network. Your programmers must be able to say "worst case, this message takes x amount of time to arrive."

Example: Factory applications often have real-time messaging applications. If a robot rotates a part, while another robot paints the part, the two robots must move in harmony. Coordinating the painting robot and the rotating robot is possible only if the people writing the software for the robots determine the maximum time required for the message to transfer.

File transfer usually is not as time-critical as real-time messaging. The time required to transfer a file (e.g., a memo or report) is not critical to the success of the overall system. The three-node example mentioned previously could be a file transfer system. The manager uses the network to relay information to the subordinate supervisors. If the message transfer takes two minutes instead of one, they have not sacrificed factory productivity. File transfer also means that the receiving computer can store the message on a disk or other media. Real-time messages are messages that the system processes quickly then discards rather than saving them on the system.

1.3.2 EMAIL

EMAIL is an embellished file transfer feature. EMAIL makes it easy and convenient for a person to send a letter-type message to another person. EMAIL provides automatic message formatting, which means that EMAIL automatically creates your layout for you. With basic file transfer, you first must build a template for the letter. You must type the headers for the field parameters (i.e., DATE, TIME, TO/FROM, SUBJECT, CC:). EMAIL simplifies all these tasks and much more.

1.3.3   Virtual Terminal

Virtual terminal allows your workstation to access a host computer that normally requires a specific terminal type. Ordinarily, you may require several terminals in your offices. IBM systems require a 3270 terminal. DEC hosts require a VT100 or VT200 terminal. It formerly was acceptable for a computer company to sell systems that require special equipment, because most users did not need to access on a regular basis more that one host computer. Today, you must have direct access on a regular basis to several computers. Virtual terminal translates terminal functions into the format that the host computer understands.

1.3.4 Network Management

You use network management equipment to monitor your network. You monitor a network so that you can take action before the system becomes inoperative. The primary uses for network management are:

- Problem Detection/Resolution
- Performance Analysis/Improvement
- Configuration Assistance
- Accounting/Usage Management for Billing Purposes
- Security Safeguards

Network management equipment can tell you that performance is lagging and can help you determine the reason for performance reduction by displaying communication activity of various nodes.

1.3.5 Directory Services

Another function that networks provide is directory services. Nodes use directory services the same way people use a telephone or address book. In the network, the number is the network address of another node with which a computer wants to communicate. All nodes in a network have a unique network address with which they are associated. A network address is analogous to a phone number. Every telephone number in a community is unique, otherwise the telephone system would not be able to connect you to the desired party with which you wish to speak.

1.4 Wide and Local Area Networks

Enterprise networks can be a Wide Area Network (WAN), a Local Area Network (LAN), or a combination of both. The difference between a LAN and a WAN is the distance between nodes and the form of technology used to deliver messages. In a sense, LANs and WANs are the same: they both deliver messages between computing devices. WANs commonly are networks built and maintained by public or private carriers, such as telephone companies, computer manufacturers, and governments. The user enterprises builds and maintains LANs.

Some WANs allows computers to communicate over telephone lines. In a WAN, communicating nodes can reside in separate buildings, perhaps even in different countries. The network is a LAN if the distance between nodes is small. A LAN usually fits within a single building. However, the distinction between LANs/WANs is becoming less important. Today, some LANs span cities, even countries.

1.5   Designing a Network

You must weigh several variables when designing a network. You want to achieve the proper functionality at the lowest cost. You want the network to perform satisfactorily, to be reliable, and you want to be able to expand your network when your network requirements grow (and they do grow).

1.5.1   Functionality Requirements

You must talk to your applications' personnel to determine what functionality your network requires. The applications' people are the network users. The network users are the reason for building a network. Listen carefully to your users—it is important to understand thoroughly their needs.

1.5.1.1 File Transfer Requirements

File transfer is an important network function. You use file transfer to relay the information that the computer stores. Such information can be product documentation, spreadsheets, memos, or graphics. You must understand, in detail, the users' requirements. It is not sufficient to know that they require file transfer. You must analyze their applications. Ask yourself if your users must send and receive files simultaneously.

Some network products allow you to do only one task at a time. Such products may force you to finish completely one file transfer before initiating a different file transfer. If your application involves transfers of both very large and very small files, this limitation may not be acceptable.

Example: Consider the example of the process management computer. This computer is responsible for sending product-build information to the manufacturing department. The process management computer also reports build activities status to a logging computer. Perhaps you connect the logging computer to a printer so that you can retrieve hard-copy prints of the work area progress on a regular basis.

It probably is unacceptable to limit the process computer to serial file transfer mode (one at a time). If the process management computer transfers a large log file to the logging computer and shortly afterwards the manufacturing department requests product-build information, manufacturing must wait until the system sends the entire log file before the process management computer can respond.

Large files take longer to transmit than small files. This can result in temporary delays in subsequent file transfers. If these delays are not acceptable then you must build a network that allows your process management computer to transfer files in parallel file transfer mode (at the same time). Build your network around products that offer the appropriate functionality for your users.

1.5.1.2 Video, Voice, and Data Transmission

Other functional requirements in the enterprise include video and voice transmission in addition to data transmission. Video and voice transmission are functions that people use, rather than machines. You can use networks for human communication, as well as communication between machines.

The concept of using video transmission has interesting potential. Instead of using a telephone or a written instruction manual to communicate information, you can send video signals directly to a recipient. These videos may contain demonstrations of how to locate a particular part of a machine under repair, display the location of a particular shelf in a stockroom, or perhaps display an engineering drawing from the library. Imaginative planners find numerous possibilities and applications.

Most companies require voice transmission to send urgent information. You normally use telephone systems to transmit voice, but voice also can be transmitted over certain networks. Broadband networks can simultaneously carry data, video, and voice. This is important, because you can install a single broadband cable network instead of three separate networks.

1.5.2 Product Architecture Impact

The industry bases some products on the concept of client and server, other products interact on a peer-to-peer basis. Some applications lend themselves towards the client/server products, while others perform better with peer-to-peer architectures.

1.5.2.1 Client-Server Model

In the client/server model, you must configure each node as either a client or a server. A client node can communicate directly to a server node, but a client node cannot communicate directly to another client node. Client/server models are hierarchical. At the top of the hierarchy is a server. The clients are at the bottom of the hierarchy (Figure 1-1). To illustrate the client/server model consider an example file server.

> **Example:** Each engineer in the department uses a personal computer for day-to-day tasks. A single computer, called a server, stores the work of each engineer and contains a master copy of commonly used software packages such as word processors. The engineers backup their work to the server on a regular basis and retrieve utility software from the server as needed. This is an ideal client/server application, because each engineer has convenient access to the other engineers' work. Each engineer uses the same version of utility software, which simplifies support.

In the previous example, the client/server model of file transfer provides the necessary functionality that the users require. However, the client/server model does not fit in every application. Client/server-based products do not allow all nodes to talk directly to each other. Real-time applications and number-crunching applications suffer a time lapse, because every data transfer is a two-step operation.

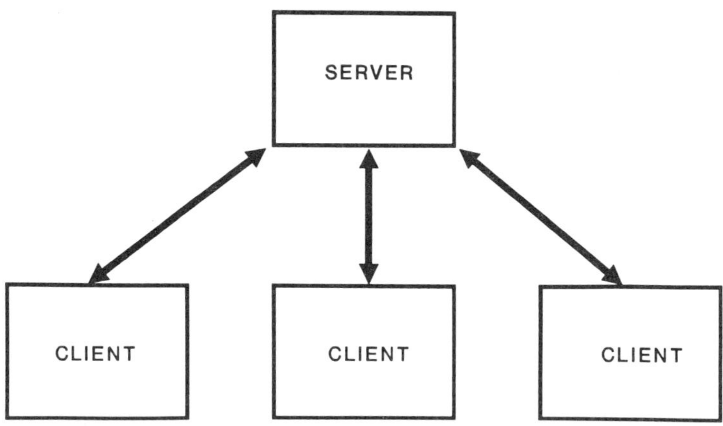

Figure 1-1: Client/Server Model

You must decide if your process can accept this type of delay. If not, you must select some other architecture for this network (i.e., a peer-to-peer architecture). Client/server architectures are useful particularly when many clients must access the same information.

Example: If you use your network for video transmission of machine repair instruction, you may want to use the client/server concept. All clients (video view stations) in the factory receive identical images for any one task. You can periodically update the tapes on the server and all clients immediately have access to the new material. This means that the network requires less maintenance.

Another place where client/server models flourish is security-sensitive applications, such as file server applications. If you force all clients to access the central server for sensitive information, you can more easily control which clients can access particular files. It is easier to monitor and configure a single server than to monitor and configure dozens of individually communicating nodes.

1.5.2.2 Peer-to-Peer Model

Products that communicate on an equal basis are based on the peer-to-peer model. This means that any node can directly communicate with another node without having to use a server (Figure 1-2). These products perform real-time applications better than client/server products. When you discuss an interaction between two peers, you use the terms *local* and *remote* to differentiate between the two.

> **Example:** One node must send information to the other node. To describe this action, you first must establish a perspective for this event. You can describe the action from the sender's or the receiver's perspective. If you decide to choose the sender, the local node sends data to the remote node. It also is valid to describe the event from the receiver's perspective, which means that the local node receives data from the remote node.

Throughout this book, the terms *local* and *remote* describe events. You must consider the perspective of the nodes to understand completely these events.

Figure 1-2: Peer-to-Peer Model

1.5.2.3 Network Functionality

You can sum-up functionality for your enterprise network as follows: Learn what applications your network users require. Ensure that your users have defined, in-detail, the applications that they use, so that you feel confident that you can select the appropriate network products that satisfy their needs.

People constantly formulate new methods to use computing devices and the networks that connect them. With imagination, you as a network designer can contribute significantly to the productivity of your organization; if you take time to understand the needs of your users before you build the network.

1.6　Network Building Costs

Different networks require different kinds of investment. Your organization must invest money, labor, and computing resources to produce and maintain a network.

1.6.1　Raw Materials

First, consider the raw materials of a network. You must have a medium for the network. You must have network hardware at each node in the network. You also must have network software for each node.

1.6.1.1 Media

Media are the physical connections between nodes. Many different kinds of media are used in enterprise networks, including:

- Coaxial Cable
- Twisted-Pair (similar to telephone wire)
- Fiber Optic

Coaxial and other forms of shielded, thick wire gained popularity during the early years of enterprise networks. These were the earliest network cable media to be standardized and widely manufactured. As a result, this wire dominates many enterprise networks today. This media is well-suited to the factory floor, because of its resistance to electrical noise, which is common in these environments.

Twisted-pair presented a more challenging technological problem and became standardized after coaxial and other heavy cables. Twisted-pair technology had to be made noise-resistant before it could be widely implemented. This cost-effective media is challenging the earlier thick cables and will ultimately replace it, except in some situations such as the factory floor.

Fiber optic, the most expensive of the medias, is commonly used for high-speed backbones. Backbones serve as major arteries between different network segments. As technology improves and prices drop, fiber will be used more often in other situations.

If you do not have a medium in place at your location, you must incur the initial expense of installing one. This can account for the greatest initial expenditure for your network.

Installing a medium is more than just stringing cable through the building. You first must test and inspect the medium before you spend the money and labor to install it. It would be irritating to install a cable network, only to find that you have continuity gaps. Such breaks in the medium mean removing sections of the first network and installing new sections.

1.6.1.2 Network Hardware

The other primary hardware investment you must make is network hardware for the nodes. Network hardware comes in many forms. For personal computers, network hardware usually is a card that slides into the chassis. Mainframe computers often have complete network interface units connected to an Input/Output (I/O) channel. The computer vendor often builds the network hardware into a product.

Network hardware is a connection between the medium and the computing device's internal environment. The network hardware cost varies. Bigger computing devices usually require more expensive network hardware than smaller computing device. A channel-connected I/O device costs more to build than a network card for a personal computer.

Performance is another factor affecting network hardware cost. High-performance equipment can cost more than the slower equipment. Network hardware usually is built around a microprocessor(s). The high-capacity microprocessor chips cost the vendor more money, as does the support circuitry that must accompany the microprocessor.

The datalink technology, the way that the network is accessed, affects hardware costs. The more mature datalink methods such as 802.3 or Ethernet, cost less than the newer datalink technologies such as 802.5 or token ring.

Network hardware often serves as a protocol engine. A protocol engine is present on every node in a network. Protocol is a set of rules that govern communication between nodes in a network. This set of rules is implemented in software and is called a *stack*. The stack software runs in the network hardware, in the node itself, or in a combination of the two.

The more sophisticated the protocol, the more processing power the system requires to implement the protocol. Network engines that run sophisticated protocols cost more, because they need more memory (i.e., Random Access Memory) and they require more microprocessor power.

Once again, you must understand the requirements of the application. If the application requires high performance, you must select the more powerful network products even though they cost more. Network hardware and network software usually are not sold together as a single product.

You ordinarily buy a card from one company and buy network software from another company. The trend is for software companies to create software that runs on several network software platforms. You usually have the ability to choose hardware from one vendor and software from another that work together.

1.6.1.3 Connecting Devices

The initial cost of raw materials is not the only investment you make. Large enterprise networks require connecting devices (e.g., bridges, routers, or gateways). Connecting devices serve two purposes.

First, the network often requires connecting devices to stretch your network beyond the normal manufacturer-recommended lengths. Every media/datalink technology has a maximum recommended length.

If you extend your network beyond the recommended length without connecting devices, you may lose communication reliability. Your network may send garbage between your nodes. Your network still functions, but the logic within the stack must retransmit packets that are corrupt as a result of the media-length violation you have committed. This retransmission activity places more overhead on your network, sometimes causing unacceptable data transmission delays.

If you extend your media too far, the datalink of your network can break altogether. Rather than exceed the network limits, you can use bridges that act as repeaters. These repeaters extend the network length without causing the problems with which you alternatively must contend.

Isolation is another reason you use connecting devices. You want to isolate faults to a single segment so that other segments do not fail. You want to reduce unnecessary traffic to segments that do not need it. Security isolation is often implemented in connecting devices.

Sophisticated connecting devices called gateways perform conversion. These devices perform conversion between networks that not only have dissimilar datalinks, but also have dissimilar network protocols.

You do not want to design networks with purposely different protocols into your enterprise, but this is almost always unavoidable. When you are confronted with this situation, you must build or purchase gateways or suffer lack of connectivity between dissimilar devices.

1.6.2 Labor

You must invest money for raw materials for your network. You must also invest labor. The first category of labor expenditure is planning. You must take the time to analyze the requirements of your applications' personnel and this analysis has cost associated with it.

You must consider the physical environment for the network. You must consider what media/datalink technology is appropriate. You must select network hardware and software. Labor investment does not end with network installation; a network requires maintenance. Cables break or eventually deteriorate. Network hardware occasionally fails. Users have questions about how to use the network, so you must supply a resource to educate your users. Also, networks tend to grow as time continues. Networks tend to grow beyond the wildest expectations of most planners, because they are useful tools for which you will always find new uses.

Do your best to consider expandability when designing your network. Some network families or product lines provide more room for growth than others. Whenever possible, select products that solve your immediate needs, but also provide ample room for growth.

Networks also consume some of your existing processing power. Some of the network software you use runs in the host computer as opposed to specific network hardware. The host computer is the programmable controller: a user workstation such as a personal computer or a mainframe that acts as a file server. You are trading your computer cycles for the capability to access remote computers.

This network software uses system memory and processor cycles. The amount of system memory and processor cycles varies greatly depending on the network family, network protocol, specialty functions supported, and many other variables.

Some network vendors are more creative than others. The more creative vendors build products that are more efficient and consume less of your system resources. Ultimately, it pays to plan, research, and compare products.

1.7   In Summary

Networks allow you to realize the potential of computing devices in your enterprise. They move data, voice, and video and include computers and other equipment. All networks are not the same: just as every application is different from the next. Unfortunately there is no pre-defined answer as to which network is best-suited for your enterprise needs—you must weigh all of the variables (i.e., functionality, performance, reliability, and cost) and choose the proper balance. You must understand the applications that may use your network. Some of the users may be machines, other users may be people. You must ensure that your network meets your requirements.

After you understand the required functionality, you must select media, network hardware, network software, and possibly other raw materials to build your network. You must invest time to plan a network and you must continue to invest labor supporting the network and its users. Planning a network is multifarious—you cannot satisfy everyone, but by weighing the variables, making allowances, and being creative, you can develop a well-balanced network that meets all your requirements.

2.1 Overview

When planning an enterprise network, you must understand certain business strategies and industry trends. This knowledge, along with your technical knowledge, helps you implement a productive and efficient enterprise network.

The strategies and trends have an impact on the functionality and cost of your enterprise network. A sound strategy can extend the life of your network. Comprehending the direction of industry trends can reduce the cost of building and maintaining your network.

When you understand these strategies and trends, you realize why vendors conduct business the way they do and you increase your prospects of successfully representing your network proposals to your management. This knowledge helps you produce a practical networking strategy that synchronizes with the industry.

2.2 Enterprise Networking Strategies

Networks within an organization were formerly the sole responsibility of individual departments. Each department manager funded and owned their respective network.

Example: The Marketing Department defined their own networking needs and built a network without regard for what the Engineering Department had planned. The Engineering Department built their network without regard for what the Production Department was doing.

The industry no longer tolerates this approach within today's enterprises. Instead, the industry demands that all departments communicate with each other or with a central network coordination team to realize fully the networking strategies and needs of the whole enterprise before building the network.

Many organizations, such as corporations and government agencies, establish upper-management task forces responsible for enterprise networking strategies. It is not uncommon to find networking chiefs with vice-president titles. Department managers often cannot build networks without upper-management task force approval.

Emphasis on enterprise networking has accelerated, because of the requirement for inter-departmental networking. Networks are a significant strategic weapon for major corporations. Information is a business commodity: companies that have exhaustive information and can access that information faster than their competition, have the highest probability of success.

It is possible to purchase software that allows your company to control information related to all operations of your enterprise instead of just one department. Your executives can access computer data that simultaneously considers all departments. This clearly is more efficient and practical than cross-referencing several computer systems' outputs for the same information.

You also must consider the value of information consistency. How much is it worth to your organization to ensure that all departments have the same information? To use this sophisticated management software, you must link the computers from each department via a data network.

Today, upper-level management must have a thorough understanding of the enterprise networking importance. Many upper-level managers involve themselves with the network installations. These managers become understandably distressed when they learn that they cannot apply the newest business applications to their organization, because the implementor installed a network that they cannot integrate easily with the other departments' networks. Upper-level managers bear the blame when their department networks must be rebuilt to synchronize with other networks in the organization.

Before you begin planning your network, take the time to understand your organization's enterprise networking strategy. Your goal is to allow nodes on your network to interwork with nodes on the enterprise network. The term *interwork* means more than connectivity; just because you physically connect two nodes with a wire, does not mean that those nodes can share data or interwork.

2.2.1   Backbone Network Interoperability

When selecting a set of technologies for your network, you must understand several interoperability issues. You may recognize that your network initially must connect to the enterprise-wide network. If not immediately, chances are that you will require enterprise connectivity at some future date.

You may think that your application is so specialized that you cannot conceive of connecting your network to the enterprise network. Occasionally this is true, but advances in communications and business software are unpredictable. New applications can arise in the future that suddenly make connecting your network to the enterprise network desirable and/or necessary. Can you afford the risk?

There are several factors that affect interoperability. The most visible aspect is media.   Other factors are network protocol, service compatibility, and administrative issues (e.g., network management and directory services).

2.2.2   Backbone Network Medias

First consider the enterprise network media. Enterprise networks have one or more main communication avenues called *backbones*. A backbone is a heavily used, distributed system of cables or other media that spans the distance of a building or group of buildings.

A backbone also implies certain software configurations (e.g., protocols). Backbones can be LANs, WANs, or the enterprise wide network can be a combination of LAN and WAN technology. Network backbones sometimes use WAN technology to interconnect to other distant LAN backbones.

Example: Suppose your company has a production facility in Denver and an engineering facility in Los Angeles. Each of the facilities has a fiber optic backbone. The two facilities can connect their backbones to each other using a WAN.

Backbone media systems are designed for high throughput and reliability. The network requires high throughput, because the backbone usually connects several departmental networks to each other. This means that ample data travels over the backbone. Common backbone applications include electronic mail and file transfer. Real-time applications are not well-suited for backbones, because backbone traffic tends to be heavy and undeterministic. Recall that real-time networks require fast, deterministic response.

Backbones must be reliable, because you cannot afford to have your enterprise network inoperative for long periods. After a backbone is in place, people tend to build highly strategical and useful business applications that operate over the backbone. Backbones are major communication arteries for your organization. You must select the most reliable technologies for your backbone medias.

2.2.2.1 Fiber Optic Backbones

Fiber optic backbones satisfy the requirements of high throughput and reliability. Fiber technology allows the highest data transfer rates of any modern media. Fiber optic cable has the theoretical capacity to transfer information at many times the rate of wire cable. The industry has not reached the performance limits of fiber optic technology. You can expect even higher transfer rates in the future.

Fiber optic backbones are reliable and immune to electrical noise. Electrical noise can disturb signals traveling over wire cable. Because light, not electrons, travels over fiber optic cable, the noise produced by electricity has no effect on fiber optic backbones.

2.2.2.2 Wire Cable Backbones

Backbones also can be wire cable. Broadband commonly is used for backbones. Broadband is more resistant to electrical noise than some other wire cables, but less resistant to noise than fiber optics.

Broadband technology has greater performance potential than many other medias, but does not have the performance potential of fiber optics. Accordingly, broadband backbones are less expensive than fiber optics.

Another wire cable that the industry uses for backbone networks is called *carrierband*. A close relative to broadband, carrierband is common to office environments, while broadband is common in automated factories. However, carrierband does have its place in the automated factory, particularity in networks with few nodes. Carrierband is less costly than broadband, but does not offer as much performance potential as broadband.

2.2.2.3 Bridges and Routers

You most likely do not want to connect your departmental network directly to the backbone—you want to use a bridge or router. The industry favors bridges and routers over direct connection, because the departmental networks are partially isolated from the backbone. You can configure bridges to transfer only the appropriate messages between your network and the backbone. This function is called *filtering*. Routers provide a more sophisticated method of isolation called *logical segmentation.*

These isolation techniques divide the enterprise into subnetworks. Each subnetwork allows direct communication between locally connected nodes. A node requires a bridge or router to communicate with a node located on a remote subnetwork. Often a departmental network equates to a subnetwork, but departmental networks can span several subnetworks.

A bridge or router filters out the correct messages and allows them to move between a network and the backbone. The correct messages are those whose origin is on one departmental subnetwork and whose destination is on a different subnetwork, where both subnetworks are connected to the backbone. Messages whose source and destination are both on the same subnetwork network do not travel through the bridge or router. This way, the subnetwork does not burden the backbone with carrying every message from every subnetwork. This strategy allows a backbone to connect a dozen or more subnetworks to each other. Without bridges or routers this may not be possible, because the total sum traffic of the networks may exceed the capacity of the backbone.

2.2.2.4 Backbone Considerations

You must consider the backbone media when planning your enterprise network. You may need to connect your departmental network to the backbone, probably through a bridge or router. Educate yourself about available products that you can use. If your backbone is fiber optic and broadband cable looks attractive for your department network, you must determine if there is a fiber-to-broadband bridge or router available at a reasonable price.

It is easier to bridge similar networks than to bridge dissimilar networks. A broadband-to-broadband bridge is easier to design than a broadband-to-fiber bridge and may cost less. If your enterprise backbone is broadband and you have the choice of fiber optic or broadband for your network, broadband may be favored, because the bridging problem is simplified and your network will be more consistent with the enterprise.

You must weigh the options: in this case, fiber optics may provide better performance, but broadband costs less and offers a smoother path to backbone connectivity.

2.2.3   Backbone Protocols and Services

A network is much more than the media. Networks depend on software to provide a protocol for data communication. Software also provides services to your network users. It is important to understand the protocol and services that the backbone provides, if you want to allow the possibility of connecting your network to the backbone.

Example: Consider a basic network that connects your Personal Computer (PC) to another PC. You installed a Network Interface Card (NIC) and Open Systems Interconnect (OSI) software in both PCs. A wire cable physically connects the two machines.

In this example, OSI is the network protocol. The protocol is the set of rules for data communication (i.e., packet size, transmission synchronization, and retransmission procedures).

The protocol defines the structure for the dialogue that occurs between the two nodes on this simple network. The communication rules are designed to provide your PC the basic capability to transfer data to another computer that supports the same protocol.

For two nodes to communicate directly, they must both have network software that implements the same network protocol. This does not mean that both computers must have the same software package from the same software company. Many companies offer OSI software for PCs.

Example: You may have OSI software from one vendor on your PC and the other computer may have OSI software written by another company. Your two computers may not be able to interwork. Just because both companies offer OSI software, does not mean that both companies have developed compatible packages.

Problems can arise if one company differently implements the standards that define the OSI software. In this case, the two computers cannot communicate, even though both software vendors claim to use OSI protocol. If you report this interoperability problem to the software vendors who sold you the two packages, chances are these vendors will help you determine which package is in error. The company whose product does not conform to the standards, has the responsibility to modify their product.

2.2.3.1 Protocol Software

You most likely have fewer interoperability problems if all nodes on your network use protocol software from the same vendor. Complete success is not guaranteed by using the same company's product. The vendor may have old versions of network software that do not interwork with the newer versions.

In this case, you must update all nodes that contain old versions by installing the newer versions of protocol software. Your risk is less by using software from the same company. Sometimes situations force you to use software from two or more companies.

Example: If you have different brands of computers in your network (PCs and mini-computers) you may need to buy network software from two different software companies. You may need to buy network software for the PCs from a company that writes PC software and network software for the mini-computers from a company that specializes in mini-computer software.

Your chances of success when using several vendors' protocol software are good if the standard the protocol is based on is mature. Most network packages from major software vendors have gone through interoperability tests in the lab before they are offered to the public. Vendors usually test their new network products with network products produced from other software vendors before releasing the final product.

2.2.3.2 Protocol Services

After you establish protocol compatibility, the next interoperability question that arises relates to protocol services. The services portion of the network software package is directly exposed to the user of the network. The user of the network is a person or a program.

End users generally are not concerned with the rules for sending data between machines, they are concerned with the interface to the network. As a user, you are concerned with the specific capabilities the network provides. Does the network allow you to send files from your personal computer to the other computer?

Perhaps, the network allows you to write a real-time application on your computer that sends messages to an application written on the other computer. In any case, both communicating computers must provide compatible services to their users if the network is to provide a useable function.

If your computer software converts data into file format and the other computer on the network does not, you may not have compatible services. If you expect to transfer files between these two nodes, both nodes must support this service. Part of the interoperability issue relates to the services provided by the nodes on the network, as well as the protocol used by the network hardware.

It is possible for you to have incompatibility even though all of your nodes support the same protocol. One reason for the incompatibility may be that one network vendor put extensions into their product. Extensions are extra protocol or services that a vendor invents and are outside of the standard service/protocol definition.

Vendors put extensions into a product to make the product more useful. Sometimes software vendors implement proprietary, non-standard extensions into their product. This works fine provided you use the same software package on all nodes that must interwork. However, a problem arises when you want to make one of these products interwork with a node that has some other vendor's software package. Unless these proprietary extensions exist on two connected nodes, the two nodes do not interwork. They have connectivity, in terms of media, but they cannot exchange information because one node supports extensions and the other node does not understand the additional services and/or protocol.

Some software packages offer you two options: you can use the proprietary extensions or you can decline the use of the extensions. This is called a *switch*. You can turn ON or OFF a switch through software. If you turn ON the switch, the extensions are active. In this case, the other nodes that do not have logic to support the extensions would not interwork with your node.

If you turn OFF the switch, the extensions are inactive. If the extensions are inactive, the product must interwork with other products based on the same protocol and services. Such a product could take advantage of the extensions when communicating to peers that understand them and could still talk to other nodes that do not, but without the benefit of the extensions.

2.2.3.3 Network Management and Directory Services

Other less visible factors to consider are network management and directory services. These functions do not directly affect interoperability, but are important to administration and maintenance of a network.

Your enterprise backbone has one or more network management facilities. Network management facilities allow people to monitor network traffic. This important capability allows network maintenance people to make decisions about network expansion. Network management facilities also provide fault detection. A network fault can mean that communication has ceased or that performance has degraded.

Some network management facilities are simple and others are sophisticated. The sophisticated packages can inform an operator which particular node is failing, others just provide implications as to the nature of the failure. When a network fails or performs poorly, it is important to solve immediately the problem.

Though directory services do not affect interoperability directly, network builders must understand the services and how they operate. Directory services provide a look-up function similar to an address or phone directory. Nodes on a network have unique addresses.

A network directory is a master list of all (or some) of the nodes on the network. When you add a new node to your network, the system makes a new entry in the directory. When one node must communicate with another node, the system queries the directory.

Directory services simplify network administration; this is true particularity for large networks. Without a master directory you must know the complete network address of any node with which you want to communicate. With a master directory, you can refer to a remote node with a logical name (i.e., Marketing Print Server).

The master directory translates "Marketing Print Server" into a network address that the network software and hardware understands. Without a master directory, you must update each node on the network when you add a new node. With a master directory, the system requires only one new entry. Because all or some nodes know how to query the directory, you must update only the directory node instead of every node on the network. Directory services and network management are two areas that present a challenge because:

- They are important to interworking and administration of enterprise networks, yet non-proprietary standards for these functions are not complete or at least are very new.

- These functions are very complex. The standards that do exist are implemented only sparsely at this time. Until the standards mature, network implementors must find creative ways to provide these functions.

If you want to connect to the backbone, determine if the network management and directory services software for your departmental network is compatible with the enterprise-wide solution.

If you conform to the backbone protocol, you probably conform to the backbone network management and directory services. Otherwise, if you select a different protocol than what the backbone uses, you must purchase or build a gateway or isolate your network management and directory services from the rest of the organization.

2.2.3.4 Protocol and Service Considerations

Consider the network technologies the backbone supports when designing your network. Ask yourself the following questions:

- Is it feasible and practical to use the same protocol and services?

- If you use the same protocols and services, will you also receive the benefit of compatible network management and directory services functions?

- Is there a particular software vendor that supplies most of the network software for a majority of the nodes in the enterprise? Can you use software from that same company?

If you decide that you cannot use the enterprise standard protocol and services (or it happens that there is not a single, dominant protocol/service standard in your organization) it is necessary to consider using a gateway to reach the backbone.

A gateway is much more complex and costly than a router or bridge. A bridge or router connects networks together at a lower level than a gateway. You use a gateway to connect entirely dissimilar networks, while a bridge or router connects two identical or relatively similar networks. Gateways are far less desirable than bridges and routers. Gateways perform conversion between networks with dissimilar protocols or services. These devices are much more expensive for vendors to build than bridges and routers. Bridges and routers also offer superior performance to gateways and require less user-maintenance.

2.3   User-Vendor Partnership

Users normally do not build networks by themselves. Networks are more often a joint effort between the network users and the people who market, build, and sell the products to the network user.

Network implementors must understand this partnership, because it affects purchasing decisions and the success of your implementation. This partnership is visible particularly to the enterprise network implementor, because these applications tend to benefit from using the latest technology. Using the latest technology implies direct interaction between users and vendors.

Suppose you discover a single vendor with a group of products that support a large portion of your networking needs. You consider a network design with these products. However, before you take the step to invest a large portion of your application into a single company's products, you must make the following considerations:

- How stable is this company? Are they going to be around for several years?

- What future product direction is this company taking? Are these products important to their long-term strategy or will they cancel these products in favor of some other product directions?

- How important are you to this company? Will they support you during the analysis of your application and continue to support you during its implementation?

If after you understand these issues you feel that the company is either too unstable or is taking a different product direction than you need, you can attempt to affect the strategies or condition of this vendor.

If you are a potentially large customer for this company, you can attempt to influence their product strategies. Perhaps if you take the time to explain your application to this potential partner, they may decide to shift their product strategy in your direction.

If the company is new or small, you can factor in the amount of prosperity that would result from your business. Your order, if sufficiently large, may be the boost that this company needs achieve stability.

2.3.1   Leveraging Vendor Support

To build a successful network for your department or enterprise, you must learn how to work with product vendors. Vendors are a source of knowledge from which you can learn. Before a vendor can build a network product, they must master the technologies of the product. Most vendors have an in-depth understanding of protocols, services, and hardware aspects of the product they sell. This knowledge comes from investment. Vendors invest in technical expertise by hiring experts or training existing engineers to become experts. If you speak to a vendor that does not appear to have a detailed understanding of the network technologies on which their own products are based, you must call someone else. Either this vendor has not invested enough or the vendor is not motivated to support your effort.

In the network industry, a kind of symbiotic relationship has evolved. You want to build successful networks and vendors want to sell network products to you. Many vendors have developed a strategy that involves more than just moving product out the door to you. These vendors want you to be successful with your network. A successful network grows, which means you will need more products. A successful network user also will become a testimonial to other potential customers for the vendor.

The amount of energy that a vendor puts into your application varies depending on several factors. Vendors have limited technical resources available for customer support. Network technology experts are costly and in high demand. Often, the same experts that design products are the same people responsible for background customer support. So when a vendor uses one of its experts for customer support, they compromise something else, including new product development.

Example: A vendor may have support people who specialize in interfacing with customers. These customer-support experts are trained to listen to users and gather questions. The support experts research the questions and answer as many as they can. Often, the support people encounter questions too detailed to answer without help from a network product design expert. The support expert explains the problem to the design person. To assist the support person, the design person must interrupt product design work.

These interruptions can affect product development schedules. Although many vendors have a keen interest in your success, they may not elect to invest too much of their product developer's time to support you. After all, their primary task is to build new products. This is why you must understand how important you are to this vendor and how important the particular products you want are to their marketing strategy.

If you are planning to purchase many products, chances are your vendor will commit substantial technical support to your effort. Because your purchase involves considerable, the vendor can justify the support. You also must consider the future. Does this vendor have a long-term commitment to the products that you plan to purchase?

You usually implement large networks in phases. You can order products at predetermined or projected intervals. In this case, the vendor has incentive to offer significant support. The vendor wants to ensure that the network's first phase is successful so that you fund the second phase, which means that they sell more product.

Vendors may have motivation to offer significant support if you plan to use their products with other similar products that other vendors manufacture. The key is interoperability.

Example: Suppose a prospective vendor offers a network product. This vendor wants to advertise that their product interworks with other compatible products. If you plan to install the prospective vendor's product into an existing network with other compatible products, the vendor may invest talent to ensure interoperability. If you are successful, the vendor is successful. You have a network with products that work together and the vendor can add to its list one more compatible product with which it interworks.

Sometimes a vendor offers support even though you are planning a small network. This is often the case with new products. When a vendor offers a new product, they are under pressure to achieve critical mass for the new product. They achieve critical mass when revenue for the new product starts to pay for the investment in building and maintaining the new product. The vendor wants to plant seeds. The seeds are the first shipments of the new product. Vendors want the first shipments to go into successful networks so that the seeds can grow and move the new product line to critical mass.

2.3.2   Product Beta Cycles

Vendors are anxious to see their new products function properly. New products enter a *beta* stage before the manufacturer mass-markets the product. A vendor prefers to live-test products at selected customer sites before the units enter the marketplace. Such a site is referred to as a *beta site*.

The goal of a beta site is to eliminate defects and shortcomings in the product while the product is in a few, limited, and controlled environments. The beta site customers run tests on these preliminary products. The vendors listen to the problems that the beta sites report and enhance the product before the product goes into general production. This way, vendors have more confidence in the stability of the new product.

Vendors actively seek friendly customers to become beta sites for their new products. Becoming a beta site for a vendor's product is a double-edged sword. On one side, you receive an immature product that is likely to have shortcomings. On the other side, you receive significant network technical support from the vendor. It is even possible the vendor may help you understand problems not related to the beta product (a fringe benefit).

2.3.2.1 Why be a Beta Site?

There are other reasons why a network user elects to be a beta site. Perhaps you want to be the first to take advantage of the latest technology and gain an information processing advantage over competition. You can decide to be a beta site to be the first car builder who reaps the benefits of the newest, fastest, or most flexible network product. Another reason to consider becoming a beta site may be that a vendor has produced a particular product that fills a gap in your existing network.

Example: Suppose you have a network based on OSI protocols. You currently have OSI connections for your personal computers, but do not yet have a product that connects your mini-computers to the OSI network. You may decide to become a beta site for a vendor who offers an OSI connection for your mini-computers. If you choose not to be a beta site, you must wait until the company releases the product for general production before you can connect your mini-computers to the other machines.

You can decide to become a beta site for a vendor that has recently designed a new connecting device (e.g., a bridge, router, or gateway). Such a connecting device may be the one piece of equipment you need to connect two isolated subnetworks. If you have a group of clients on a broadband network and a group of servers on a baseband network, you can decide to beta test a vendor's broadband-to-baseband bridge so that you can connect your clients to the servers on the baseband network.

2.3.2.2 Beta Site Responsibilities

Before you commit to becoming a beta site, you must know if you are willing to provide your share of support to the beta project. As a beta site user, you have implied responsibilities; just as the vendor has implied responsibilities.

You must provide a test environment for the new product. Because this product is new and largely untested, you must be prepared for the product to malfunction and possibly fail during beta test.

Vendors test new products in their own laboratories before they enter beta, but most vendors do not have the kind of environment to stress-test sufficiently their products. A user environment can test the seams of a new product in a way that the vendor cannot. Vendors that build products do not abuse or misuse the product the way a new user does. As a new user, you try things with the new product that vendors may not think to try.

Suitable environments for beta tests vary. Some large network users have dedicated laboratories solely for the purpose of testing new products. These network users test new products and learn their true capabilities before ordering large quantities. Some companies require all new products, beta or mature, to be tested in such an environment before approving a large order.

Other users test beta products on live production networks. A production network is a network that you use actively for day-to-day operation. You must take precautions to ensure that the beta equipment does not impair the production network if you encounter an error.

One precaution you can take is to configure the beta device to interact with otherwise idle production equipment. Such idle equipment may be undergoing program changes or other maintenance. Another popular technique for beta testing equipment on production networks is to do the testing at night or on weekends when potential problems have a lesser impact.

Most vendors help with your beta testing. Many send technical personnel to your site and assist during installation, configuration, and operational testing. Successful beta testing means the vendor can begin production.

Vendors occasionally ask you to test the product documentation as well as the product itself. This means that they ask you to do certain tasks without direct vendor technical support. Instead, you must rely on beta documentation. The documentation may lack information or be confusing, just as the equipment may contain flaws. Imminently your company benefits from this exercise. If, after successful beta test, your company decides to purchase more equipment from the vendor, your company benefits if the documentation is correct and easy-to-understand.

2.3.3   Non-Recurring Expenses (NRE)

Occasionally a user pays a vendor to design and build a new product. You may have a specific need for a product that does not exist in the marketplace. Perhaps you have an unusual requirement for a unique connecting device. You may be able to persuade a vendor to work as your partner to co-fund research and development for such a product. Such a product may have a limited market demand outside of your company.

These efforts are called Non-Recurable Expense (NRE) projects. The vendor charges a one-time, non-recurring fee to proceed with product design that otherwise would not make good business sense. Sometimes the user that helped finance the research and development markets the product of such a partnership.

A network user can elect to provide NRE funds to a vendor if the need for the product relatively is urgent. The NRE is an incentive for the vendor to shift design priorities and build this product ahead of schedule. NRE often is justified, because many user companies are not well-suited to network product development. Such companies would rather pay a vendor to build a new product instead of building it themselves.

2.4   Network Standards

Trade magazines for the network industry are full of articles related to network standards. The factory automation industry was the first to drive a large-scale standards effort for networks. A brief history of this standards movement will give you a feel for how massive this effort is and will help you to understand how other industries are progressing.

Those involved with factory automation have a fascination with productivity. After all, the automation goal is to build better products for less cost. Since the beginning of the Industrial Age, man has sought to improve the manufacturing process by using new technologies. However, the sole act of using the latest and greatest equipment does not guarantee that you realize the full potential that technology has to offer. Understanding and applying industry and government standards for networks is vital to realizing the full potential of your computer systems.

The desire to improve manufacturing processes has caused many technologies to mature at a faster than normal rate. It seems that as soon as the industry discovers a new scientific method, someone, somewhere, tries to apply this method to manufacturing engineering.

History has displayed that even simple concepts can improve production and quality or reduce production costs. Today factory engineers apply complex concepts in the form of robots and computerized workcells.

Previously, factory people may have discovered that applying new technologies did not bear the expected maximum potential, because these people lacked the entire perspective. The assembly line turned a demand for skilled craftsman into a demand for unskilled, methodical piece-workers.

Man plunged into the assembly line age without considering the social impact on the workers. Large sweat shops replaced smaller specialty shops. The workers' morale diminished, pride in workmanship became a managerial quality issue, and the formation of unions offset the economical savings.

2.4.1   Interoperability Problem

A similar lesson was learned during the early 1980's.   Advances in microprocessor technology allowed people to develop robotic technology and use programmable controllers to an advantage. The industry hastened to exploit this valuable technology.   Soon, the industry was building real products using computer-controlled motion and scheduling.

Computer Integrated Manufacturing (CIM) came to life in the factories. The industry automated workcells one at a time, using equipment from different vendors.

Example: A computer from one company controlled a paint workcell. Another computer from another company controlled the welding workcell. Yet another computer from a third company controlled the inspection area. The complex nature of CIM equipment forced the industry to use equipment from several companies.

Today, the industry still implements enterprise automation as a multi-vendor solution. No one single vendor can supply a complete enterprise automation solution. The industry improved significantly quality, production, and cost-effectiveness at the workcell level, but also discovered a problem that was not anticipated.

After being successful at automating the workcells, someone conceived that the ability to connect the automated workcells to area controllers must be available. It became imperative to connect multiple dissimilar devices that several companies made. The industry wanted to build more complex workcells to take further advantage of automation technology and realize the potential that the computerized automation offers. These complex workcells demanded that the industry integrate different brands of computers.

The industry realized that some day it would be possible to integrate the entire manufacturing processes within the organizations. The industry envisioned a factory with few human workers. Computers could track inventories, sales, and production, and paperwork could be reduced to a fraction. The industry calls this a paperless factory.

The industry discovered that integrating the complete manufacturing process meant making computers from different vendors communicate with each other. Making computers talk to other brands of computers is a complicated task.

It consequently was an arduous and time-consuming task to make a robot controller from one company communicate to a programmable controller from a different company. The industry painfully realized that communication techniques varied significantly from one vendor's product to the next.

When the industry first started to experiment with robots and other computerized equipment, they had no idea that the integration problem would be so complex and expensive. They had focused their technical skills on real-time motion control, electronic imaging, voice recognition, and computerized vision. They were astonished by the communication problem. The industry knew that integration was the next step, but the industry underestimated the effort.

The first attempts at integration quickly alerted the industry to the reality of the difficulty of integration. It took weeks or even months to design methods to connect devices from different vendors. The cost of making computers from different vendors communicate to each other was so high that factory automation started to lose momentum.

During this period, *General Motors*, the United States leader in the factory automation effort (in terms of dollars invested), estimated that the cost of integrating these islands of automation would account for up to 50% of the entire cost of CIM systems. In other words, the communication systems to link workcells together was going to cost as much as the robots, programmable controllers, automatic machining tools, and other equipment. Much of this cost would be spent on communication experts.

The systems required experts to create gateways between the different proprietary communication systems in the workcells. The integration requires experts that understand several communication methods and these experts represent a large labor expenditure. This put a damper on the dreams to build the Factory of the Future.

2.4.2   Birth of Standards for Factory Automation Networks

The Factory of the Future required that the manufacturing process become a centralized, integrated operation. Until the industry could reduce the cost of connecting these workcells, the automated factory would remain a subject for science fiction instead of becoming reality.

Major manufacturers started to divert investment dollars away from computerized automation to study the interoperation problem. Several companies arrived at the same conclusion at about the same time. Factory automation was at an impasse that had to be crossed before they could go any further.

How could they reduce the cost of communication systems in the automated factory? They needed to address this issue before factory automation could again become a cost-effective investment. Companies such as *General Motors, John Deere, McDonnel Douglas, Boeing,* and others decided to assemble task forces to analyze the problem.

These task forces determined that there were several things they could do to reduce the cost of integrating factories. To start, they could study communication in today's factory and compare it to communication in tomorrow's factory. They could educate themselves about the new communication technologies. They could understand network topologies and how to manage networks within networks. Finally, and most importantly, they could build a strategy to overcome the interoperability problem.

During the early 1980's, the task forces within the major manufacturers worked independently of each other. Very little technology exchange occurred between the various companies. Networks were already understood to be a corporate strategic issue and information systems were private property. Nobody wanted to disclose their secrets to the competition. This closed-mouth attitude continued even though many companies were trying to solve the same problem.

Many companies determined that the best way to solve the interoperability problem was to create data communication standards. If they defined suitable standards, vendors could build products that would communicate to each other, the integration task could be brought to a workable level, and factory automation would become a cost-effective, long-term investment.

However, a single company could not produce the standards. A multi-company consortium had to develop the standards. Vendors build products based on standards—if many potential customers support the standards.

2.4.2.1 1984 Integration Effort

In 1984, an historic event occurred. Several major manufacturers met to address interoperability. This meeting occurred at a two-day workshop at *McDonnel Douglas Corporation*. This meeting had representation from 56 companies and represented a new era of technology sharing. These companies agreed to exchange information about integration efforts. The need to establish industry standards out-weighed the risk of giving away company secrets.

The agenda of this meeting was to select a set of technologies on which to base factory data communication standards. The technologies had to address the needs of the automated factory. Networks in the automated factory must be able to handle large traffic loads, must be deterministic, and must be able to function amidst considerable electrical noise. The protocols and services also must be robust enough to handle a very wide variety of applications.

General Motors had already invested considerable time and money defining such a group of technologies. This group of technologies was called *Manufacturing Automation Protocol* (MAP). The consensus of the *McDonnel Douglas* workshop attendees was to support MAP as the factory communications standard.

A tremendous amount of work had to be done. The young MAP standard had to be expanded, formalized, refined, and published. In September 1984, the MAP Users Group was formed at *General Motors' Technical Center* in Warren, Michigan. The charter of the MAP Users Group was to bring the MAP standards to maturity. The Users Group also would influence vendors to build products based on these standards.

2.4.2.2 Manufacturing Automation Protocol

MAP is successful, both directly and indirectly. MAP is directly successful, because vendors accept the standard and build products that are MAP-conformant. This means that factory network builders can select from a variety of products from several vendors and expect those products to communicate with each other.

Before MAP, vendors purposely defined proprietary communications protocols. Vendors wanted to be able to control their existing installed base. Vendors wanted to control whether or not customers could connect rival vendor's equipment to their networks.

By controlling connectivity, vendors were assured of revenue when users wanted to expand their networks. Proprietary networks meant that users would prefer to purchase more proprietary equipment instead of other vendor's equipment. Vendors knew that users did not want to attempt gateway construction. Instead, users would more often go to their current product vendor for additional equipment. This strategy effectively "locked" the user into one particular product line.

The MAP effort is successful at convincing vendors to discontinue this pattern of proprietary communications. During 1986, *General Motors* announced that only MAP-compatible equipment would be considered for future computer purchases. Other companies followed the lead. The message to vendors was "comply to the standards or lose our business." To a large extent, the vendors heard this message. Vendors still produce proprietary products, but many also produce products that conform to MAP or other industry standards. The attitude in the industry is that standards are the way of the future. Most major product vendors already produce or have plans to produce, products that conform to MAP or other standards.

MAP is indirectly successful for the acceptance of other data communication standards. MAP was the first user-defined set of standards to influence computer vendors to create compatible equipment. MAP enters history as the first large-scale example of computer users dictating product characteristics to computer vendors.

The early success of MAP prompted users to work together to support other, new data communication standards. MAP standards specifically address networks in the factory, but factory network users were not the only ones who recognized the interoperability issue. Office and government network users also desired to see standard data communication networks replace proprietary networks.

2.4.2.3 Other Standards

MAP initiated the effort. Two years after creating MAP, office network users formed the Technical and Office Protocols (TOP) User's Group. The charter of TOP was similar to the MAP charter. TOP wanted to define data communication standards for the engineering and office environments. TOP also wanted to influence vendors to build TOP-conformant products.

The United States government announced Government OSI Profile (GOSIP) standards during the late 1980's. The government was creating a mandate for its numerous agencies (i.e., Department of Defense, Department of Agriculture). These agencies make extensive use of networks and WANs.

The office community and the government community had the same goal as the factory automation community. The goal was to define standards, publish documents that vendors could use to build products, and influence vendors to produce products that conform to the standards.

2.4.3   Standards Protocols vs. Standards Profiles

MAP, TOP, and GOSIP are called standards profiles. A standards profile is a collection of standards protocols. Standards protocols are defined by a number of organizations such as the International Organization for Standardization (ISO), the Institute for Electrical and Electronics Engineers (IEEE), the American National Standards Institute (ANSI), and the Consultive Committee for International Telephone and Telegraph (CCITT).

These organizations are responsible for defining protocol standards. They produce documentation that delineates standard rules for data communication. As such, these protocols by themselves are insufficient documentation for computer vendors to build products.

These standards contain numerous options. If vendors were to build products based solely on these standards, the chances are highly probable that the products would not interwork. One vendor would implement one set of options and another vendor would implement a different set of options. Each vendor could build incompatible products and still conform to standards.

These standards purposely omit implementation details from their documents. Their charter is to document protocols in an abstract manner. It is necessary to define implementation specifics before these abstractions can be applied usefully. That is why protocol profiles are essential. A protocol profile is an unambiguous sub-set of protocol standards and a set of implementors' agreements. As protocol profiles, MAP, TOP, and GOSIP specify the details necessary to build products.

Data communication vendors first must understand the protocol standards, which the standards' organizations produce. The vendors then must understand the standards profile (i.e., MAP, TOP, or GOSIP) and properly implement the product. Products that different vendors build to conform to the standards and also conform to the same profile must interwork with each other.

There is not an absolute distinction between a standards protocol organization and a standards profile. Sometimes a standards group defines certain implementation details. A standards profile sometimes also contains raw protocol abstractions. A standards profile document contains protocol rules if there is no available standard protocol available to reference. This happens if the industry is waiting for a protocol standards group to finish publishing a particular protocol. The profile temporarily satisfies a demand in the protocol standards. Later, as true protocol standards become available, the temporary documentation that the profile defined can be replaced by the protocol standards group documentation. This practice is applied carefully, because it can result in an interoperability problem.

> **Example:** Suppose a profile group decides to publish protocol documentation for network management, because it is waiting for protocol standards groups to finish their work. Vendors base their products on this temporary network management protocol. Later, the protocol standards groups publish a bonefide network management protocol specification. As vendors implement the new network management protocol, they produce products that do not interwork with the earlier products that implemented the old, temporary, network management protocol.

Profiles contain implementation details and specify specific options within a set of protocols, but profiles, like protocol standards, include options.

Example: A profile may offer a set of media/datalink technologies from which the network builder can choose. A profile is more specific than a protocol standard, but a profile that is too dogmatic may not be useful to certain industries.

The MAP profile specifies two datalink technologies: broadband and carrierband. Broadband offers features appropriate for factory backbones; whereas carrierband is more appropriate for certain smaller networks (e.g., automated workcells).

So a vendor can choose to build a MAP-conformant broadband product or a MAP-conformant carrierband product. Both are MAP, but one product is appropriate for backbone applications, while the other is appropriate for smaller networks. The MAP profile specifies two options, because two options are appropriate for factory automation.

Protocol standards documents offer a wider variety of options than profiles. Protocol standards groups tend to define universal documents without focus on any one environment. Profiles tend to offer options that are appropriate to a particular environment.

Another important organization to factory network standards is the National Institute of Standards and Technology (NIST). This group was formerly the National Bureau of Standards (NBS) and was renamed during the late 1980's. NIST is the sponsor for the OSI Implementors' Workshop (OIW). OIW does not fit into either the standards protocol category or the profile category. OIW has served as a forum for the building of implementors' agreements.

MAP and TOP profiles often reference OIW documents. These workshops are held to resolve ambiguities in protocol standards. OIW participants define implementation specifics. OIW, at the request of industry organizations, such as profile organizations, addresses protocols that are nearly ready to be implemented in products. Implementors' agreements often are referenced by several profiles.

Example: MAP and TOP could both reference the same implementors' agreements. This method has the advantage of insuring that MAP and TOP products can interwork with each other. This means that the standards become even more powerful, because vendors can build products that conform to a larger user market.

2.4.4   Conformance Testing

Industry has defined data communication standards to make it possible for vendors to build products that interwork with other vendor's products. However, documentation usually is not enough. Even though a significant amount of effort is spent resolving ambiguities in standards documentation, it is possible that one vendor may interpret one paragraph, or even one sentence, differently than the next vendor.

When you consider that a vendor must reference hundreds, often thousands of pages of documentation, the chances of one or more discrepancies is fairly high. A live-test can bring such discrepancies into view. Conformance testing allows vendors to test their new products and demonstrate, through operation, that their products conform to the standards on which they are based.

Conformance testing has become an important part of data communication product development. You want to gain a level of confidence before you purchase a product. This confidence is a reflection of your attitude towards the vendor. Vendors are anxious to make their standards-based products interwork with other standards-based products. However, interoperability is a complex issue. Even the most carefully planned product may have problems interoperating with other vendors' products.

Data communication products are based on protocols, which are sequences of events that can occur in an huge number of permutations. Because there are so many permutations, a protocol test suite is very expensive to build. The software required to test the permutations requires a large development effort. Such tests are so expensive to build that many vendors would have difficulty making a business case to build data communication products.

Conformance testing is accomplished by national and international agencies, such as the Corporation for Open Systems (COS) and the Industrial Technology Institute (ITI). User groups, such as MAP and TOP, sometimes contract these agencies. Vendors pay a fee to have their products "conformance tested" at a testing agency. Such fees can run thousands of dollars a day. Vendors often pay the fee because some users, such as the government, insist on conformance testing before they purchase a product.

Vendors also pay to have their products conformance tested, because this testing can indicate flaws before the product goes into production. It is less expensive to fix a problem during product development than to fix a problem after mass-producing the product. If an error exists in many products, they must apply the correction to all of the products. If they discover the problem when the product is in the prototype stage, the correction applies only to the prototypes.

A conformance testing facility consists of hardware and very complex software. This hardware and software is configured as an actual network node. The node is a control node that conforms to a standard protocol. The vendors try to make their new product interwork with the control node constructed by the testing agency.

Writing control node software is very complex. The node is supposed to be the perfect implementation of a protocol. Much care and quality control must be applied to control node development. After all, the control node is used as a measure of other products' conformance to a standard.

Control nodes also must execute many protocol events. Often, a control node exercises hundreds, even thousands, of pre-planned protocol exercises with the product under test. These protocol exercises are called *scenarios*. It is impossible to create enough scenarios to test every possible real-world network event. However, it is possible to create enough scenarios to test the majority of all likely permutations.

It can take hours or days for a set of scenarios to execute. This can be expensive for the vendor, because fees are based on the number of days the tests require. If the product has problems, the time required to pass conformance testing can increased. If the control node detects an error by the product under test, the control node can log the error and continue. At the end of the test run, the vendor can be given a list of the errors. The vendor fixes the errors, then the tests are re-run. This process continues until no errors are detected by the control node. When no errors occur, the product has passed conformance testing.

Sometimes vendors can purchase or lease a conformance testing system from a conformance testing agency. Such systems include a hardware workstation and software to execute scenarios. Often vendors have two choices: purchase a conformance testing system or take their chances at the conformance testing agency. Occasionally, the vendor will wait for the conformance agency to put a testing system into product form rather than take their chances at the agency itself.

2.5   In Summary

The network industry has business issues, as well as technical issues. It is beneficial to you the network builder or implementor to understand business strategies and industry trends. You must understand the your enterprise strategies before deciding on which technologies to use. You and your vendors can work as partners. Both partners can help each other if you understand each others' objectives.

The introduction of standards for networks has lowered significantly the cost of interworking products from different vendors. Industry and government network users are actively vital in defining and driving standards for networks. The organizations describe documentation called profiles, which reference base standards.   Implementors   produce   agreements   that   make   real-world implementations possible. Conformance testing is a complicated, expensive process that ensures that new products correctly execute standard protocols.

Chapter 3

Data Communications

3.1   Overview

To build a network, you need network products. It is a combined effort between you and your vendors that results in designing and constructing the network products that you require. A single network product serves no useful purpose, but a network family defines a group of products that you can use efficiently. Data communication is the concept on which designers base network families.

A network family is a group of products that communicate with each other. That may seem simple, but communication is complex. People have infinitely more sophisticated thought processes than computers; people can detect and interpret body language and can put a statement into context. People are able to apply past experiences when communicating with other people. Computers are not able to understand these complex communication processes, so people have developed methods to describe communication in more simple terms. The industry calls such a method a *model.*

Designers have developed abstract models to define communication between computers. These models describe a well-defined set of data communication events that are simple enough for computers to execute. These models are complex, but compared to communications between people, these models are simple.

A network family is a group of products that the designers base on a common data communication model. Computer vendors and standards organizations develop data communication models.

An example of a vendor-developed model is the IBM-defined Systems Network Architecture (SNA). An important model developed by a standards organization is the Open Systems Interconnect (OSI) model. The International Organization for Standardization (known as ISO, because of its French name) defined the OSI model. ISO first published the OSI model in 1979. Many products that you use in enterprise networks are based on the OSI model.

The demand is high for products based on the OSI model, because using such products can simplify significantly the interoperability problem. Integrating two vendors' OSI-based products is easier than integrating two products based on separate proprietary models.

3.2　Layered Architecture

Developers design data communication models with regard to product development. A useful model is one that you can use in product design. Because communication is a complex process, a model that defines communication also is complex. Such a model is easier to understand if you divide it into several sections. The OSI model, like other data communication models, divides communication functions into groups. The industry calls these groups *layers*. Each layer is responsible for a well-defined set of functions.

The concept of a layered architecture is similar to the structure of a company. Each company employee is responsible for a certain set of functions. Like employees, each layer of a data communication model has distinctive functions. Data communication models divide functions into layers for several reasons. Network product developers, network users, and people who define network standards benefit from a layered architecture.

Example: The designers divided the OSI model into seven layers. A network product vendor could assign one engineer to each layer. In this way, each engineer must design only one layer. Before an engineer can design a layer, the engineer first must master the standards associated with that layer. It takes less time to master one layer than to master the entire model. A layered architecture makes it possible for a team of engineers to work in parallel, which means that each engineer can focus on a relatively small portion of a complete product.

As a network user, you also benefit from a layered architecture. Network behavior is easier to predict if you build the network with products that a developer based on layered architectures. Network behavior is easier to visualize, because you can consider individually the functions of each layer. A network that is easier to visualize also is easier to debug and administer.

Another group that benefits from a layered architecture are the people that make the standards. Standards organizations divide themselves into committees; each responsible for defining one layer of the model. This allows them to define the standards more quickly and efficiently. Similar to the design engineers, the committee members must master one layer instead of the whole model. In this way, several committees can work in parallel.

Learning the OSI model is simple, because the design engineers based the OSI model on a layered architecture. It is easier to learn one layer at a time than to attempt to comprehend the entire model. In reality, it is useless to understand only a single layer of a data communication model. Product vendors, network users, and the people who define standards usually understand two or more layers of a given model. Each layer of a data communication model interacts with other layers. Though it is common to find experts regarding one layer, such an expert usually has at least a basic understanding of other layers.

3.3   OSI Model Layers

Design engineers divided the OSI model into seven layers. Schematically, the OSI model resembles a stack of pancakes (Figure 3-1). Many people refer to network software as a *stack*. Except the Application and Physical layers, each layer communicates with the layers above and below it in the stack. Application is the top layer and communicates only with the layer below (Presentation). Like Application, Physical only communicates with one layer (Datalink).

The Application layer communicates with the program (Application Process) that uses the network. An Application Process can be a real-time program, a file transfer program, or some other kind of program that accesses the network. A network user can write the Application Processes or product vendors can write and market the Application Processes.

Example: A vendor-written process can be a menu-driven utility that your computer operator uses. You may decide to purchase an application rather than write it yourself. One example of a vendor-written package is a virtual terminal Application Process that allows your operator to access a variety of different hosts from a single personal computer.

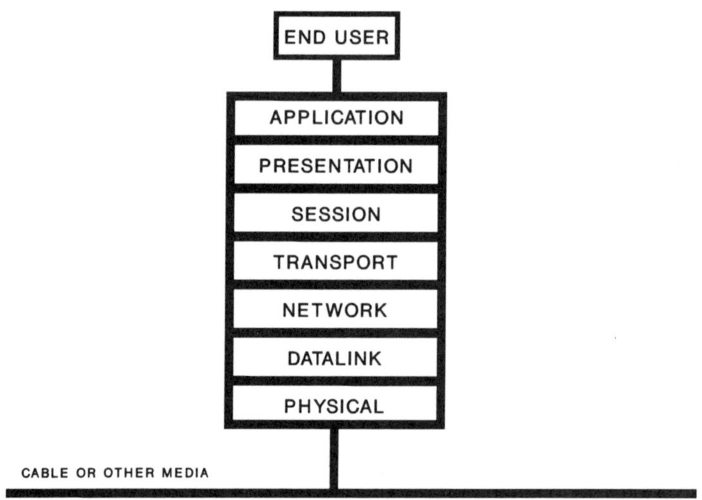

Figure 3-1: OSI Model Layers

3.3.1 Upper Layers

Designers call the Application, Presentation, and Session layers the *upper layers*. The OSI model implements the upper layers in software. These layers provide the functions that are closest to applications that use the network. These layers perform the final processing of data coming in from the network and going out to the network:

- The Application Layer (Layer 7) describes standard file transfer, electronic messaging, and virtual terminal services.

- The Presentation Layer (Layer 6) puts data into a format that the host computer understands.

- The Session Layer (Layer 5) performs dialogue control.

People who write network application software must know more about the upper layers than the other layers.

3.3.2   Middle Layers

Beneath the upper layers are Transport and Network layers, which the industry calls *middle layers*. Like upper layers, the OSI model implements the middle layers in software.

- The Transport Layer (Layer 4) ensures that the system accurately sends and receives the data.

- The Network Layer (Layer 3) is responsible for forwarding data to the proper destination. Engineers call this function: *routing and relaying*.

Both layers are responsible for detecting errors in transmitting and\or receiving data.

3.3.3   Lower Layers

The industry refers to the Datalink and Physical layers as the *lower layers*.

- The Datalink Layer (Layer 2) is responsible for transforming data into electronic pulses and vice-versa.

- The Physical Layer (Layer 1) interfaces directly with the media of the network (e.g., wire or fiber optic cable).

Datalink converts computer information into electronic signals. The higher layers perform software functions, while Datalink is the first layer that must be implemented partially in hardware. The Datalink layer prepares ones and zeroes to go "on the wire." Data is "on the wire" if it can be observed from the cable or other media.

The model closely links the Physical layer to the Datalink layer.   The Datalink layer converts software messages into hardware signals, but at this point, these signals are not ready to go on the wire.

The Datalink layer produces low voltage, low power signals. The Physical layer converts these low-level signals into stronger signals. The Physical layer also can perform other electronic encoding functions (e.g., modulation and demodulation). The Physical layer often is a modem. The term *modem* stands for MOdulation\DEModulation. Modulation and Demodulation means conversion of digital signals into analog signals and vice-versa.

The Physical layer performs the final step necessary to allow electronic signals to travel over a media. Conversely, the Physical layer converts strong, incoming signals into low-level signals so that the Datalink layer can convert them back into software messages. Experts often refer to the cable or media as *Layer 0*.

3.4   Service and Protocol Properties

A stack has two distinct sets of properties: service properties and protocol properties. Service properties define the relationship between a stack and the Application Process that uses the stack. A stack provides a service to an Application Process, which is why the industry calls it a *provider*. A network comprises two or more Application Processes, each using the services that their own stack provides to achieve data communication. Protocol properties define the relationship between two stacks. One stack communicates with another stack according to a well-defined protocol.

Example: Imagine two Application Processes named DIAL and ANSWER. DIAL and ANSWER are two pieces of software that exist on two nodes in a network. DIAL is the program that initiates the communication session, while ANSWER is the program that responds. This is analogous to a phone conversation.

The initiator is the one that dials a number, while the responder is the one that picks up the ringing phone. For simplicity, assume that this network only has two nodes (Figure 3-2). You can use DIAL and ANSWER to demonstrate several data communication concepts, starting with the concept of service and protocol.

DIAL and ANSWER each have their own stack. DIAL's stack is labeled STACK-D and ANSWER's stack is labeled STACK-A. STACK-A and STACK-D are service *providers*. DIAL and ANSWER are service *users*. DIAL's goal is to have a conversation with ANSWER.

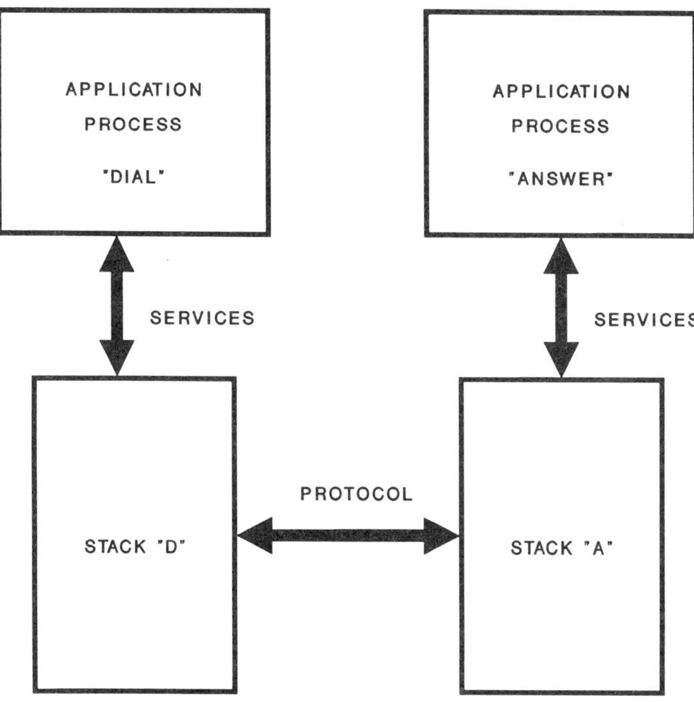

Figure 3-2: Protocols and Services

Assume that DIAL is a personal computer (client) and ANSWER is a print server (a computer attached to a printer). DIAL periodically sends documents to be printed to ANSWER. DIAL uses the services that STACK-D provides to deliver documents to ANSWER, while ANSWER uses the services that STACK-A provides to receive the documents from DIAL.

The relationship between an Application Process and a stack is a master-slave (user-provider) relationship. In the example, DIAL is the master and STACK-D is the slave. DIAL instructs STACK-D to deliver messages and STACK-D carries out those instructions. The situation is the same for ANSWER and STACK-A. ANSWER is the master and STACK-A is the slave. ANSWER expresses a willingness to accept incoming messages. STACK-A, according to the instructions of ANSWER, delivers incoming messages to ANSWER.

As a service provider, a stack is a slave to an Application Process. However, from a protocol angle, a stack is a peer to another stack. STACK-D communicates with STACK-A using the rules of a protocol. The OSI protocol defines a peer-to-peer relationship between stacks. STACK-D and STACK-A perform services as a slave, but STACK-D and STACK-A have protocol functions that they execute as a peer.

The service and protocol concept goes beyond the context of Application Process and stack. The OSI model defines three relationships for any given layer (Figure 3-3). Each layer of the stack is both a user and a provider of a service. Each layer is also a protocol peer to a remote layer in a remote stack. Each layer is a service user, a service provider, and a protocol peer, all at the same time.

Example: The Application layer of STACK-D provides a service to DIAL. The Application layer of STACK-D is also a *user* of the services that the Presentation layer of STACK-D provides. Furthermore, the Application layer of STACK-D is a peer to the Application layer of STACK-A.

The Presentation layer, like the Application layer, has three personalities: user, provider, and protocol peer. The Presentation layer is a provider to the Application layer. Presentation is a user of the services that the Session layer provides. STACK-D's Presentation layer is a peer to STACK-A's Presentation layer.

ISO produced the OSI specifications to reflect this multi-personality aspect of a layer. When you order documentation for a particular layer, you normally order at least two documents. One document describes the services the layer provides, while the other document describes the protocol or peer relationship between the layer and its peer layer on some other node.

Example: *ISO 8072* describes the services that the Transport layer provides while *ISO 8073* describes the Transport protocol or the relationship between two Transport peers. If you want the specification for the services that the Transport layer uses, you must order Network layer documents. The services that the Transport layer uses are the services that the Network layer provides.

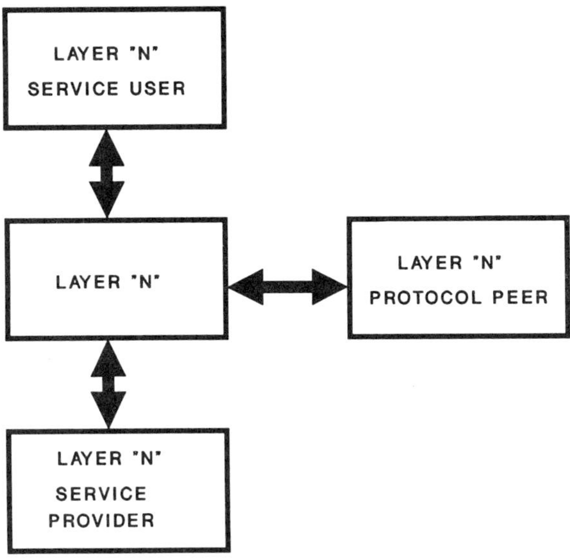

Figure 3-3: Layer "N" Relationships

3.5　　**Connection-Orientation**

The OSI model and other network models describe logical connections between two stacks. These connections are functional rather than physical. A network may have 12 nodes attached physically to a network, yet none of them is logically connected to any other until messages are exchanged. Your telephone is physically connected to every other phone on the block, but a phone call does not exist until you dial a number and somebody picks up the other phone. Logical connections between stacks are like phone calls.

A connection is like a circuit between two electrical devices, such as a battery and a light bulb. In an electrical circuit, electrons flow in a circular motion between the battery and the light bulb. In a data communication circuit, messages travel between nodes. Experts call this communication function the *connection mode data transfer*.

When the system transfers data without first establishing a connection, it is a *connectionless mode data transfer*. A connectionless mode transmission is analogous to sending a letter. You mail a letter without first announcing your intention to do so. A data communication connection goes through three phases:

- Connection Establishment Phase
- Data Transfer Phase
- Connection Termination Phase

In connection mode protocols, the system must establish a connection before it can transfer data between two nodes. This is similar to a telephone conversation between two people. Before two people can speak, one first must establish a telephone connection.

The process of establishing a data communication connection is the *Connection Establishment Phase*. After the network establishes a connection between two nodes, it can send messages between the nodes: this is the *Data Transfer Phase*. When the nodes finish sending messages to each other, the network closes the connection: the *Connection Termination Phase*.

3.5.1   Connection Establishment Phase

To demonstrate data communication connections, return to the example of the DIAL\ANSWER network.

Example: When a secretary wants to send a document to the printer, DIAL desires to begin communications with ANSWER. The system loads DIAL with the document file. Before DIAL can send the file to ANSWER, the system first must establish a connection.

DIAL tells its provider (STACK-D) that it wants to communicate with an Application Process named ANSWER. STACK-D must determine on which remote node ANSWER exists. In this example network, there are only two nodes. STACK-D can make the deduction that ANSWER is on the only other node: the node that uses STACK-A.

In a real network with dozens of nodes, ANSWER can be on any one of many nodes. STACK-D must look-up the network address associated with the Application Process named ANSWER. STACK-D performs a network address look-up by using a function called *Directory Services*. This is analogous to looking up a phone number in a telephone directory.

After STACK-D obtains the network address of the Application Process named ANSWER, (STACK-A) the connection establishment process begins. STACK-D sends a *connect request* to STACK-A. STACK-A receives the connect request and informs ANSWER that a remote Application Process wants to establish a connection. STACK-A informs ANSWER that the name of the requesting Application Process is DIAL. ANSWER informs STACK-A whether or not it will participate in a data communication session with DIAL. If ANSWER does not want the connection, STACK-A sends back a negative response to STACK-D. Otherwise, if ANSWER does want the connection, STACK-A sends a positive response to STACK-D. Note that STACK-A does not make the decision to accept or reject the connect request. The Application Process makes the decision. STACK-A simply reports to its user that a request has arrived. The stack, as a provider, must wait for the Application Process to decide whether or not to accept the connect request.

Meanwhile, STACK-D waits for a response from its peer (STACK-A). After the response arrives, STACK-D informs DIAL of the result. If the result is positive, the system establishes the connection. If the result is negative, the system does not establish the connection. If the system does not establish the connection, DIAL can repeat the connection establishment sequence and try again or DIAL can wait for awhile and retry later.

3.5.2   Data Transfer Phase

Assume the system establishes the connection. You have completed the Connection Establishment Phase and entered the Data Transfer Phase. This means that either Application Process can send messages to the other. When DIAL wants to send assembly instructions to ANSWER, DIAL gives the message to STACK-D and STACK-D delivers to message to STACK-A. After STACK-A receives the message, it gives it to ANSWER. The opposite scenario is possible during the Data Transfer Phase. The system allows ANSWER to send a message to DIAL using the services that STACK-A provides.

Example: ANSWER may want to report the status of a printing job in progress. The system allows ANSWER to send messages to DIAL even though DIAL initiated the connection.

3.5.3   Connection Termination Phase

An Application Process can destroy the data communication connection at any time.

Example: If DIAL has sent a document for printing to ANSWER and ANSWER has sent a printing job status to DIAL, DIAL can decide to close the connection. DIAL informs STACK-D that it is finished with the connection. STACK-D sends an abort message to STACK-A. STACK-A informs ANSWER that the system closed the connection at DIAL's request. This is analogous to a person telling someone that they are ready to hang-up the telephone.

Sometimes a stack initiates the Connection Termination Phase without the Application Process telling it to do so.

Example: Suppose STACK-D and STACK-A are communicating during the Data Transfer Phase when an employee accidently trips over the cable between the two nodes. Sometime later, STACK-D and STACK-A detect that something has gone wrong.

Two OSI stacks periodically send heartbeat messages to each other to let each other know that they are still alive. If the heartbeats stop coming in, the stacks assume that something has happened to the network. In this case, the stacks themselves initiate the connection termination phase. Both stacks report to their Application Processes that the connection terminates. The industry appropriately calls this a *provider abort*, because the stack (provider) has closed the connection.

Connection orientation occurs between the layers of the two stacks.

Example: The Application layer on STACK-D establishes a connection with the Application layer on STACK-A. The Presentation layer on

STACK-D also establishes a connection with the Presentation layer on STACK-A.

Each of the higher layers establish a connection with its peer layer on the other node. When all of the layers have established their connections, it becomes possible for the Application Processes to transfer data. According to the OSI model, each connection at each layer is independent of the other. The Application layer of STACK-D does not communicate with the Presentation layer of STACK-A. Instead, layers communicate on a peer-to-peer basis. The Application layer of STACK-D only communicates with the Application layer of STACK-A.

3.5.4   Connectionless Mode Transmission

In theory, connection establishment is optional at every layer except the Physical layer. The Physical layer supports a physical connection, but does not describe a logical connection as the higher layers do. ISO produced parallel standards at each layer above Physical for both connection-oriented and connectionless services and protocols. Although most real-world implementations provide connection-oriented Application, Presentation, and Session layers, the middle and lower layers are implemented both ways.

Because connections are optional at most layers, it is important to ensure that all nodes in a network have implemented these layers in the same way. If STACK-D has a connection-oriented Network layer, STACK-A also must have a connection-oriented Network layer. Otherwise STACK-A does not interwork with STACK-B. A connection-oriented layer does not interwork with a connectionless layer. The connection-oriented Network layer would be trying to establish a connection, but the connectionless Network layer would not know how to establish a connection. This is one example of why profiles and implementors' agreements are important. Profiles and implementors' agreements address options such as connection and connectionless mode transmission.

A layer that supports connectionless mode transmission sends messages to its peer using a *datagram*. A datagram is a message that the system sends without a connection being present. This is analogous to sending someone a postcard. In a way, this is as if the two peer layers were always in the Data Transfer Phase. A datagram is not guaranteed to reach its destination. A guaranteed message delivery mechanism is part of connection mode transmission. A connection-oriented layer can retransmit a packet if an error occurs during data transmission, but the system sends a datagram as an atomic, independent event.

Connections manage groups of messages. Layers that participate in a connection monitor and manage data transmissions. Layers that provide a datagram service yield to their user (the next higher layer) to monitor data flow, ensure data integrity, and retransmit as required.

3.6   Four Basic Service Primitives

The OSI model defines four categories of service primitives. The industry defines these primitives as the:

- Request
- Indication
- Response
- Confirmation

A service user generates two of these primitives (Request and Response). The provider delivers the other two (Indication and Confirmation) *to* a service user. The system passes service primitives between a user and a provider, while the system exchanges protocol between two peers.

3.6.1   Confirmed Service

When a service user issues a service primitive, it usually results in a protocol exchange between the two service providers. Figure 3-4 shows that a Request service primitive that DIAL issues, causes STACK-D to send a protocol message to STACK-A. After receiving this protocol message, STACK-A issues an Indication service primitive to ANSWER. Figure 3-5 shows what happens when ANSWER acknowledges the Indication service primitive. The Response service primitive causes STACK-A to send a protocol message to STACK-D, which issues a Confirmation service primitive to DIAL.

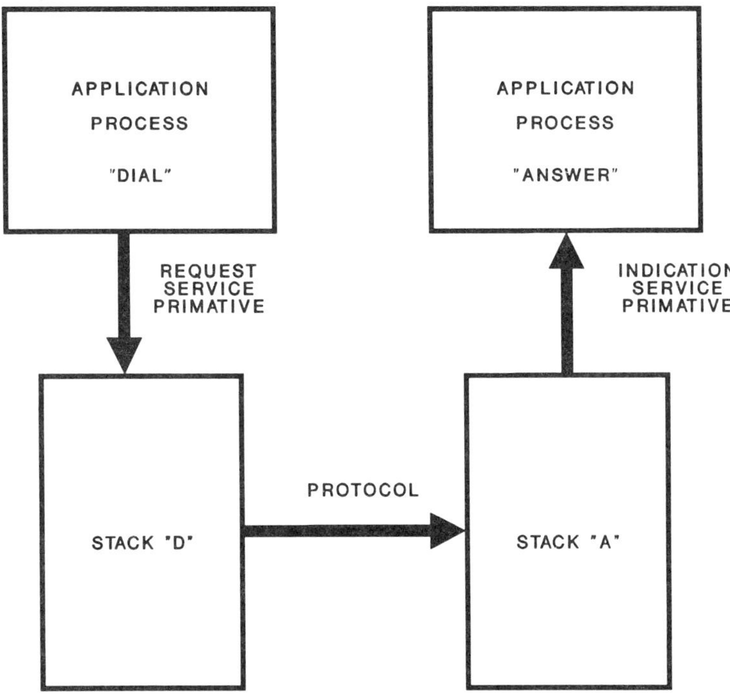

Figure 3-4: Request and Indication Primitives

A peer-to-peer event, such as connection establishment, proceeds as follows:

1. A user issues a Request primitive.
2. The system delivers an Indication to the peer user.
3. The peer user issues a Response.
4. The system delivers a Confirmation to the user that issued the request.

Note that even though four primitives are visible to the users, only two protocol messages have crossed the network. Each message has two service primitives with which it associates. The system sends the first message as a result of the initiating user issuing a connect request primitive.

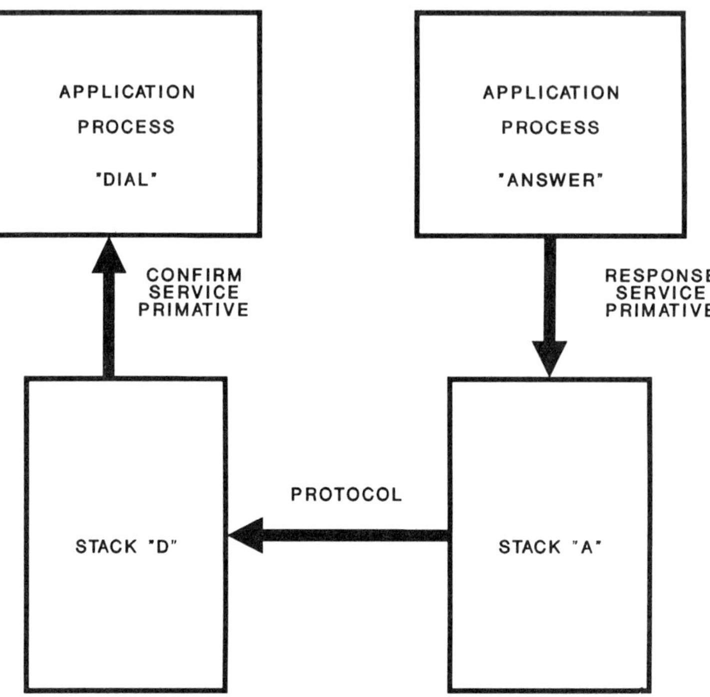

Figure 3-5: Response and Confirm Primitives

When the first message reaches the destination stack, the system presents an indication primitive to the peer user. The system sends the second message as a result of the responding user issuing a connect response primitive. When the second message (sent in the opposite direction of the first message) reaches the originating stack, the system presents a confirm primitive to the originating user. The industry calls this four-primitive scheme: a *confirmed service*. The service is confirmed, because the receiving stack sends a response. The system delivers this response to the sender as a confirm.

3.6.2   Unconfirmed Service

There is an alternate scheme called *unconfirmed service*.   Unconfirmed service means that only the first two service primitives are involved.   The sender issues a Request that results in an Indication at the receiving side.

The receiver, in an unconfirmed service, does not issue a Response. A two-primitive event does not provide confirmation to the sender.   The complete unconfirmed corresponds to Figure 3-4. Both confirmed and unconfirmed events are important to the OSI model and to other network family models.

Consider the Transport layer of the OSI model.   During connection establishment, the system uses the confirmed service scheme. However, during the data transfer phase, the system uses the unconfirmed service scheme.

At the start of the connection establishment phase, the initiator issues a T_CONNECT REQUEST service primitive that the system receives on the responding side as a T_CONNECT INDICATION.

The responding side issues a T_CONNECT RESPONSE that the system receives on the initiating side as a T_CONNECT INDICATION. This is an example of the use of confirmed service. This event has two associated protocol messages: a Connect Request message and a Connect Acknowledge message.

Alternatively, Data transfer is an unconfirmed service. A sending node issues a T_DATA REQUEST that results in a T_DATA INDICATION on the receiver. However, the receiver does not issue an explicit confirmation.   The system completes the entire event with the Request and Indication primitives.

3.7   Data Integrity

A network family model must have mechanisms to ensure that the system correctly sends data from one node to the other. Support for end-to-end data integrity has two aspects: error detection and error recovery.

3.7.1   Error Detection

A common error detection technique involves using a checksum. A checksum is a special field in a data packet. The sending node calculates the value of this field and records the data in the data packet at a well-known position.

The calculation involves adding each of the bytes of data together producing a modulus value. The result is a sum or checksum of the numeric values of the data bytes. The receiving node, on receipt of the data packet, performs the same calculation that the sending node performed. The result of the calculation must be the same as the checksum value in the packet.

> **Example:** Suppose the well-known position for the checksum is the end of a data packet. The first part of the packet is the data, the second part of the packet is the checksum. The sender performs the calculation on the data portion of the packet and places the result of the calculation into the checksum portion of the packet.
>
> The system sends both the data portion and the checksum portion as a single message to the receiving node. The receiving node, on receipt of the packet, performs the calculation on the data portion of the packet. If the result of the calculation is different than the value in the checksum portion of the packet, the receiver has detected a checksum error.

A checksum error means that the message was not sent properly. Perhaps a glitch occurred during transmission of the packet. A *glitch* is a short burst of electronic noise (e.g., noise from nearby electric motors or turbines).

A healthy network occasionally produces a checksum error: a single error does not mean network failure. A checksum error also could mean that the cable between the nodes is deteriorating. A checksum error also could mean that the system contains a failure in support hardware (i.e., a tap, splitter, or connector).

A close relative to the checksum is the Cyclical Redundancy Check (CRC). The difference is the calculation algorithm. A checksum is a simple addition algorithm, while a CRC is a polynomial algorithm. The polynomial algorithm is superior, because the result of the calculation is more likely to produce a non-ambiguous value. The tradeoff is that a CRC requires more processing time to produce than a checksum. A possible failing network or a nearby interference can cause a CRC error.

Checksums and CRC checks are one level of data integrity checking. A different level of data integrity checking is called *sequencing*. Checksum and CRC checks can detect an error within a packet, but cannot detect that an entire packet has been lost. Sequencing is a technique to ensure that an entire packet has not been lost.

If the system uses sequencing, each packet sent has a sequence value in a well-known position. The sender places the sequence number into the well-known position. The receiver tracks the sequence numbers for each packet received. If a packet comes in out-of-sequence then a packet is lost or some other error condition occurred. For example, if the receiver received packets with sequence numbers of 1, 2, and 4, packet number 3 is missing. The industry says that the network lost or dropped packet-3.

Some network models allow packets to be sent out of order. Such models provide for such packets to be properly re-ordered at the receiving node. In this case, an out-of-sequence packet would not be an error.

Another error detection mechanism is associated with heartbeats. As previously discussed, two OSI stacks periodically send short heartbeat messages to each other. In the OSI model, these heartbeats occur at the Transport layer. The term for a heartbeat at the Transport layer is *Acknowledgement* or ACK.

Example: Figure 3-6 shows an example exchange of Protocol Data Units (PDUs) between two Transport layers. After establishing the connection, data can be transferred in both directions.

The system exchanges ACKs between data transfers so that both sides know the other is still alive. If the period between ACKs exceeds a certain time limit, the Transport layer assumes the network has failed.

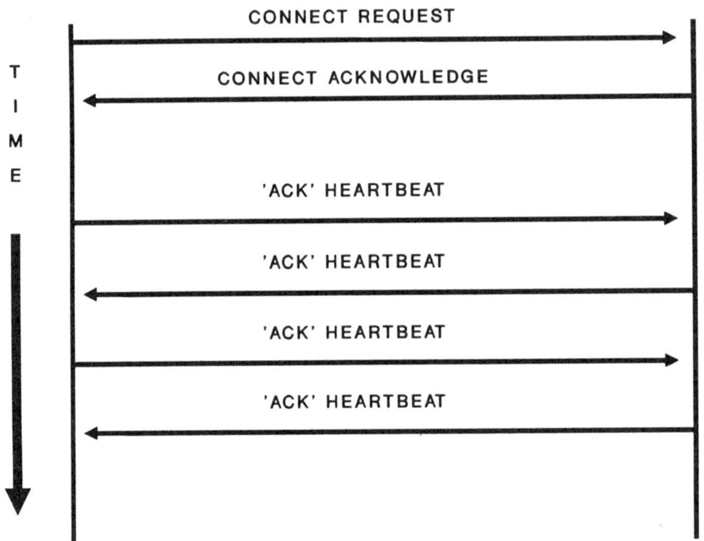

Figure 3-6: Transport Layer Heartbeats

3.7.2   Error Recovery

Ensuring data integrity is more than error detection: error recovery also is part of ensuring data integrity.   One error recovery mechanism is called *retransmission*. If the receiver detects a checksum or CRC error, the receiver can request that the sender retransmit the corrupt packet. Retransmission also is used to correct an out-of-sequence error. If a receiving node detects that the network dropped a packet, the receiver can request that the sender retransmit the missing packet.

The system uses a similar mechanism to re-establish a connection that the system aborted due to failure to detect heartbeats. If a Transport layer aborts a connection, because the acknowledgements have not been received, the Transport layer user (Session layer) can elect to attempt to re-establish the Transport connection.

The system design hides these data integrity mechanisms from the Application Processes. This means that checksum errors, CRC errors, out-of-sequence errors, and timeouts are not visible to the Application Processes. The stack can handle error detection and error recovery without intervention from the Application Processes. If the errors are unrecoverable (e.g., severed cable between nodes), error recovery is not possible. In this case, the system informs the Application Processes that problems have occurred.

If recoverable errors occur, the Application Processes continues to function, but network performance degrades, because of the overhead associated with error recovery. This performance degradation occurs, because it takes time to retransmit a packet or to re-establish a connection. This means that a network could be quite unhealthy and the Application Processes would continue to run, but would run slower.

If a worn network component (i.e., a connector) was causing a growing number of checksum errors, the Application Processes would not detect this condition. Such a condition can be detected though Network Management mechanisms. Network Management Processes are special Application layer processes that monitor network errors. A Network Management Process can be configured to alert an operator if network errors exceed some pre-defined limit.

3.8   Protocol and Service Data Units

Peer layers communicate with one another by exchanging Protocol Data Units (PDUs). A PDU is a single interaction between one layer on one stack and another layer on another stack. The Application layer of STACK-D sends PDUs to the Application layer of STACK-D. Such a PDU is called an *Application PDU* (A-PDU). Presentation layers exchange Presentation PDUs or P-PDUs.

A PDU comprises two parts: Protocol Control Information (PCI) and (possibly) user information (Figure 3-7). PCI exchanges between two layers for the purpose of executing the communication protocol. User information is the actual data being transferred between the two peer users of the layers. The system sends some PDUs without user data (perhaps to perform sequencing functions). However, all PDUs contain PCI.

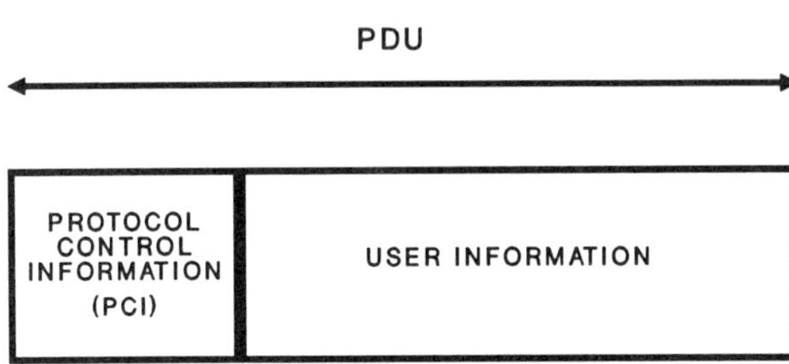

Figure 3-7: PDU Format

Example: DIAL, as an Application Process, wants to send a memo for printing to ANSWER. The memo represents user data. DIAL informs STACK-D that it wants to open a communication session with ANSWER.

The Application layer of STACK-D starts the Connection Establishment phase by building an A-ASSOCIATE PDU. This A-ASSOCIATE PDU contains PCI and does not contain any user data. The PCI contains information that the local Application layer needs to communicate to the remote Application layer to establish a connection.

The Application layer of STACK-D gives the A-ASSOCIATE PDU to the Presentation layer. The Presentation layer does not look at the information within the A-ASSOCIATE PDU. Instead, the Presentation layer treats the A-ASSOCIATE PDU as user data.

The Presentation layer builds a Connect Presentation PDU with PCI intended for the remote Presentation layer. Note that the Connect Presentation PDU serves a similar function that the A-ASSOCIATE PDU serves. The system uses both primitives to establish a connection with their peer layer. However, each layer uses a different naming convention for similar functions.

Conceptually, both layers send a connect request. The Presentation layer also adds the user data (A-ASSOCIATE PDU) to the Connect Presentation PDU. The Presentation layer delivers Presentation PCI and user data to the Session layer as a complete Connect Presentation PDU.

The Session layer behaves like the Presentation layer. The Session layer treats the Connect Presentation PDU as user data. The system constructs a Session Connect PDU. The Session layers builds Session PCI and adds the Connect Presentation PDU to form a complete PDU. This process continues as each lower layer of the stack receives a PDU from its service user. Each layer, in turn, adds PCI to the PDU that the next higher layer received, forming a new PDU. Finally, the Physical layer puts the packet onto the wire.

When the remote stack receives the packet, the whole process repeats in reverse order. Each layer strips out their PCI and delivers the user data to the next higher layer. Finally, the remote Application layer receives the original PDU, the A-ASSOCIATE PDU that the initiating Application layer constructed.

The OSI model describes the relationship between a service provider and a service user as the (N-1) relationship. A service user is layer (N) and the service provider is the next lower layer: layer (N-1). An (N) layer delivers PDUs to the (N-1) layer. Figure 3-8 shows that the (N-1) layer treats the (N) PDU as user data. The (N-1) layer refers to this user data as a Service Data Unit as shown in Figure 3-9. The (N-1) layer adds PCI to the (N-1) SDU to form an (N-1) PDU.

3.9   Segmentation and Concatenation

The concepts of Segmentation and Concatenation are important to the OSI and other network family models. These terms describe special relationships between SDUs and PDUs. Segmentation and Concatenation can be described in concise terms using the concept of (N) and (N-1) entities.

Segmentation is the function that an (N) entity performs to transmit an (N) SDU using two or more (N) PDUs (Figure 3-10). Concatenation is the function that an (N) entity performs to put more than one (N) PDU into one (N-1) SDU (Figure 3-11).

All messages sent between one peer layer and the other peer layer are (N) PDUs. However, an (N) PDU can contain only a portion of an (N) SDU, in which case a subsequent (N) PDU would contain the next portion of the (N) SDU. This is called *Segmentation.*

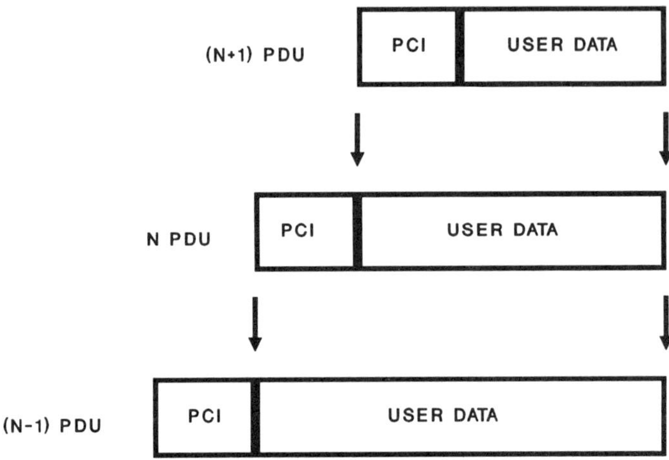

Figure 3-8: PDU becomes User Data for Layer N-1

The system sends a segment of the entire (N) SDU one piece at a time, each piece contained within an (N) PDU. The system requires segmentation when a complete message is too large to fit within a single (N) PDU.

Example: If the Datalink technology between two nodes is IEEE 802.3 (similar to Ethernet) then the maximum Datalink PDU size is 1514 bytes (at the Datalink layer, the industry calls PDUs: *packets*). Fourteen of those 1514 bytes are PCI, that leaves 1500 bytes available for the SDU. If the Datalink user (the Network layer) wanted to send a message (PCI and user data) whose combined total was larger than 1500 bytes then the Network layer must segment the message into several Network PDUs.

The other remote Network layer must combine the user data within the Network PDUs back into a single Network SDU. This process is called *reassembly*. Reassembly is the inverse of segmentation.

Concatenation, on the other hand, means that a single (N-1) SDU contains more than one (N) PDU. If the Network layer wanted to send several small

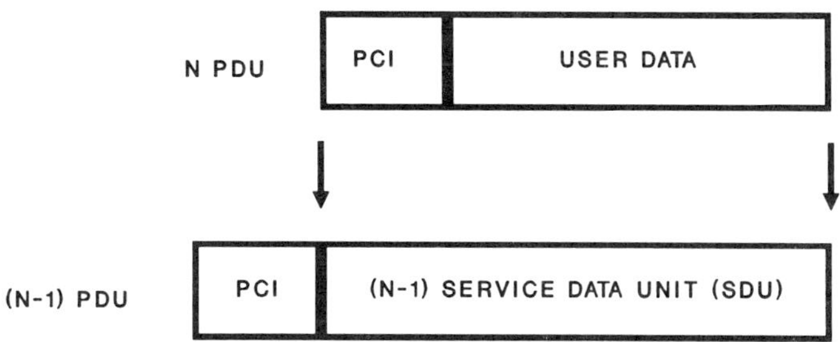

Figure 3-9: Layer N PDU becomes Layer N-1 SDU

messages then the Network layer could combine the messages and deliver them to the Datalink layer as a single message. The Datalink layer treats the combined messages as a single SDU (in the example of an 802.3 Datalink the total length of the Datalink SDU must be 1500 bytes or less.) Such combining of (N) PDUs within a single (N-1) SDU is called *concatenation*.

The other remote Network layer must divide the data in the (N-1) SDU back into several (N) PDUs. This process is called *separation*. Separation is the inverse of concatenation.

3.10 Flow Control

Network family models must address Flow Control. Flow control is a mechanism(s) to prevent one node from sending data quicker than the other node can receive it. Flow control also ensures that a service user does not issue service requests faster than the service provider can handle. The OSI model addresses both flow control situations.

3.10.1 Flow Control between Two Peers

The first situation is an issue between two network peers. For example, consider a network with two nodes. One node is a mainframe and the other node is a personal computer.

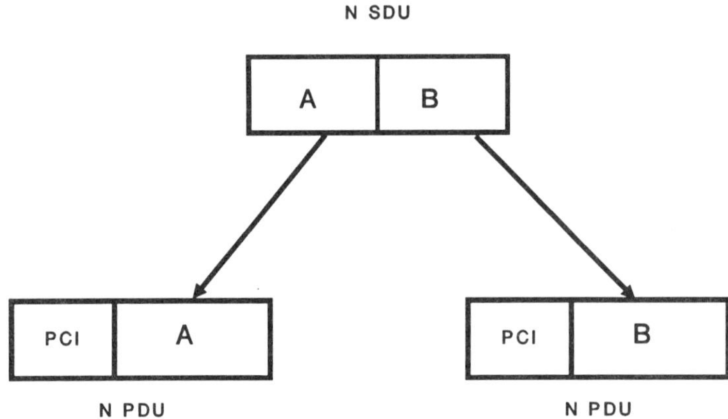

Figure 3-10: Segmentation

If the mainframe was allowed to send data as quickly as possible, the personal computer would not be able to keep up with it. The personal computer may try to store or queue up the incoming data, but eventually the mainframe computer would overrun the personal computer.

When the personal computer ran out of memory, it would not be able to continue to queue up any more incoming data. In this case, data may be lost, because the personal computer had no place to store it.

A Flow Control mechanism to prevent the previous situation is a peer-to-peer mechanism. Protocol conventions implement such mechanisms. The OSI Transport model, for example, has a Flow Control protocol convention called Credit Windowing. The system allows the sending Transport layer to send data to a peer Transport layer only if the sending Transport layer has enough credits.

A credit is permission to send a given amount of data. A receiving Transport layer issues credits to a sending Transport layer using well-defined protocol mechanisms. If the receiving Transport layer is not able to keep up with a sending Transport layer, the receiving Transport simply stops issuing credits. The sending Transport must wait until the receiving Transport layer sent more credits. This method of slowing down a sender often is called *throttling*.

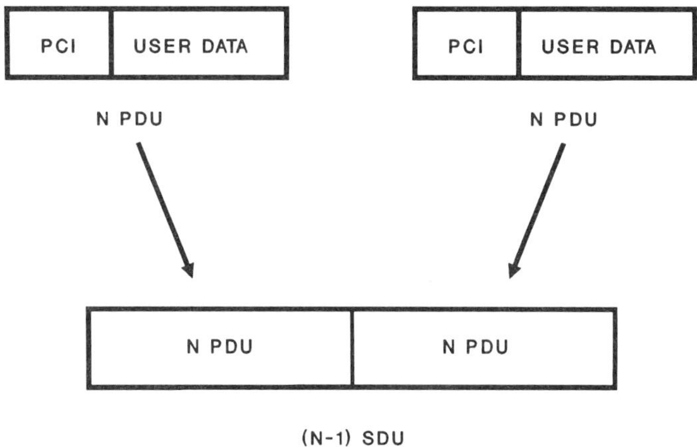

Figure 3-11: Concatenation

3.10.2 Flow Control between Service User/Provider

The other Flow Control mechanism that the OSI model mentions, regards the service user/provider relationship. If an Application Process was allowed to send an unlimited number of requests to a stack, the stack could incur an overrun condition. For example, if an Application Process started making requests for the stack to send large packets and the stack was not able to transmit the large packets quicker than the amount of time the Application Process required to issue another send, eventually the stack may run out of memory.

The OSI model does not define explicitly the mechanisms to handle the previously-mentioned situation. However, the OSI model does mention such mechanisms. The OSI model calls such a mechanism an implementation issue, which means that the implementor must construct the solution. Implementation issues also are called *local issues*. Local issues are outside of the scope of the standards, which technically means that any solution the implementor develops is conformant, even if the solution does not function well. The standards provide a description of the intent of the local issues, but do not define exactly how to implement the functions. The way one vendor implements a local issue can be a differentiator between another vendor's product.

3.11   In Summary

Communication is a complex process. Network product vendors and standards organizations developed abstract models that define communication between computing devices. The OSI model is an important model to enterprise network implementations. Designers based the OSI model and other data communication models on layered architectures. These models address several general data communication concepts. The industry defines a communication model in terms of services and protocols. Most abstract models define connection orientation. The OSI model defines confirmed and unconfirmed events. A network family model must provide mechanisms to ensure data integrity, which involves error detection and recovery. The industry defines data units in terms of PCI and user data (SDU). A PDU contains PCI and optionally contains SDU. Finally, the OSI model addresses segmentation, concatenation, and flow control.

Chapter 4

Network Families

4.1 Overview

A network family has aspects related to architecture and functionality. The architectural aspect of a network family defines how each individual component contributes to the entire communication process. Some products allow application processes to communicate with other application processes. Other components support routing and relaying and some products provide lower-layer bridging functions to interconnect subnetworks with different technologies.

Different network families provide different kinds and levels of functionality. Most network families define some kind of file transfer and real-time communication capability. However, the interfaces to these functions vary considerably from one network family to the next. Some network families, such as CCITT X.25, are solely a data transport on which you or a product vendor must add value. Other families describe high-level functions with an assortment of available interfaces.

4.2 OSI Profiles—MAP, TOP, and GOSIP

These three profiles have much in common. All three represent a statement by network users. Network users have joined to influence network product vendors to produce standards-based products. The rationale is to simplify the task of making products from various computer vendors interwork with one another.

The factory automation industry drives MAP. The technical and office computer users drive TOP. The United States government endorses GOSIP. However, network users within all three industries have the hope that some day all three profiles will be completely compatible. Industry participants desire a single, unified profile. The goal of these participants is to achieve enterprise connectivity. If these three profiles merge into one, the enterprise connectivity movement strengthens. One large profile receives more attention and support than three separate profiles.

MAP, TOP, and GOSIP have very similar architectures. All three profiles describe nodes with OSI stacks. They each have a root document that defines a profile. These profiles reference ISO standards documentation and implementors' agreements. In part, a profile is a subset of a larger data communication model. Profiles are useful, because base standards, such as ISO, are too broad and abstract on which to base products.

These profiles also reference implementors' agreements. Implementors' agreements address specific technical options that are beyond the scope of profile and standards documentation. When you study documentation for one of these profiles, you start with the root profile document. The next step is to read the ISO standards documents to which the root document refers. Finally, you read the implementors' agreements that the root document specifies.

To understand a technical detail about a profile, it is necessary to understand what the root document, the ISO base standards documents, and the implementors' agreements state about that detail. MAP, TOP, and GOSIP reference the National Institute of Standards and Technology (NIST) OSI Implementors' Workshop (OIW) agreements.

The OSI profile root documents describe two basic kinds of nodes: end systems and intermediate systems. An end system is a node where an application process resides. End systems are the nodes that perform information processing. An intermediate system is a router. A router acts as a relay. So, an intermediate system does not interface to an application process. Instead, you use a router to expand or logically divide an existing network.

A router physically isolates one subnetwork from another, which prevents network mishaps from collapsing the entire network. Routers also interconnect networks with different datalink and physical aspects. Routers are tools you use to provide security to selected nodes and to make large networks more manageable.

It is possible for a node to be both an end system and an intermediate system. Such a node provides an application process interface and also behaves as a router. Another example of a combination end system/intermediate system is a router with an application interface that provides access to network management functions. In this case, the router is capable of communicating with other routers for the purpose of gathering network-wide statistics or solving network-wide problems.

The OSI profiles define several options at the various layers of the stack. For example, the root profile documents describe a variety of physical medias. Each profile also specifies several application layer configurations, called Application Service Entities (ASE).

This allowance for options means that you construct a MAP-, TOP-, or GOSIP-compliant node using building blocks. You select a block for the Application layer, Physical layer, and other layers to form a complete seven-layer node. A compliant node interworks with another similarly constructed node. A compliant node does not interwork with another compliant node comprised of different building blocks.

The profiles allow such options, because of the variety of network requirements in our enterprises. Enterprises require small LANs, as well as large WANs. Enterprises also require a variety of application layer functions. It is necessary to provide options even though such options mean that one compliant node does not necessarily interwork with another compliant node.

It would be convenient to have a profile that defines products that interwork with any other compliant product. You would not have to understand the various options available—any MAP-compliant product interworks with any other MAP-compliant product. However, this hypothetical profile describes a product appropriate for some applications, but unsatisfactory for other applications.

4.3   OSI Model Layers

Each layer of the OSI model has a general set of functions. Together these functions address the basic data communication concepts. Before you examine the building blocks of the OSI profiles, you must explore the layers of the OSI model in more detail.

- Application Layer
- Presentation Layer
- Session Layer
- Transport Layer
- Network Layer
- Datalink Layer
- Physical Layer

4.3.1 Application Layer

The purpose of the Application Layer is to provide an interface into a
network. Because the Application Layer provides services to application
processes, there is no higher layer. In a classic OSI network, the Application
Layer is the only layer to provide directly services to application processes.
(Some real-life implementations allow application processes to interface to lower
layers, and bypass the Application Layer.)

One way an Application Layer provides services to an application process is
via an Application Programming Interface (API). Some products provide an
externalized API for you. Other network products provide an operator or batch
interface written on top of an internal API. Some products offer both an external
API and an operator or batch interface.

A configuration of a particular Application Layer contains one or more
Application Service Elements (ASE). Each ASE performs a specific task, such as
association (connection) control, file transfer, or electronic messaging. When an
Application Layer contains more than one ASE, they work together to perform
a function for an application process and conceptually, each ASE appears to be
a sub-layer.

4.3.2 Presentation Layer

The purpose of the Presentation Layer is to provide services to the
Application Layer. Specifically, the Presentation Layer is responsible for
negotiating the representation of data. After negotiation of data representation
completes, the Presentation Layer executes translation to and from the agreed on
format and the format understood by the local application entity.

When we discuss representation of data, we reference two categories of
syntax: Transfer Syntax and Abstract Syntax. Transfer syntax refers to the
encoding techniques used to pass information.

Example: If two people agree to communicate using spoken words,
including single syllable and double syllable words, then they agree to a
transfer syntax. Note that the transfer syntax does not define the meaning
of the words. Only the two people conversing know what the words

represent. If you take this example a step further and say that the two people agree to hold a conversation that progresses with alternating single syllable and double syllable words, and that the single syllable words represent file name and the double syllable words represent file data, then they agree to an abstract syntax. Again, knowledge of the abstract syntax does not imply knowledge of the content of the words.

You can implement a given abstract syntax using any one of a variety of transfer syntaxes. Knowledge of the transfer syntax does not imply knowledge of the abstract syntax. Two peer Presentation Layers negotiate use of a particular transfer syntax. If the chosen transfer syntax represents a format different than that the local application entity understands then a transformation function occurs. This transformation can be part of the Presentation Layer or be a separate operating system service accessible by the application entities.

In the previous example, the two people conversing represent two Application Layers. The Application Layers know the meaning of the data; the two Presentation Layers do not. However, the Presentation Layers know the names of the abstract syntaxes they negotiate.

Two peer Presentation Layers negotiate abstract and transfer syntax. The Application Layer specifies to the Presentation Layer the name of the abstract syntaxes it requires. For example, if the Application Layer initiates a file transfer, it gives the name of a file transfer abstract syntax to the Presentation Layer. The Presentation Layer negotiates use of this abstract syntax with the other Presentation Layer. Neither Presentation Layer knows the meaning of the abstract syntax, they simply perform the mechanics of negotiation on behalf of their respective Application Layers.

Presentation Layers also negotiate one or more transfer syntaxes for use with each abstract syntax. The initiating Presentation Layer proposes a file transfer abstract syntax and suggests one, two, or more transfer syntaxes. If the other Presentation Layer can support the abstract syntax along side any of the suggested transfer syntaxes then it chooses one transfer syntax and informs the initiating Presentation Layer of its choice. Data exchange occurs when two peer Presentation Layers agree on an abstract syntax and an associated transfer syntax.

The Presentation Layer also offers an application entity the same set of functions the Session Layer provides. Presentation offers these services as a pass-through function. This means that the Presentation Layer makes certain services available to the Application Layer that the Session Layer performs.

4.3.3   Session Layer

The purpose of the Session Layer is to provide direct services to the Presentation Layer and indirect services to the Application Layer. The key function of the Session Layer is dialogue management. Dialogue management includes the functions of synchronization and interaction management.

The synchronization function allows a sending Session Layer to group information into logical portions. Markers called synchronization points, or *sync points*, separate logical portions of data. If for some reason, the underlying network fails, the Session Layers can re-establish the connection later and continue the data transfer at some pre-established sync point.

A Session Layer connection has two levels of synchronization called *major synchronization* and *minor synchronization*. The Session Layer records minor sync points and reports them to the Session Layer user (such as the higher layer) in the form of a serial number. A Session Layer user can remember a serial number and request that data transfer resume at some prior sync point. A minor sync point serves as a marker, but the Session Layer must report only the serial number of the sync point to the Session Layer user.

Major sync points are similar to minor sync points with one important difference, a Session Layer that sends a major sync must wait for a confirmation from the peer Session Layer before sending any more data.

Interaction management describes certain rules for data exchange. These rules describe a token. When a Session Layer sends data to the other Session layer, it first acquires the token. This concept is similar to the talking stick children use at a campfire. One child may speak while in possession of the talking stick. When the speaking child passes the stick to the next child, the right to speak belongs to the next child.

The management of the token depends on the mode of interaction in place. The mode of interaction can be Two-Way-Simultaneous (TWS) or Two-Way-Alternate (TWA). TWS means that either Session Layer can send data at any time. TWA means that only one Session Layer at a time has the token that represents the right to send data.

Two Session Layers negotiate a mode of interaction during the connection establishment phase. The Session Layer is the lowest layer in the OSI model that has the concept of graceful connection close.

A Session Layer engaged in a connection with a peer Session Layer can close the connection using a release, which guarantees no loss of data during the connection close. Alternatively, a Session Layer can close a connection using an abort, which means immediate close. Closing a connection using the abort procedure can result in data loss.

The Session Layer, like the Presentation Layer, also offers an application entity some of the same functionality the lower layer provides. Again, this functionality occurs as a pass-through function.

4.3.4 Transport Layer

The purpose of the Transport Layer is to provide services to the Session Layer. The Transport Layer provides also a service called *expedited data transfer*, which the upper-layers pass through to an application entity.

The primary responsibility of the Transport Layer is to ensure reliable transfer of data between two nodes. The Transport Layer ensures data integrity using mechanisms that are invisible to the upper layers. The Transport protocols define ways to recover from lost or out-of-sequence packets. The upper-layers do not participate in the error recovery procedures.

If two peer Transport Layers cannot recover from an error then they inform the upper-layers. This could happen if the physical connection between two nodes becomes severed.

The Transport Layer provides two kinds of flow control. Peer-to-peer flow control ensures that a sending Transport Layer does not overrun a slower receiving Transport Layer. The other kind of flow control performed by a Transport Layer ensures that a Transport user (such as the Session Layer) does not overrun the capabilities of the local Transport Layer. There are no well-defined mechanisms for the latter form of flow control. An implementation provides user/provider flow control in any matter.

There are two categories of data transfer between two Transport Layers: normal data transfer and expedited data transfer. Normal data transfer allows exchange of both large and small messages. Expedited data transfer allows limited exchange of high-priority data.

Normal data transfer dictates that a Transport Layer sends messages in the same order they receive them from the Transport user. An expedited message bypasses this rule and is sent ahead of turn. You use expedited data transfer to send short, urgent messages. An example use is to report an urgent incoming message from corporate headquarters.

A Transport Layer user can use multiple Transport connections at the same time to accomplish a single task. A Transport Layer can use more than one Network Layer connection during a single Transport Connection. This function, called *multiplexing*, occurs without the upper-layer's involvement.

The Transport Layer does not have the concept of graceful close of a connection. The only way for a Transport Layer to close a connection is to send a T-DISCONNECT REQUEST. Any data transfer in progress can be lost by the receiving Transport Layer.

There are five distinct classes of Transport protocol labeled Class-0, Class-1, Class-2, Class-3, and Class-4. Class-0 Transport, the most basic class, performs the most simple functions. Each next higher class provides increasing sophistication with Class-4 being the most sophisticated. Class-4 tends to be the most popular form of Transport in the United States, while Class-0 and Class-2 are popular in Europe.

4.3.5   Network Layer

The purpose of the Network Layer is to provide services to the Transport Layer. The primary function the Network Layer performs is to route and relay messages between peer end systems. The Network Layer provides a way for Transport Layer PDUs to cross subnetwork boundaries. A subnetwork can be a LAN or a remote attachment such as X.25.

These route and relay functions are transparent to the Transport Layer. This means that two peer Transport Layers communicate with each other the same way whether they connect directly by wire a few feet apart or by miles of cable with several relay nodes between them.

There can be several paths between two nodes. The Network Layer is responsible for selecting the best path to use when more than one path is available. The Network Layer can consider several things when choosing the best path:

- Connection Priority
- Path Expense
- Path Performance

Some connections have higher priority than others.

Example: A connection between mainframe computers is more vital to an organization than the connection between two rarely used personal computers. So, the Network Layer chooses a relatively expensive, higher performance route for the mainframe connection.

4.3.6   Datalink Layer

The purpose of the Datalink Layer is to provide services to the Network Layer. Datalink Layer functions include packet construction, sequencing, error notification (and possibly error recovery), and flow control.

The Datalink Layer hides the nature of the underlying Physical Layer from the higher layers. This means that a Network Layer behaves the same regardless of the physical medium, whether it is baseband wire, broadband wire, or fiber optic cable. Because datalink and physical technologies cover a wide spectrum, the complexity and inner mechanisms of the Datalink Layer vary considerably.

It is the responsibility of the Datalink Layer to construct properly packets. This involves framing and ordering of bits in preparation to go on the wire. For example, some Datalinks represent an eight-bit byte with bit zero as the most significant bit and bit seven as the least significant bit. For other Datalinks the inverse is true.

Some Datalink technologies require sequencing of control information and data. Again, such activities are transparent to the higher layers. Some datalink technologies have built-in recovery mechanisms. If an unrecoverable error occurs the Datalink Layer informs the Network Layer.

Different datalink technologies have different data transfer performance capabilities. Such capabilities include packet size and transfer speed or throughput. The Datalink Layer must perform flow control between the Network Layer and the physical network.

4.3.7 Physical Layer

The Purpose of the Physical Layer is to provide services to the Datalink Layer. The function performed by the Physical Layer is to maintain a bit stream between two nodes.

Maintenance of a bit stream means keeping the physical connection intact. This duty is electrically passive or active. A passive physical connection means that the wire does not amplify or modify the signal a node generates. An active connection, such as broadband, means that signals modify after a node sends them. A broadband network has a device attached to the cable called a *headend demodulator*. The headend amplifies signals that nodes send. This gives the physical medium an active role in the electronic transmission of signals.

A Physical Layer PDU consists of a single bit if the transmission technology is serial or a group of bits if the transmission technology is parallel. A physical connection can allow full-duplex or half-duplex transmission of Physical Layer PDUs. Full-duplex means that two peer nodes can both send and receive signals at the same time. Half-duplex means that only one peer node can send at a time.

In real world implementations, the boundary between the Datalink and Physical layers is weak. It is difficult to point and say where the Datalink Layer ends and the Physical Layer begins. The functions performed by the Datalink and Physical Layers are usually built into the same hardware components.

4.4   OSI Profile End System Specifications

The MAP, TOP, and GOSIP root documents describe options at each layer of the OSI model. All three profiles are evolving. Each root document continues to grow as committees add more options.

4.4.1   Upper-Layer Options

The upper-layers include the Application, Presentation, and Session Layers. To start, there are no options available at the Presentation and Session Layers. All three profiles point to *Iso 8326* (Session Service) and *Iso 8327* (Session Protocol) for the Session Layer. For the Presentation Layer, *Iso 8822* (Presentation Service) and *Iso 8823* (Presentation Protocol) apply. The options at the Application Layer are numerous (Figure 4-1).

4.4.1.1 Association Control Service Element (ACSE)

ACSE represents functionality useful to other Application Layer components. The OSI profiles point to *Iso 8650*, Service Definition for ACSE and ISO 8649, Protocol Specification for ACSE. The primary function of ACSE is to establish and terminate Application Layer connections called *associations*. Part of this function involves exchange of application context identifiers. An application context identifier describes the complete nature of an application entity. For example, an Application Layer can contain a file transfer component such as File Transfer, Access and Management (FTAM) and contain also ACSE.

During the association establishment procedure, the initiating ACSE informs the responding ACSE partner of this composition. This way the partner Application Layer knows what protocol syntax it must support if it decides to accept the association.

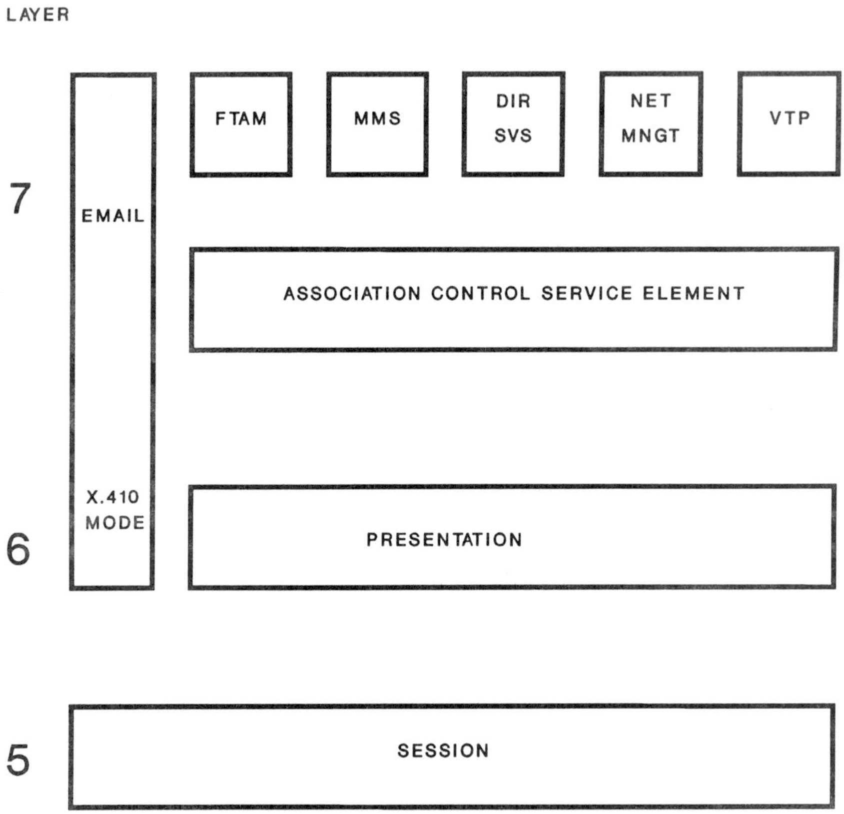

LAYER

7

EMAIL

| FTAM | MMS | DIR SVS | NET MNGT | VTP |

ASSOCIATION CONTROL SERVICE ELEMENT

X.410 MODE

6

PRESENTATION

5

SESSION

Figure 4-1: Osi Upper Layers

4.4.1.2 File Transfer, Access and Management (FTAM)

File transfer is a function useful to many enterprise LAN environments. The ability to move files from one computer to another computer made by a different vendor gives you the ability to exchange memos, print documents, and download manufacturing information from a CAD/CAM/CAE station.

Iso File Transfer, Access and Management (FTAM) describes two roles in the file transfer process: one node is an initiator and the other is the responder. The initiator is responsible for giving file handling instructions to the responder. All file actions occur at the request of the initiator and the responder executes the file actions. This is analogous to the client/server model; an FTAM initiator is a client to an FTAM responder or server.

It is possible for an FTAM node to function both as an initiator and a responder. However, for any one FTAM session, one node is an initiator and the peer node is a responder.

The ISO FTAM concept of the virtual filestore addresses several complex issues regarding file transfer between computers from different vendors. Different vendors' computers handle files in different ways. For example, some personal computers have file naming rules that state that a file name is 1-8 characters long with one period and a 1-3 character extension. Some mini-computers have very different file naming rules. For example, some mini computers allow file names to be 32 characters long with a 1-9 character extension.

The problem arises in the case where the mini-computer, as the FTAM initiator, sends a file to a personal computer that acts as the responder. If the mini-computer sends a request that specifies a 32-character file name, what does the personal computer do with that file name? The personal computer only allows 8-character file names. ISO defined the virtual filestore to describe how FTAM nodes from various vendors handle this naming difference and other file related differences.

FTAM makes the distinction between a real filestore (system) and a virtual filestore. In the earlier example, the mini-computer and the personal computer have their own real filestores. The personal computer filestore is maintained by one operating system and the mini-computer filestore is managed by a different operating system. These two real filestores are managed very differently. However, when the two machines participate in an FTAM session they agree to make their respective filestores appear to be compatible. They perform a mapping function that gives the appearance of a single, network-wide virtual filestore.

The virtual filestore is a model of a filestore that all FTAM nodes on a network must support. This imaginary file system is robust enough to perform as many as possible of the functions real filestores perform. The virtual filestore is a powerful mechanism capable of addressing the different ways computers manage files. For example, consider again the file naming problem. The mini-computer sends a file that has a 32-character file name. The mini computer must first ensure that this local file name adheres to the rules of the FTAM virtual filestore.

If the name does not adhere then the mini-computer must create a name that does conform. The mini computer does not have to change the name of the file in the local filestore. However, the mini computer must keep a table that the local FTAM user uses to translate the local file name to the name used during FTAM sessions. FTAM uses the virtual file name during FTAM sessions.

In this case, the 32-character file name is compatible with the virtual filestore rules, and the mini-computer does not perform mapping. The personal computer cannot store a file with a 32-character file name. So the personal computer FTAM must make an entry into a table that maps the 32-character virtual filename into a 1-8 character real filename for use in its local file system. To maintain consistency throughout the enterprise network, the personal computer must keep this table in case the mini computer (or some other FTAM initiator), at some later time, attempts to perform further actions on this file.

4.4.1.3 Electronic Mail—(X.400)

Electronic mail (EMAIL) is a useful function for inter- and intra-enterprise communication. Originally, EMAIL was used solely by people to send messages to one another. However, EMAIL is also useful for machines as well as persons.

The first EMAIL systems were little more than file transfer systems. However, implementors discovered drawbacks to using file transfer to send messages to each other. For example, a sender never knew if the recipient received the message. Also, if the destination computer was not active or not currently connected to the network, the message could not be delivered. Often implementors wanted to send copies of a memo to several people, which meant that you had to transfer the file several times, which seemed cumbersome.

Over time, EMAIL has evolved to address these and other issues. The CCITT X.400 recommendation describes an EMAIL architecture and protocols and is commonly used throughout the world. ISO has aligned with CCITT to enhance further X.400. This means that ISO and CCITT have agreed to produce a single standard (but they each use their own document numbering system). ISO and CCITT do this to avoid the situation where two standards organizations define separate international standards.

The X.400 standard describes three basic entities:

- User of the Service
- User Agent (UA)
- Message Transfer Agent (MTA).

Figure 4-2 shows the relationship between these entities. The user can be a person or a program. The UA is responsible for accepting input from the user and for delivering incoming messages to the user. Also, the UA interfaces to the MTA. One UA can service one or multiple users.

The MTA is responsible for sending mail to its destination node. This can require traversing several intermediate MTAs along the way. After the message reaches the destination MTA, the MTA gives the message to the destination UA and finally the destination user. An MTA has the capability to store a message it receives from another MTA. This way, if the destination user is not currently able to receive the message (perhaps the workstation is OFF) the MTA can save the message until the user is ready to receive.

X.400 can handle translation between different text and graphic formats. For example, an MTA can convert an ASCII message into an EBCDIC or even a voice message (using a voice synthesizer.)

4.4.1.4 Virtual Terminal

Virtual Terminal (VT) addresses the differences between terminals and consoles produced by computer vendors. Today's enterprises contain computer systems from IBM, DEC, Hewlett Packard, and others. The various computer systems often require terminals that are not compatible with other vendors' equipment. This means that you must have several computer terminals in your work areas; one for each of the host computers that you use.

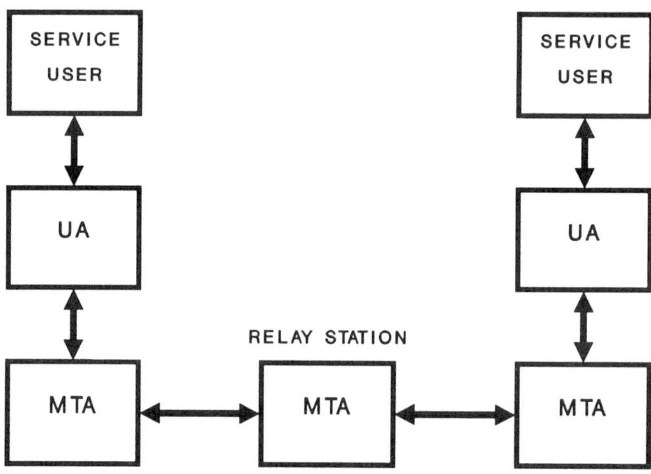

Figure 4-2: X.400 Architecture

For example, some terminals are character-oriented. This means that every character you enter is sent immediately to the host. Other computers require screen-oriented terminals. A screen-oriented terminal allows you to enter data on various parts of the screen. After you press Enter, the entire screen of data transfers to the host. A computer that requires a screen-oriented terminal does not work with a character-oriented terminal and vice-versa.

Other differences between terminals and consoles include escape sequences and other special characters. For example, one terminal type requires a carriage return and a line feed to bring the cursor to the beginning of the next line. Other terminals require only a carriage return character.

Virtual terminal defines an abstract, model terminal that functions similarly to the virtual filestore defined by FTAM. Vendors map the behavior of their proprietary terminal to the behavior of the virtual terminal. This way, a computer host from one vendor functions with a terminal from a different vendor. If the terminal is a dumb terminal, without an internal processor and memory, then the host performs the mapping function.

The virtual terminal standard makes it possible for workers to get rid of the various terminals in the work area and replace them with a single workstation, such as a personal computer. If the personal computer supports virtual terminal, you can use it to operate any host computer that also supports virtual terminal.

4.4.1.5 Directory Services—CcITT X.500

Directory Services serves as the telephone directory for a network. The directory serves an important purpose in today's complex enterprise networks—it gives you a tool to simplify finding information about a network object. A large network can have hundreds, even thousands of objects. Each object can have multiple information items important to other network objects. Directory services allow you to reference those objects with user-friendly names.

A network application must access several kinds of information, including the following:

- Network addresses of application programs
- Aliases or alternate names of application programs
- Postal addresses
- Telephone numbers
- Teletex addresses
- Organization identifiers

The directory services standard defines two roles: Directory User Agent (DUA) and Directory System Agent (DSA). The Directory Information Base (DIB) is a depot that stores information about directory objects.

One or more DSAs manage the DIB. DSAs are responsible for reading from and writing to the DIB. An application entity that uses information from the DIB serves as a DUA. A DUA makes a request to a DSA and the DSA performs the operation on the DIB.

The DIB, sometimes called the Directory, is not a general purpose database, although a general purpose database can serve as the Directory. Instead, the Directory stores information about well-defined objects—specifically objects that relate to network communications.

In a real network, the Directory can be distributed over several nodes. In this case, two or more DSAs cooperate to manage the distributed database (Figure 4-3). If a DUA makes a request to a DSA, that DSA is capable of asking for help from a second DSA if it cannot find the information in its own database. The first DSA can instead give a suggestion to the DUA in the form of a hint. If the first DSA does not have the information the DUA requires, it can suggest some other DSA.

4.4.1.6 Network Management

The purpose of network management is to make your networks more efficient and reliable. Network management also helps you to find and fix network problems. Finally, network management allows you to monitor network traffic for accounting, planning, and security purposes.

Network management describes three roles: network manager, manager application, and agent application. A manager application provides an interface to the network manager, such as a person.

A network manager is a separate entity than the network manager application. The network manager uses the services the manager application provides as a tool to perform certain tasks.

An network agent application collects and reports information to the manager application. Network management agent applications can exist on various nodes in the networks, including end systems and intermediate systems. In this case, the network manager application queries the network agent application. The total of the information the network manager application gathers is made available to the network manager.

The exact nature of the information gathered by network management and the exact procedures the network manager performs with this data, is still under study. IEEE has defined objects, such as number and kind of packets, that a network management system accumulates. Other objects to monitor include information about bad packets, such as CRC errors and underruns.

The term *network manager* implies a certain amount of network management expertise. The network manager application and the various network agent applications provide the tools for the network manager to perform highly

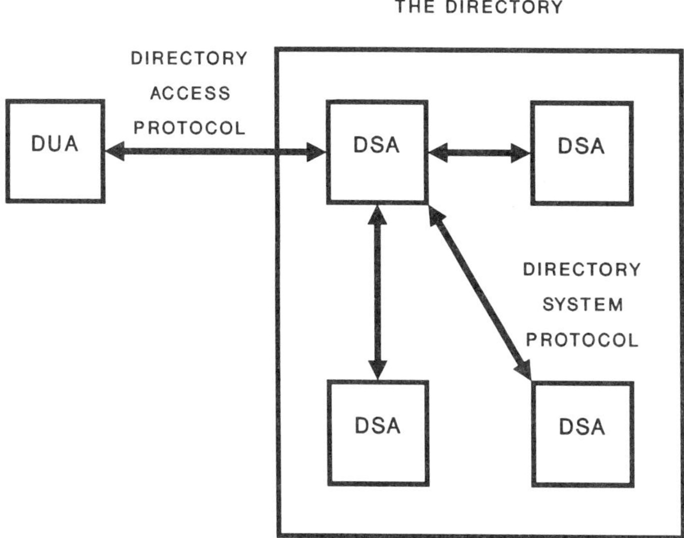

Figure 4-3: X.500 Directory Model

sophisticated functions. Today, a network manager is a person. However, in the future, you will use expert systems as tools to help you perform the duties of the network manager.

4.4.1.7 Manufacturing Message Specification (MMS)

This ASE describes a set of semantics to allow devices on the factory floor to communicate. *Iso 9506* Part 1 defines the MMS Service Definition, while *Iso 9506* Part 2 defines the Protocol Specification. This standard provides a way for you to define complex data structures, such as those required by robots and other motion control devices. You also can define complex events, such as process control tasks. Mechanisms define how to coordinate tasks and report status of events. You have a simple file transfer service available. MMS is particularity useful in automated factory environments.

4.4.2   Middle-Layer Options

Compared with the upper-layers, the middle-layers do not have as many options. For the Transport Layer, the OSI profiles point to *Iso 8072*, the Transport Service Specification and *Iso 8073*, the Transport Protocol Definition. As mentioned previously, the Transport Layer describes five different protocol classes numbered 0 through 4, so even though the OSI profiles only specify one set of standards there are options available within that set.

Two Transport Layers negotiate a particular protocol class during the connection establishment phase. For example, if a Transport Layer initiates a connection and specifies protocol Class-4, the responding Transport Layer can suggest Class-0 instead. If the initiating Transport Layer can support Class-0, it can accept the alternate class the responder suggests.

The actual protocol class two Transport Layers negotiate and subsequently agree on is transparent to the upper-layers. The differences in protocol classes apply to error recovery mechanisms and multiplexing functions and do not affect the services the Transport Layer performs.

The Network Layer is a bit more complicated, because a way had to be found to support WAN connectivity. X.25 is widely accepted as the best way to support wide area implementations. *Iso 8348*, the Network Service Definition and *Iso 8473*, the Protocol for Providing Connectionless-mode Network Service, are the choices for Local Area Network applications.

You use X.25 for long distance connections and ISO Network Layer for short, LAN connections. Industry calls this variation of the ISO Network Layer the Connectionless Network Layer Protocol (CLNP). X.25 describes a connection-oriented Network Layer, while CLNP is connectionless.

A connection-oriented Network Layer provides different services than a connectionless Network Layer. This creates a problem for the Transport Layer: the Transport Layer must know how to use both sets of services to accomplish its tasks or a mapping function must occur to make the connection-oriented X.25 appear to be a connectionless Network Layer.

The OSI Profiles decided to define a function called the Subnetwork Dependant Convergence Function (SNDCF) to make X.25 appear like CLNP, so the

Transport Layer does not need to know whether the underlying Network Layer is X.25 or CLNP.

4.4.3   Lower-Layer Options

Many options are available for the Datalink and Physical Layers for the same reason that many options are available for the upper layers—today's enterprise networks have a varied set of applications and environments. One datalink/ physical technology can suit certain environments, but may not suit other environments.

The boundary between the Datalink Layer and the Physical Layer is a subject for discussion (or argument) between network experts. Real-life implementations place both layers in a single hardware/mechanical package. However, the Datalink Layer has two sub-layers and the boundary between these sub-layers is clear. The upper sub-layer, Logical Link Control (LLC), is relatively simple in function and implementation. The Lower sub-layer, called Medium Access Control (MAC), is somewhat more complex.

The OSI Profiles reference IEEE standards for the LLC and MAC sub-layers as well as the Physical Layer. IEEE 802.2 defines the simple services and protocol LLC performs, regardless of the MAC sub-layer and underlying Physical Layer. The MAC sub-layer associates directly with the Physical Layer. It is useful to think of the MAC sub-layer as part of the Physical Layer.

The OSI profiles specify three MAC/Physical Layer configurations:

*   IEEE 802.3
*   IEEE 802.4
*   IEEE 802.5

IEEE 802.3 derives from the earlier Ethernet standard. 802.3 uses a technique called Carrier Sense, Multiple Access with Collision Detection (CSMA/CD) to manage network access. IEEE 802.4 and 802.5 use token-passing schemes to perform the same task. 802.4, also known as *token bus*, describes a logical ring through which a logical token circles. 802.5, or *token ring*, also describes a logical token, but also requires an actual physical ring (Figure 4-4).

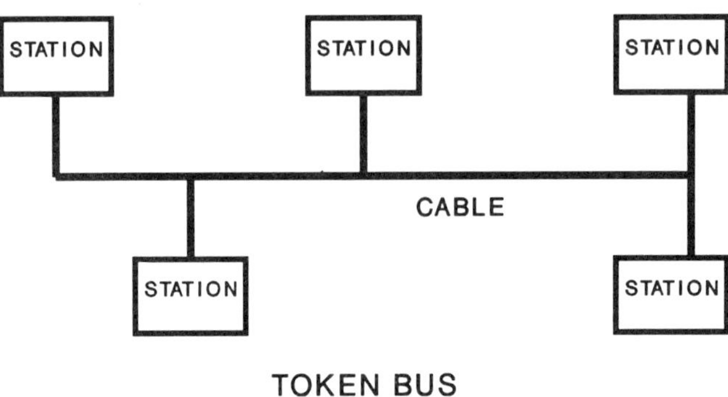

TOKEN BUS

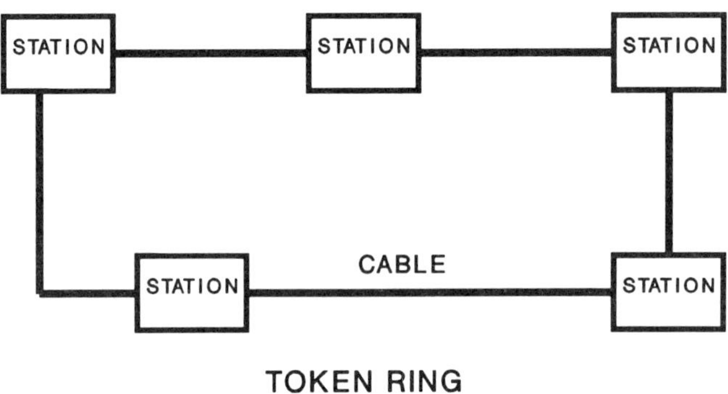

TOKEN RING

Figure 4-4: Token Topologies

A datalink/physical configuration consists of an IEEE 802.2 LLC sub-layer on top of an IEEE 802.3, 802.4, or 802.5 MAC/Physical Layer pair. X.25 describes different datalink/physical technologies that provide a point-to-point connection. Various cable choices exist for a MAP, TOP, or GOSIP node:

- Baseband
- Broadband
- Carrierband
- Twisted-Pair

You also can use fiber optic cable, but be careful because some product vendors implement separate fiber technologies that do not interwork with each other. Work is in progress to unify how the IEEE MAC/Physical pairs operate over fiber optic mediums.

4.5   OSI Profile Intermediate System Specifications

An intermediate system is a Network Layer relay or router. Such routers implement layers 1, 2, and 3 of the OSI model. Routers interconnect two or more subnetworks (Figure 4-5).   Routers can connect similar or dissimilar subnetworks. For example, a router can provide connection between an IEEE 802.3 subnetwork to an IEEE 802.4 subnetwork or a router can connect an IEEE 802.5 subnetwork to another IEEE 802.5 subnetwork. Routers also connect an X.25 WAN to a LAN. Such a router performs the SNDCF mapping function to hide the connection-oriented nature of X.25 from the end systems. MAP, TOP, and GOSIP also define other connecting devices called *repeaters*, *bridges*, and *gateways*. A repeater is a Physical Layer device. You can use a repeater only if the subnetworks it connects are identical. A bridge is a Datalink Layer device.

A bridge can connect two subnetworks with different Physical Layers. However, both subnetworks must have similar Datalink Layers. Both Datalink Layers must support the same packet size and addressing schemes. For example, you use a bridge to connect two 802.4 subnetworks, one that uses broadband cable and one that uses fiber optic medium.

A gateway (as the OSI Profiles define them) connects an OSI profile network to non-OSI profile network. As a seven-layer device, gateways are the most complex and expensive connecting device. You only use a gateway between two nodes that have entirely different stacks that otherwise do not interwork.

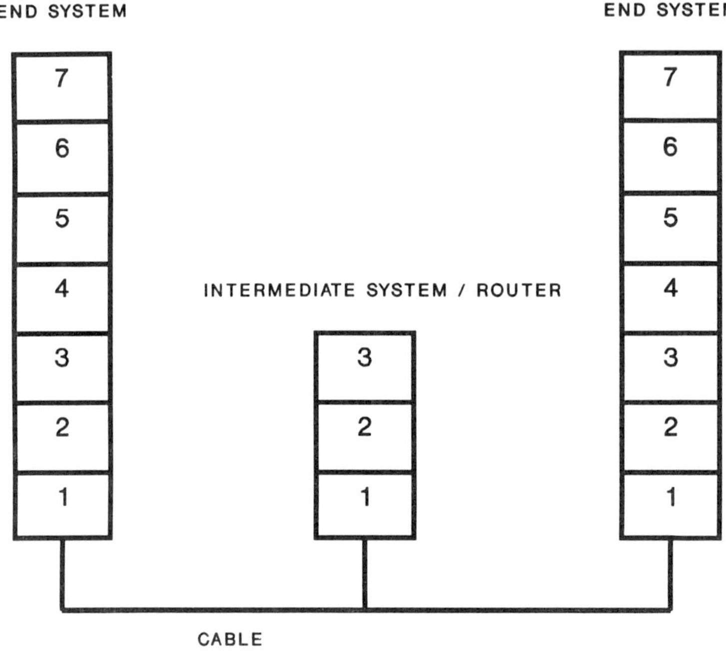

Figure 4-5: End System and Intermediate System

4.6   CCITT X.25

Our enterprises have requirements for local and wide area data communications. X.25 is an important WAN technology throughout the world. However, X.25 applies to more than remote communications.

The United States views largely X.25 as a WAN technology and views LANs as the norm for short distance connectivity. In Europe, people use X.25 for both local and wide area networks.

In Europe it is common to find two computers in the same building, within several feet of each other, connected via X.25 instead of via a LAN. In Europe,

X.25 is dominant and LAN technology is just growing. The opposite is true in the United States: LANs are common, but X.25 is growing.

CCITT first published recommendations for this layer 1, 2, and 3 protocol in 1976, and publishes updated recommendations every four years. The original purpose was to prevent different European countries from developing their own, incompatible network standards. Since then, organizations throughout the rest of the world have begun to implement X.25 networks.

X.25 often combines with other network product families. X.25 exists in SNA, TCP/IP, and OSI Profile based networks. Because X.25 is important to several network families, this section treats it as a family of its own. Other network families allow this useful technology, even though X.25 does not fit neatly into their architectures.

4.6.1   X.25 Function—Interface Specification

CCITT X.25 describes, in a detailed manner, how to access a network. In contrast to the OSI Profiles, X.25 describes data flow between nodes, but does not describe how to use data. For example, X.25 does not describe file transfer or electronic mail, although you commonly implement these functions on top of the core X.25 capability.

X.25 assumes that the network is a black box, managed and operated by a public or private carrier, such as AT&T or a national government. A carrier network uses very similar technology that telephone networks use. Most telephone companies and long distance service companies also offer X.25 service. These carriers charge a fixed monthly rate plus variable costs based on number of connections established and the amount of data transmitted.

Because a carrier manages the network, X.25 must describe only the behavior of equipment that accesses the network. CCITT describes this behavior in terms of an interface. This interface describes Physical Layer characteristics such as connectors, voltages, and cables. The interface also describes Datalink and Network Layer functions, such as packet framing, error detection, and recovery exist. This interface is a specification that applies to a point-to-point network. In a way, X.25 describes a simple LAN that you use to access a WAN.

This point-to-point interface describes two nodes called Data Terminal Equipment (DTE) and Data Circuit-terminating Equipment (DCE). The DTE is the user equipment that accesses the network, while the DCE is the carrier equipment. The term *Data Terminal Equipment* is an indication of the perception the world had about networks during the 1970s; networks were viewed as a way to connect terminals or consoles to computers. Today, you view networks as ways to connect any computing machine to any other computing machine. However, the term DTE remains with us (and most likely will remain with us for some time.)

4.6.2   X.25 Architecture

X.25 was one of the first networks based on the OSI reference model. The DTE-DCE interface uses the lower three layers, with options available at the Physical Layer (Figure 4-6).

The Network Layer implements Packet Layer Protocol (PLP). This connection-oriented protocol serves as the highest layer in the X.25 model. PLP provides full-duplex data transfer, flow control mechanisms, and negotiation of options in a similar manner that the Transport Layer does in the OSI Profiles. Because this interface is a point-to-point connection, PLP does not perform any routing functions.

The Datalink Layer is Link Access Procedure Balanced (LAPB). Like PLP, LAPB is connection-oriented. Mechanisms ensure data integrity, provide sequenced transmission of packets, and support flow control, error detection, and recovery.

The Physical Layer offers options. In Europe, X.21 is popular. X.21 defines a digital technology. In the United States, X.21 BIS is more popular. X.21 BIS is very similar to the RS-232-C standard. CCITT describes another set of options, called the V-series, to address a variety of physical and performance requirements.

4.6.3   X.25 in a LAN Environment

You can implement X.25 without the presence of a network carrier. For example, a proprietary device can simulate a public or private network and instead provide a LAN solution. Such a device must provide only the standard

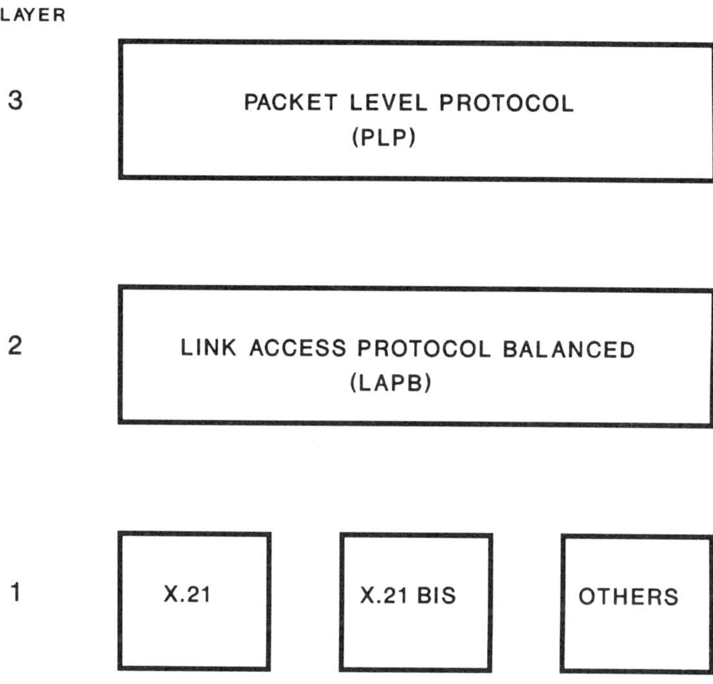

Figure 4-6: X.25 Architecture

DTE-DCE interface to its user-devices. This alternate use of X.25 exists, because of the popularity of the DTE-DCE interface. If a machine can connect to a carrier DCE it can also connect to a LAN-based DCE.

Yet another implementation can use X.25 strictly as a point-to-point connection. In this case, one device assumes the part of DCE and the other assumes the role of DTE. Vendors often do this in laboratories where they develop X.25 products. After all, it is much less expensive to develop products in this configuration than to use a real carrier network.

4.7 TCP/IP

TCP/IP represents two sets of protocols: Transmission Control Protocol and Internet Protocol. This network family enjoys significant success in the United States and has a growing install base throughout the world.

Originally developed to connect computer systems within the United States Department of Defense (DOD), TCP/IP is so popular that you can equip virtually every brand of computer to communicate with other TCP/IP nodes.

One TCP/IP network, called the Internet, connects thousands of users from the academic, commercial, and government communities throughout the United States. The Internet allows various sizes and makes of computers to exchange files and send electronic mail to each other.

In part, Universities developed the Internet, which was formerly known as the Advanced Research Projects Agency Network (ARPANET). As a result, many of these universities became linked using TCP/IP. The protocols were defined and developed at a time when SNA and other proprietary protocols were predominant in industry.

Eventually the DOD formed its own TCP/IP network known as the Defense Data Network (DDN). The DDN has stringent security requirements that cannot be met with the growing ARPANET.

TCP/IP is common in today's enterprises, because of the connectivity solution it offers to the various computers. Most industry experts feel that OSI profile networks will slowly replace TCP/IP, as OSI products become more generally available.

Although TCP/IP is very attractive to network implementors, it has two disadvantages to the OSI suite:

- The United States government originally drove the TCP/IP standard, while OSI is an international standard and has more world-wide support.

- Although TCP/IP has several useful functions it does not offer the robustness of OSI.

4.7.1   TCP/IP Architecture

Unlike X.25, the TCP/IP creators did not base their protocols on the OSI Reference Model.   In fact, ISO Transport was developed after TCP/IP, and borrowed some of the concepts of the earlier academic/government work. Figure 4-7 shows the TCP/IP architecture.

Like OSI, TCP/IP defines a peer-to-peer relationship. Another similarity to OSI is the concept of protocols and services. In contrast to X.25, TCP/IP defines the activities that occur on the network.

The IP protocol relates to the Network Layer of the OSI model. IP is a connectionless service in contrast to the connection-oriented X.25 PLP layer. Because IP sends datagrams, higher layers such as TCP must perform the end-to-end data integrity. Much of IP deals with routing and relaying.

TCP provides a transport mechanism similar to the ISO Transport Layer. This protocol offers a Reliable Stream Transport Service to the application functions. As the name implies, data transfer is reliable or guaranteed to transfer without errors.

Like ISO Transport, TCP describes a connection establishment phase, a data transfer phase, and a connection termination phase. TCP functions include flow control, error detection and correction, and urgent data delivery, which is similar to ISO expedited data delivery.

The TCP/IP suite describes a datagram service called User Datagram Protocol (UDP).   Like TCP, this function uses the services provided by the IP level. However, UDP does not provide a guaranteed delivery service like TCP does. UDP can deliver corrupt messages or can lose messages entirely.

As for the lower layers, TCP/IP does not require any particular media or datalink technology. What TCP/IP requires is a network interface in the form of a device driver that satisfies a set of services the IP Layer requires. In practice, the common datalink/physical technologies used are IEEE 802.3, 802.5, and X.25.

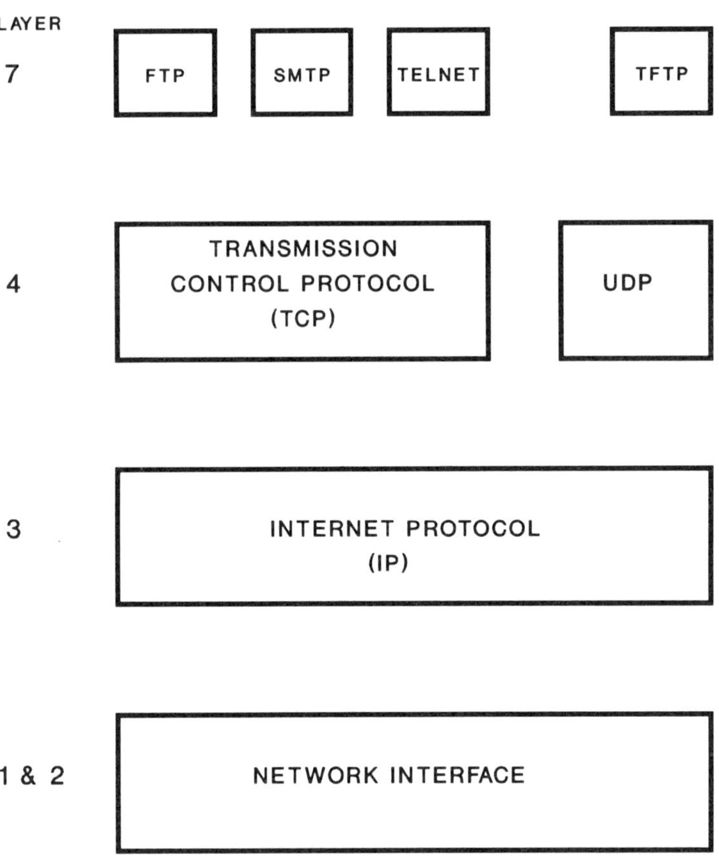

Figure 4-7: TCP/IP Architecture

4.7.2 TCP/IP Application Level Services

In the TCP/IP world, application functions use the TCP layer to perform file transfer, EMAIL, and virtual terminal. Each of these functions has options, so you can choose a specific set of options that best meets your needs.

4.7.2.1 File Transfer

TCP/IP offers two forms of file transfer: File Transfer Protocol (FTP) and Trivial File Transfer Protocol (TFTP). As the name suggests, TFTP provides a scaled-down version of FTP.

FTP is capable of providing reliable file transfer, while TFTP provides a best-guess function. FTP uses the services of TCP, while TFTP uses the UDP services. FTP provides some conversion capability, such as from ASCII to EBCDIC character sets. TFTP only allows transfer between two nodes, while FTP can do third-party transfers.

The decision to use FTP instead of TFTP is a trade-off between functionality and system resources. If memory and processor cycles are not an issue then you should use FTP. If you have memory constraints then TFTP applies more appropriately.

4.7.2.2 Virtual Terminal

TCP/IP describes a virtual terminal function called *TELNET*. TELNET allows you to establish a TCP connection with a remote node and to pass keystrokes to the operating system of that remote node. This makes it appear as though you are attached directly to the remote node.

This powerful function allows you to have a single terminal and access several computers instead of having several terminals. The relationship between the terminal node and the remote computer is a client/server relationship. For a local client node to access a remote computer a server process must be active on the remote node.

TCP/IP describes a specialized version of virtual terminal called *RLOGIN*. RLOGIN takes advantage of certain UNIX operating system functions such as RSH. RSH allows you to pass a command to a remote system without having to execute the complete user login process.

4.7.2.3 EMAIL

TCP/IP describes two EMAIL facilities called Mail Transfer Protocol (MTP) and the newer Simple Mail Transfer Protocol (SMTP). The main difference is that

SMTP only addresses how the Internet delivers messages from one node to the other.

When you use SMTP, you specify a series of recipients for a given message. You also complete a FROM field that determines where SMTP reports errors. SMTP performs address look-up and optionally informs you if the address of a peer changes.

4.8   Systems Network Architecture (SNA)

SNA is different than the other network families, because it is a proprietary standard that a company developed, rather than a standards group or government/academic concern.   As such, SNA pertains specifically to IBM products and does not address interconnection to non-IBM products.   However, because IBM products are very common in our enterprises, an understanding of SNA is important to the study of modern enterprise networks.

One variety of SNA functionality appears similar to OSI and TCP/IP—Logical Unit 6.2, referred to as LU 6.2.   LU 6.2 describes a peer-to-peer relationship that resembles architecturally the industry/government standards.

4.8.1   SNA Architecture

SNA describes how devices connect to one another and how these devices communicate. Traditional SNA makes the assumption that somewhere in your network an IBM mainframe exists.   The newer LU 6.2 can exist without the presence of a mainframe. SNA describes three basic categories of nodes:

- Physical Unit (PU) Type 5
- PU Type 4
- PU Type 2

LU 6.2 describes an additional PU Type 2.1. A Type 5 PU is a mainframe. A Type 4 PU is known as a front end that directly attaches to a mainframe using a high-speed I/O channel. A Type 2 PU is called a *cluster controller* (Figure 4-8.) A Type 2.1 PU has some of the characteristics of each of the PU Types 5, 4, and 2.

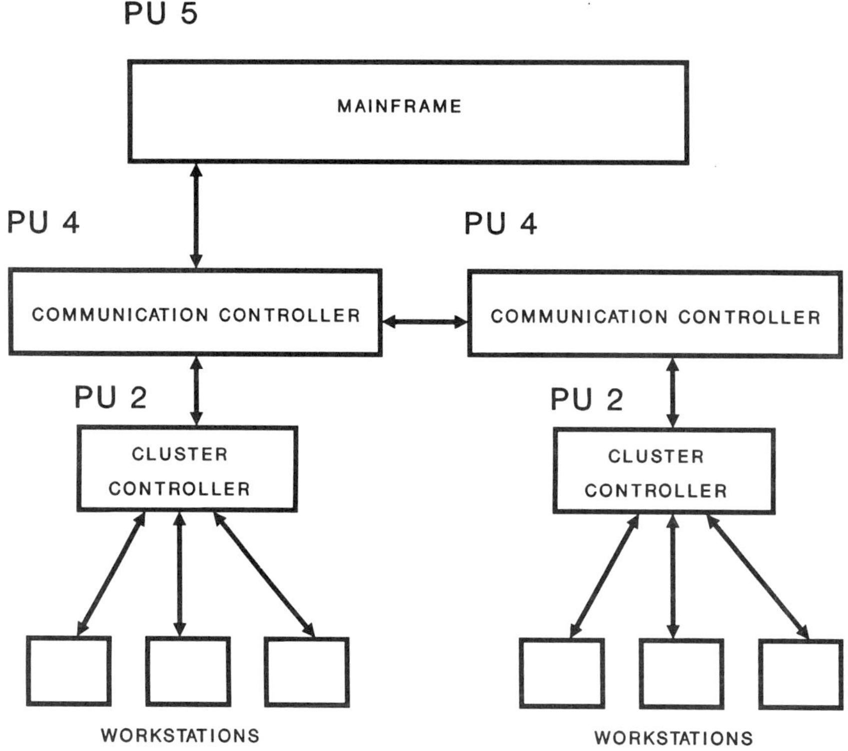

Figure 4-8: SNA Architecture

A PU Type 5 (mainframe) contains a special function called the System Services Control Point (SSCP). The SSCP is the main administrative program in the network. A control point handles directly or indirectly all messages in an SNA network. In LU 6.2, a PU Type 2.1 contains a miniature control point and so it does not require a mainframe (Figure 4-9). A PU Type 5 is master of a section of an SNA network called a *domain*. Two PU Type 5s connect to one another over a cross-domain connection.

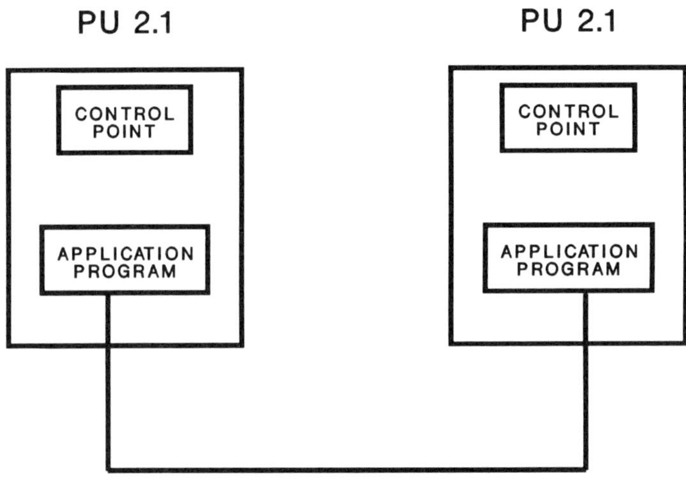

Figure 4-9: SNA LU 6.2

In an SNA network, terminals or consoles can attach to a PU Type 4 (front end) or to a PU Type 2 (cluster controller). You use a terminal or console to perform functions on the local mainframe or to operate remote mainframes over a cross-domain connection.

4.8.2   SNA Functions

Traditional SNA describes how terminals and consoles communicate to mainframes. Traditional SNA also describes inter-process communication between programs on same or separate mainframes. LU 6.2 adds to these functions the ability for application programs on workstations to communicate with each other on a moderate peer-to-peer basis.

For terminals and consoles, SNA describes a data flow called *3270 datastream*. The various IBM terminals (e.g., 3278 and 3279) support the 3270 datastream. Personal computers with special software can mimic terminals. This is called *3270 emulation*, because the personal computer is emulating or simulating a 3270 terminal. This is useful, because you do not require both a

3270 terminal and a personal workstation—you can switch back and forth between personal computer functions and mainframe access.

In your enterprise, assume you require 3270 to start and monitor mainframe activities. Alternatively, you can use LU 6.2 to provide real-time communication. You can use LU 6.2 nodes (specifically PU type 2.1 nodes) without having an IBM mainframe to do message and connection control. The primary disadvantage to OSI is that SNA is proprietary and tends to influence you to purchase more IBM brands when some other brand of computer may more closely suit your particular application.

4.9   In Summary

The enterprise network implementor has several network families to use as building blocks. The OSI profiles are becoming the predominant standard; slowly replacing TCP/IP and SNA. X.25 is used commonly for wide area connectivity with the other network families. Each network family has its advantages and disadvantages. The first step to understanding a network family is to learn the architecture and functions of that family. Other considerations are cost, complexity, and interconnection.

Chapter 5

Upper-Layer Components

5.1   Overview

Network applications' people work with upper-layer components more than the middle- or lower-layers. The high interface or upper-layers of a network product define the functions a network performs for computers or people. Upper-layer applications include file transfer and electronic mail. Other upper-layer functions include association establishment/termination.

5.2   Iso File Transfer, Access and Management (FTAM)

The ability to move file information between computers is the most common network application. Iso produced the FTAM specifications with the goal to address a wide spectrum of file operations, as various real file systems describe a significant variety of file handling concepts. As a result, FTAM remains one of the richest, robust, and complex network standards.

FTAM is a sub-layer of the Application Layer, the highest layer in the OSI model. *Iso 8571* describes FTAM and contains five parts. *Iso 8571* part onc provides a general introduction to the standard. Part two describes the virtual filestorc, which is the backbone of the FTAM model. Part three describes the FTAM services available to the user elements. Part four details the FTAM protocol. Finally, part five provides a framework for conformance evaluation of FTAM products.

The NIST implementors' agreements produced during the middle 1980's provides the basis for the first industry-wide implementations of FTAM. Early versions of MAP and TOP referenced this version of FTAM. However, this first FTAM, Phase I, did not result in many implementations outside of trade shows and evaluation laboratories. In December of 1987, NIST produced the Phase II FTAM agreements, which vendors and users implemented on a larger scale than the earlier version. Some vendors have plans to release the next generation, Phase III FTAM products during 1992.

5.2.1   Initiator and Responder Roles

A responder performs all FTAM operations at the request of an initiator. Standards documentation uses the terms *initiator* and *responder* to describe construction of connections or sessions. Generally, after the connection establishes, both peer nodes have the same set of actions available. In the FTAM standard, the roles of initiator and responder continue beyond the connection establishment phase. During an FTAM session, certain actions are valid for the initiator and (with few exceptions) a different set of actions are valid for the responder.

An initiator can request a file read operation, which means that file data moves from the responder to the initiator. An initiator also can request a file write operation, which means that file data moves from the initiator to the responder. The terms read and write represent the direction of data flow from the perspective of the initiator.

Example: A workstation on your desk is an FTAM initiator and an file server is an FTAM responder. The workstation requests a file that contains marketing information from the file server. This is an example of a file read. When you send a file from your workstation to the file server, a file write occurs. In this second action, the workstation is the initiator and movement of data is from the file server to the workstation, which represents a read. In FTAM terminology, the node that receives data (a file) is a receiver and the node that sends a file is a sender.

An FTAM node functions as either an initiator or a responder, or functions as both a receiver and a sender. An FTAM entity performs one of the following file transfer roles during a single file transfer:

- Initiator Receiver
- Initiator Sender
- Responder Receiver
- Responder Sender

An FTAM vendor can produce a product that functions in one or more of the above four roles. Some products perform all four functions. As a network planner it is important to understand the FTAM roles that a product can perform.

Example: A stand-alone file server implementation performs only the responder-sender and responder-receiver roles. This product does not provide a means of initiating a file transfer.

The roles two FTAM nodes play determines whether they interwork. An initiator-sender interworks with a responder-receiver, but does not interwork with a responder-sender. Figure 5-1 shows a matrix describing interworking between the four kinds of ftam roles.

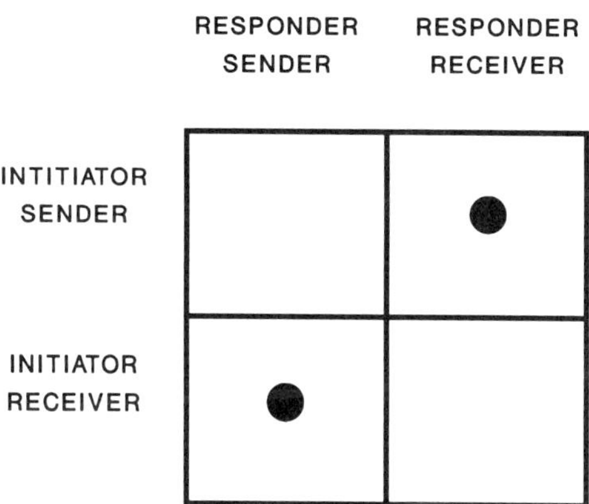

Figure 5-1: FTAM Role Compatibility

5.2.2   FTAM Regimes

An initiator and responder perform a series of negotiations and exchange information before a file operation occurs. An environment forms with constraints and capabilities that relate to the negotiation. This environment has phases or *regimes*. FTAM defines four regimes:

- Association Regime
- File Selection Regime
- File Open Regime
- Data Transfer Regime

The regimes nest within one another and form the structure shown in Figure 5-2. First the Association regime forms, which represents a certain level of agreement between the two nodes. Next, as more of the total environment establishes, the FTAM relationship proceeds to the next regime.

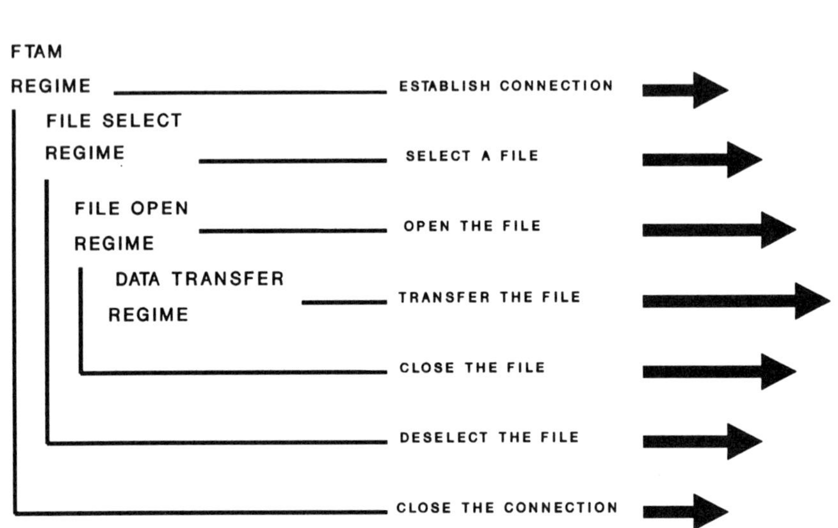

Figure 5-2: FTAM Regimes

The association regime corresponds to the connection establishment phase the layers below use. The initiator sends an F-Initialize to open an FTAM connection to the responder (Figure 5-3). If the FTAM responder sends a positive response to the FTAM initiator then the association regime begins.

The F-Initialize contains two fields called INITIATOR ID and PASSWORD. The initiator uses these fields to establish its privileges within the filestore controlled by the responder. If the responder does not recognize the INITIATOR ID and PASSWORD sent by the initiator then it rejects the F-Initialize request. A responder rejects an F-Initialize request if the INITIATOR ID and PASSWORD do not match a pre-configured security scheme.

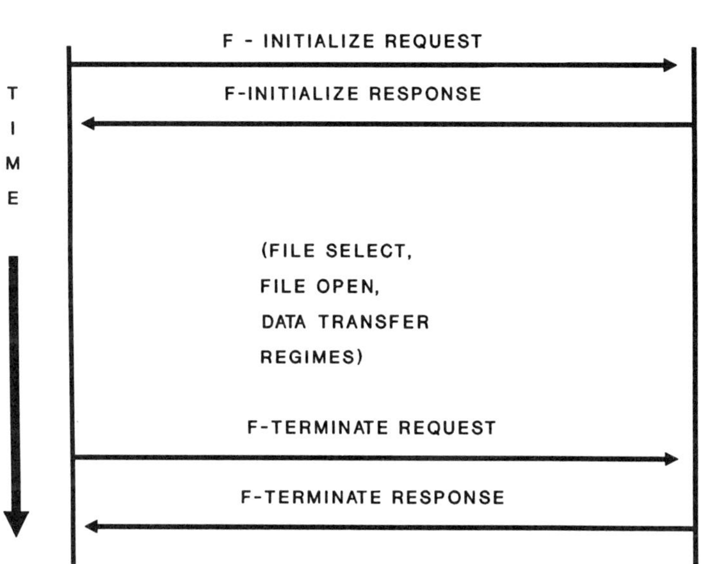

Figure 5-3: F-Initialize Regime

During the association regime, the initiator can begin initialization of the file selection regime (Figure 5-4). The initiator has two choices: Select a file or Create a file. Select means the target file already exists, while create produces a new file.

The file open regime comes next (Figure 5-5). The initiator opens the target file with parameters that specify the actions the initiator must perform on the file. Optional actions include read, write, or erase. After opening the file, FTAM optionally enters the data transfer regime (Figure 5-6). During the data transfer regime the initiator either reads the file or writes to it.

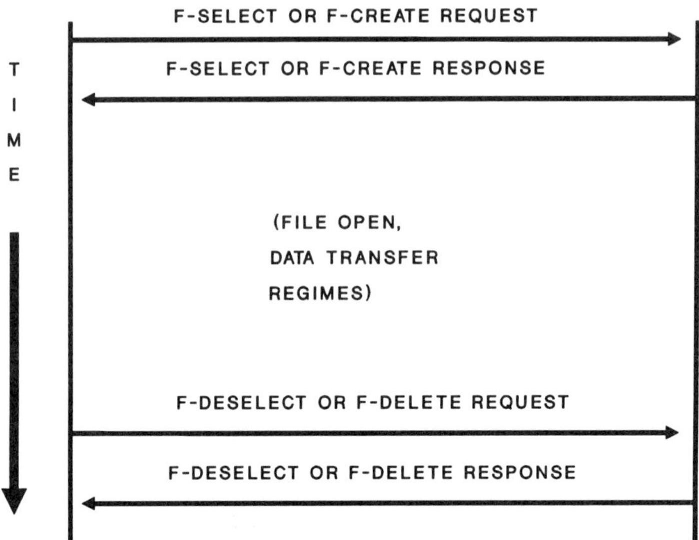

Figure 5-4: F-Select Regime

After reading or writing the file, the initiator normally closes the data transfer regime, the open regime, the select regime, and finally the association regime. However, the initiator or responder can drop out of all regimes at once by aborting the session. This happens during a failure such as a severe memory shortage.

The time period when two nodes establish a new regime is a *phase*. Each phase involves an exchange of FTAM protocol messages as shown in Figures 5-3 through 5-6.

The FTAM initiator and responder concatenate the primitives exchanged during the file select and file open phases. This process called *grouping* helps to simplify the FTAM state machine. Grouping occurs also during the file de-select and file-close phases. During grouping, multiple FTAM messages travel in a single F-PDU.

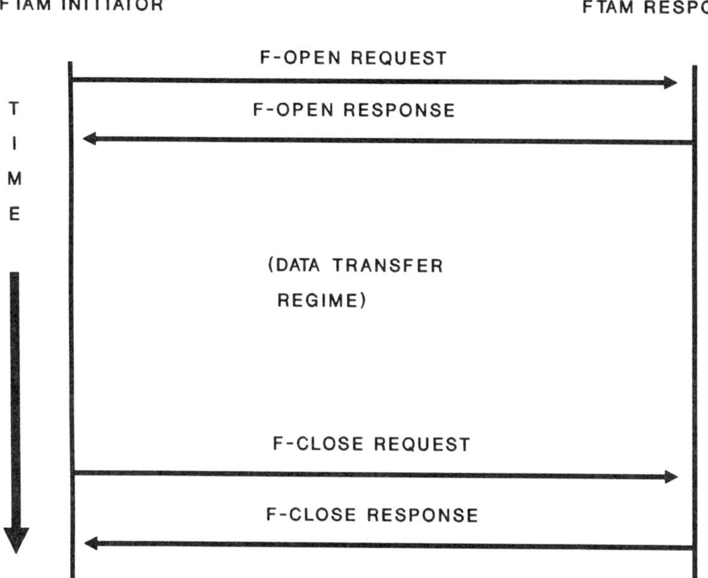

Figure 5-5: F-Open Regime

The responder treats concatenated primitives as a single logical action, in terms of success or failure. The responder reports either that all of the requests succeed or all of the requests fail. If all the requests succeed, then all of the implied regimes form. Otherwise, if one or more of the initiator requests fail then none of the regimes form and the FTAM state returns to the same state prior to the grouped requests.

5.2.3 FTAM Document Types

Within a single implementation, an ordered group of ones and zeroes represents a computer file. If you copy this file to an identical make and model of computer, the ordered group of ones and zeroes remains the same or very similar. However, if you copy the file to a different make or model of computer then a conversion must occur or certain vital characteristics change. Often this change means you lose information.

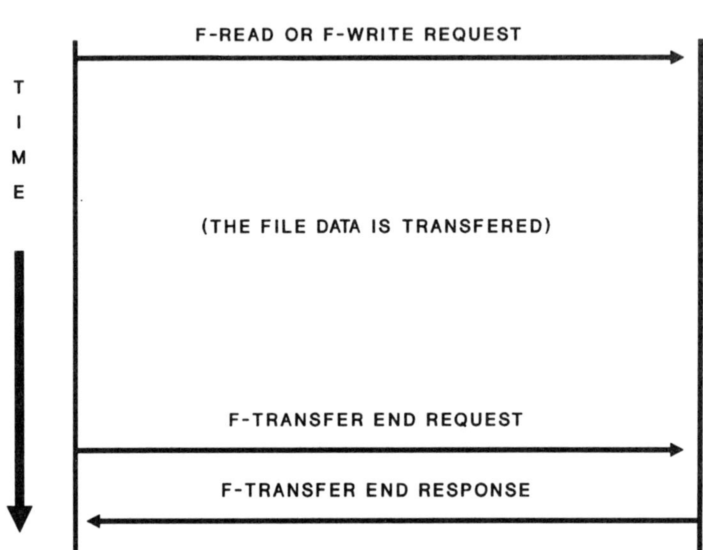

Figure 5-6: Data Transfer Regime

Example: Consider a memo consisting of text information. If you create this memo on a computer that encodes text information in EBCDIC format, the hexadecimal representation of the letter *A* is *C1*. Other computers encode text information in ASCII format and represent the letter *A* as hexadecimal *41*. If you copy a text file between these two systems without conversion, you lose the meaning of the file.

FTAM addresses differences in file representations by defining certain document types. A document type describes a class of virtual files in terms of syntax and semantics. FTAM allows you to copy the file between the two dissimilar systems without any loss of file meaning.

Example: Assume that the EBCDIC machine is an FTAM initiator and the ASCII machine is an FTAM responder. The EBCDIC machine sends a text file to the ASCII machine. During the file select and file open phase, the initiator informs the responder that it will send a file of type FTAM-1 (textual file). The EBCDIC machine first must convert the file into the exact format defined by FTAM-1 before it performs the file write operation. When the ASCII machine receives the file, it performs a similar translation. For this write operation, the format of the data during transmission is FTAM-1, regardless of the format before or after the transfer.

FTAM describes several document types, according to characteristics such as text versus binary and structured versus unstructured. A binary file, perhaps containing a word processing program, transfers between two FTAM nodes without any conversion, other than record lengths or other file system implementation constraints.

The concepts of structured and unstructured files relates to operations that involve part of a file as opposed to an entire file. You always must treat an unstructured file as a whole. A structured file is one that you can view as a group of records. You can append a structured file, which means that you can add data to the end of it. To append an unstructured file, an initiator creates a new file after it locally concatenates data (outside an FTAM regime) and then transfers the new file using FTAM procedures. Table 5-1 lists some of the FTAM document types defined by ISO and NIST OIW.

For an FTAM initiator to interwork with an FTAM responder, they must both support one or more identical document types. An initiator-sender that supports only FTAM-1 and FTAM-2 interworks with a responder-receiver that supports either document type, but does not interwork with a responder-receiver that supports only FTAM-3.

Table 5-1: Iso and Nist Document Types

Iso-Defined Document Types	
Type	**Description**
FTAM-1	Unstructured Text
FTAM-2	Sequential Text
FTAM-3	Unstructured Binary
FTAM-4	Sequential Binary
Nist-Defined Document Types	
Type	**Description**
NBS-6	Sequential
NBS-7	Random Access
NBS-8	Indexed Sequential
NBS-9	File Directory

5.2.4   Service Classes and Functional Units

During FTAM regime establishment, the initiator and responder negotiate service class and functional units. Functional units relate to the kind of file operations the initiator can request, such as file read, write, create, delete. Service classes group certain functional units into sets to simplify the negotiation process.

Table 5-2 lists the functional units and service classes that an initiator proposes during the regime establishment phases. A responder can support some, none, or all of the proposed functional units, which means it can negotiate a subset of functional units.

However, a responder must not propose additional functional units. An initiator proposes one or more service classes during the association establishment phase. As with functional units, a responder can negotiate a subset of service classes available for the forthcoming select and open regimes.

Table 5-2: FTAM Functional Units and Service Classes

FTAM Function Units	
Kernel	Enhanced-File-Management
Read	Grouping
Write	FADU-Locking
File-Access	Recovery
Limited-File-Management	Restart-Data-Transfer

FTAM Service Classes
Unconstrained
Management
Transfer
Transfer-and-Management
Access

5.2.5   Using the Lower-layers

FTAM requires the presence of the ACSE Presentation and Session Layers to carry out its functions. What lies beneath these layers is not important to FTAM. In other words, the underlying network can be X.25 or it can be a connectionless network running over 802.3 or 802.4. The initial connection establishment phase requires the ACSE sub-layer. After the FTAM association regime forms, ACSE remains inactive until one node closes the connection.

FTAM uses the Presentation Layer as a mechanism to negotiate abstract and transfer syntaxes appropriate for the desires of the initiator. FTAM uses the Presentation Layer mechanisms to specify the abstract syntaxes associated with the document types of the files that the initiator intends to manipulate. The Presentation Layer also negotiates the transfer syntaxes associated with each abstract syntax.

The Session Layer provides services that allow FTAM to perform a recovery function. During the forming of the association regime, an initiator suggests a value for a field called *checkpoint window*. The checkpoint window value indicates how often the Session Layer inserts synchronization points into the data stream during file transfer. If during a file transfer a message gets corrupted or lost, the two FTAMs can resynchronize at an earlier Session sync point. This is especially valuable during the transfer of very large files. Instead of retransmitting the entire file the process restarts at a checkpoint.

5.3   Iso Association Control Service Element (ACSE)

ACSE as an Association Service Element is an Application Layer sub-component often used with another Application Service Element. *Iso 8650* and *Iso 8649* respectively define the ACSE protocols and services. The primary function of ACSE is to provide two peer application entities a complete point of reference, describing their identities and contexts.

ACSE performs functions during the association establishment process, then remains basically idle until the association dissolves. ACSE does not provide a data transfer service. FTAM uses ACSE during association establishment, but uses the Presentation Layer for data transfer.

5.3.1   Association Establishment

The association establishment process is a confirmed service. This means that an initiator issues a request PDU and the responder issues a response PDU. An association begins when an ACSE user, such as FTAM, issues an A-ASSOCIATE primitive to the ACSE provider. This primitive, as the primary ACSE service primitive, contains several parameters. These parameters allow the initiating Application Layer to describe its expectations for a subsequent association to the responding Application Layer.

Example: If the initiating ACSE is working on behalf of FTAM then the responder needs to know this. If FTAM does not exist on the responder then obviously it does not make sense to establish an association.

Another piece of information ACSE provides is an invocation identifier. In a multi-processing environment, it is possible that several copies or invocations of an application entity can be active. The invocation identifier is a tag or key that distinguishes one process from another.

The A-ASSOCIATE primitive results in an ACSE-Associate-Request (AARQ), which the initiator sends to a responding node. The AARQ carries the information represented in the A-ASSOCIATE primitive and optionally user data. The user data can contain upper-sublayer information. The user data portion of an AARQ carries the FTAM Initialize PDU.

5.3.2   Association Termination

ACSE terminates an association two ways—either gracefully or abruptly. The graceful close service is A-Release service, while the abrupt close is the A-Abort service.

* **A-Release**—A confirmed service and requires a response from the peer. The peer can refuse the close, which means that the association remains active.

* **A-Abort**—An unconfirmed service, which means that the association closes immediately. Use of the A-Abort service can result in lost data.

The A-Release and A-Abort services report information regarding the reason for association termination and the entity that orders the close. ACSE can request a close in the event of a local environment problem or an ACSE user can terminate the association, because the association is no longer needed or because there is a local error.

5.4   Iso Presentation Layer

As layer six in the OSI model, Presentation provides mechanisms for negotiation of abstract syntax and transfer syntax. ISO defines the Presentation protocols in document *Iso 8823*, the services are described in *Iso 8822*. Abstract and transfer syntax are concepts that allow standards to address the different ways computers represent information.

A Presentation Service Access Point (PSAP) identifies a user of the Presentation Layer. For a local Presentation Layer user to connect to a remote peer it must know the PSAP of the peer. The local node can get this information from the directory or this information can exist in the local database via an operator interface.

5.4.1   Presentation Definition Context Set

An integral aspect of the Presentation Layer is a structure called the Definition Context Set (DCS). During a Presentation connection the DCS contains the names of one or more abstract syntaxes that the peer Presentation Layer users can use (e.g., FTAM). Each Presentation Layer maintains an identical view of the DCS. This way, one Presentation Layer can refer to entry number three in the DCS and the peer Presentation Layer knows which abstract syntax the other is referencing. Note that the DCS is an abstraction or view of a list as opposed to an actual well-defined data structure somewhere in some computer's memory.

The procedure for constructing the DCS begins at connection establishment time. Like the other upper-layers, Presentation defines a confirmed connection establishment process. Part of the P-Connect Request PDU contains a structure called a Presentation Context Definition List (PCDL). This represents an effort on the part of the initiating Presentation Layer to propose a DCS for the forthcoming Presentation connection. The responding Presentation generates a

P-Connect Response PDU that contains an identical Presentation Context Definition List, as well as a Definition Result List (DRL). The DRL contains a list of answers to each of the proposed abstract syntaxes. The DRL can indicate that the responder can support none, one, or more of the suggested entries in the PCDL the initiator supplies. The abstract syntaxes that the responder reports favorably to become the official DCS.

The contents of the DCS can change later in the connection. A Presentation Layer can issue an Alter-Context primitive, which contains one or more proposed additions or deletions to the existing DCS. The peer Presentation Layer must accept the proposed changes before they become official.

5.4.2   Data Exchange Between Presentation Layers

Presentation provides a data transfer service to its users. User data is grouped into sets called Presentation Data Values (PDVs). All information within a single PDV belongs to the same abstract syntax. However, a single Presentation Data PDU can contain multiple PDVs, each associated with a different abstract syntax.

The Presentation Layer or the user-application formats local data into the format of one of the entries in the DCS. Some products offer a Presentation Layer that performs the conversion with very little effort by the user. Other implementations provide a more simple Presentation Layer that forces the user software to do the conversion. ISO does not define how conversions are performed. Instead, ISO defines the Presentation protocol as a mechanism for negotiation of abstract and transfer syntaxes.

5.4.3   Other Presentation Layer Features

Like the ACSE sublayer, the Presentation Layer Connect PDU can optionally carry user data. A P-Connect PDU carries the AARQ PDU as user data in a P-Connect PDU, just like the AARQ carries the FTAM F-Initialize PDU. Like ACSE, the Presentation Layer also offers two levels of connection termination services. The confirmed Presentation Release procedure guarantees that any data transfer in progress at the time of connection termination will not be lost. The abrupt P-Abort service can result in lost data.

5.5　Iso Session Layer

ISO Session describes several mechanisms to manage dialogues between two peers. The activities of Session require an underlying network that is reliable, as Session does not provide error detection functions. The level of dialogue management the Session Layer performs relates more closely to buffering and synchronization than to data integrity, which is the responsibility of the layers below Session.

Iso 8326 describes the Session services, while *Iso 8327* defines the Session protocols. These documents describe a rich set of mechanisms that the Session Layer makes available to the higher layers. Although the functions are rich, the protocols by comparison are simple. Session by itself does not perform dialogue management. Instead, Session provides a mechanism for the Application Layer to control dialogue management.

A Session Service Access Point (SSAP) identifies a user of the Session Layer. For a local Session Layer user to connect to a remote peer it must know the SSAP of this peer. The local node can get this information from the directory or you can enter this information in the local database via an operator interface.

5.5.1　Negotiation of Session Layer Functional Units

Like the other upper-layers, the Session Layer describes a confirmed connection establishment phase. During connection establishment, the connection initiator proposes a group of functional units for the forthcoming connection. The responder can negotiate down to a subset of the proposed functions, but cannot add to the list the initiator generates.

5.5.2　Kernel Functional Unit

The most basic functional unit, the kernel, always must be in the initiator's proposed list and all responders must support it. The kernel functional unit describes how sessions form, how normal data transfers, and how connections terminate.

A Session connection can function with the kernel functional unit and either the duplex or half-duplex functional unit, and no other functional units. In this case, very little of the Session dialogue management capability is available to the Application Layer.

5.5.3   Duplex and Half-Duplex Functional Units

The initiator must propose either the duplex or half-duplex functional unit, but cannot propose both. In half-duplex mode, a *data token* controls the right to send data. In duplex mode, the peers have no restrictions and always have the right to send data.

5.5.4   Negotiated Release Functional Unit

The Session Layer describes abrupt connection termination called an *abort*. Optionally, a connection terminates in an orderly manner using the release procedures. In addition, if the release functional unit is active, a node can refuse a release request. If not active, a node always must accept a release request.

5.5.5   Expedited Data Functional Unit

If this functional unit is present then a Session entity can send a limited amount of data at a higher priority than the normal data flow. The underlying Transport Layers must negotiate and agree on expedited data transfer for the Session Layers to use this functional unit.

5.5.6   Typed Data Functional Unit

This functional unit pertains to a Session Connection where half-duplex dialogue control is active. Typed data describes a way for a node to send data even if the data token belongs to the other node. A Session Layer can override the half-duplex mechanisms if the typed data functional unit is active.

5.5.7   Activity Management Functional Unit

Activity management describes how two Session Layers divide dialogue into logical groups. During a Session connection, there can be two unrelated data exchanges called Activity A and Activity B. During the Session connection, data associated with Activity A can transfer and data associated with Activity B also can transfer. Only one activity at a time can be active. An activity can suspend and then resume at a later time.

5.5.8   Capability Data Exchange Functional Unit

The activity functional unit must accompany this functional unit. If no activities are active, the Session Layer at either end can send a limited amount of capability data. This is a confirmed or acknowledged data exchange.

5.5.9   Major and Minor Synchronize Functional Units

These functions allow a Session Layer user to insert checkpoints into the normal data flow. The Application Layer uses these checkpoints to restart a data transfer at an earlier reference point. A peer must acknowledge a major sync point before more data can transfer. Minor sync points do not require an acknowledgement before data transfer continues.

5.5.10   Resynchronize Functional Unit

When the resynchronize functional unit is present, aspects of a Session connection can change. The resynchronize functional unit allows data transfers to restart at an earlier sync point and allows tokens to assume new values.

5.5.11   Exceptions Functional Unit

The exceptions function makes it possible for two Session Layers to recover from a severe error, such as a protocol error, without terminating the connection. This functional unit requires the half-duplex functional unit.

5.6 CCITT EMAIL—X.400

CCITT first published the X.400 EMAIL or Message Handling System (MHS) recommendation in 1984. A group of standards, numbered from X.400 through X.430 describes MHS. The MHS Layer corresponds to the ISO Application Layer.

In 1988, the industry significantly enhanced the standard both functionally and architecturally. This section focuses on the 1984 standard, as most real-world implementations currently operate at that revision level. The industry will migrate eventually to the newer standard. The end of this section provides a description of the differences between 1984 and 1988 X.400.

5.6.1 Architectural Details

The primary X.400 components are the Message Transfer Agent (MTA) and the User Agent (UA). The MTA delivers and receives messages, providing a service the UA. The UA provides an interface to the user, either a person or an application program. A user of X.400 serves as either an originator or a recipient of a message.

Collectively, a group of cooperating MTAs comprises a Message Transfer System (MTS). A collection of interworking UAs, along with an MTS, comprise a Message Handling System (MHS). An MHS, along with the users of the system comprise a message handling environment. Figure 5-7 illustrates a message handling environment, showing the various relationships between the components. Figure 5-8 shows the X.400 protocol relationships.

X.400 divides a message into two parts: Message Content and Message Envelope. The content is the message that the originator sends to the recipient. The envelope is information the MHS uses during transfer of the content.

X.400 defines a Management Domain (MD). An MD contains one or more MTAs and optionally one or more UAs. Two forms of MD exist: Administration MD (ADMD) and Private MD (PRMD). The difference is whether a public administration manages the MD (ADMD) or a private organization manages the MD (PRMD).

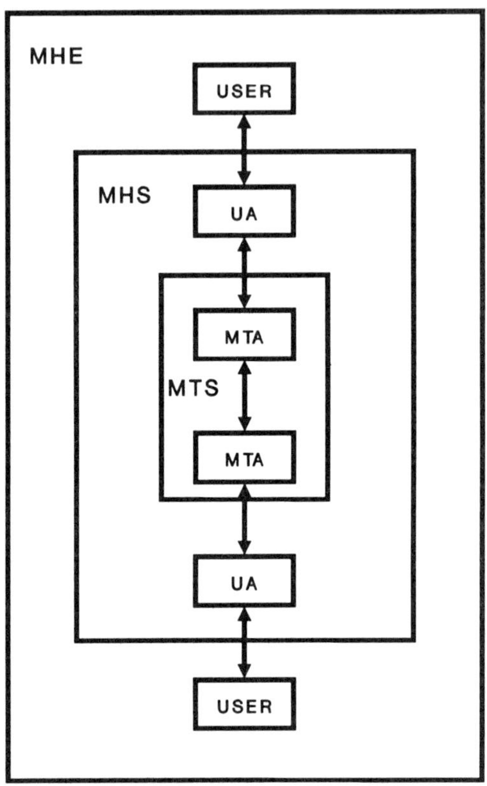

Figure 5-7: X-400 Components

According to the CCITT specification, an ADMD can act as a relay between PRMDs, but a PRMD does not relay messages between ADMDs. The original concept was that ADMDs would serve at the boundaries of countries. In practice, ADMDs can also serve as boundaries between companies. PRMDs do route between other PRMDs, in spite of the intention of the standards. The restriction is political, rather than technical—nothing in the protocol prevents a PRMD from being a routing domain. When an ADMD interacts with a PRMD the ADMD is responsible for ensuring that the PRMD performs properly such activities as logging and accounting, in addition to the basic message transfer service.

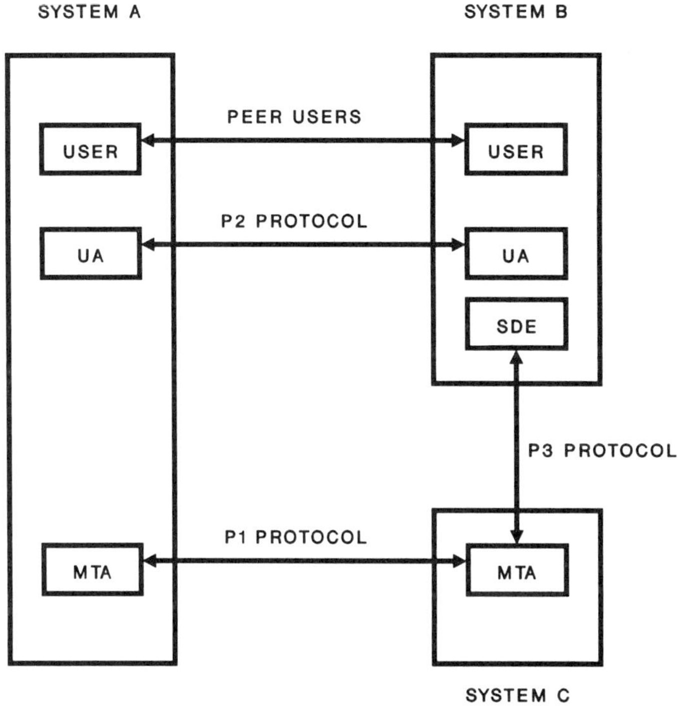

Figure 5-8: X-400 Protocols

5.6.2 Message Transfer Layer

CCITT recommendation X.411 describes the services and protocols associated with an MTA. In the X.400 model, the Message Transfer Layer (MTL) performs the functions of the MTA. The MTL is a sub-layer of the Application Layer.

An MTL offers several services to a User Agent Entity (UAE). The MTL transfers messages to/from a UAE. A UAE can also request a probe, which means that the MTL determines if a message can be delivered to a specific destination UAE.

A UAE can request optionally notification if a particular message is undeliverable. When a UAE requests delivery of a message it can specify several pieces of information, including:

- Delayed delivery (do not deliver until a specific date and time).

- The original form of the encoded information.

- Conversion rules (i.e., either allow/disallow conversion or force a specific conversion).

- Alternate recipients of the message.

When an MTL delivers a message to a UAE it can specify:

- Conversion rules.
- Message transfer submission date and time.
- The date and time the message was delivered.
- The names of the other UAEs designated as recipients of the message.

A UAE can cancel delivery of a message previously submitted for delayed delivery. A sending UAE request optionally that the MTL report when a message transfers, and whether any conversion occurs during the delivery.

The MTL services fall into two categories: those that an MTL performs locally and those that require interaction between two peer MTLs. The service to delay delivery of a message is local, and does not require a peer protocol to execute. Although the MHS services seem rich, the underlying protocol between two peer MTLs is simple, as many of the services are executed locally. When MTL-MTL interaction occurs, two MTLs execute the P1 protocol.

P1 describes Message Protocol Data Units (MPDUs). An MPDU is either a User MPDU (UMPDU) or a Service MPDU (SMPDU). SMPDUs carry the actual messages between MTLs, while MTLs use SMPDUs to perform control functions, such as error reporting.

X.400 defines only one UMPDU. This UMPDU transfers during message delivery to one or more destinations. Two SMPDUs exist: Delivery Report MPDU and Probe MPDU. Delivery Report reports delivery or non-delivery status of a message. Probe conveys information about whether a message is deliverable.

5.6.3   User Agent Layer (UAL)

CCITT X.420 describes the UAL. Users of X.400 use the Interpersonal Message Service (IPM Service) that the UAL provides. As with the MTL, the UAL is a sub-layer of the Application Layer of the OSI model.

The services provided by the UAL include the basic ability to send and receive messages. A user element interfaces to UAL, which also provides access to the services the underlying MTL layer provides. The UAL is the direct interface to the user element and provides mechanisms for the user element to access the MHS. The UAL can provide an editing capability to the user element. Such a capability allows a user to create a message, indicate the recipient(s), or specify delayed delivery.

To provide these services the UAL uses the services of the MTL and also executes a peer protocol called the P2 protocol. P2 like P1 describes very few protocol primitives. Although the services available to the user element vary, most of the services are local issues, and do not require that the communication stacks perform a complicated protocol. The impact on interworking is two-sided. The protocol is rather simple, so the chances for protocol compatibility is higher than FTAM, which has a very complex protocol. The optional fields within the P2 PDUs are numerous and is where most X.400 interworking problems exist, because both stacks must implement the same optional fields.

Two PDUs pass between UALs:

- Interpersonal Message User Agent PDU (IM-UAPDU)

- Interpersonal Message Status Report User Agent PDU (SR-UAPDU)

The IM-UAPDU carries a message from an originator to a recipient. The UAL sends the SR-UAPDU either to another UAL or to a user element and reports receipt or non-receipt of a message.

5.6.4   Submission and Delivery Protocol—P3

CCITT realized that there are real-world implementations in which the UA and the MTA exist on two different computers. An architecture can consist of a single MTA on a mainframe computer and several UAs on personal computers. CCITT produced a standard to describe how a UA communicates with a remote MTA. This service, Remote Operations, uses the P3 protocol.

The Submission and Delivery Entity (SDE) operates when a UA resides remotely from an MTA. The SDE delivers messages from the UA to the MTA. The SDE does not perform the operation requested by the UAE. Instead, the SDE makes the services of the MTA available to the UAE.

X.411 describes P3 as a peer protocol between an SDE and an MTA. Interactions between the SDE and MTA are *operations*. The entity that provides the mechanism for an SDE to communicate with an MTA is the Remote Operations Service. ROS is another sublayer of the Application Layer.

An operation has a formal definition including an operation identifier field, a result field, and an error field. Three Operation PDUs (OPDUs) support remote operations:

- Invoke OPDU
- Return Result OPDU
- Return Error OPDU

The invoke OPDU requests activation of an operation. Return result reports successful completion, while return error reports unsuccessful operation.

5.6.5   Reliable Transfer Service (RTS)

CCITT X.410 describes how MHS makes use of the Reliable Transfer Server (RTS), the OSI Presentation Layer, and OSI Session Layer. MHS has few requirements of the Transport, Network, Datalink, and Physical Layers. One detail worth noting is that the ISO Transport expedited data service is not used. In general, all that MHS requires of the middle and lower layers is that they support the services the Presentation and Session Layers require.

The RTS like ROS, performs a general rather than specific purpose. RTS is responsible for establishing Application Layer associations and for moving APDUs between application entities. These APDUs contain P1 or P3 messages.

This service is similar to the ACSE services. 1984 X.400 describes use of RTS instead of ACSE. RTS provides confirmed association establishment and termination services and provides an unconfirmed data transfer service. Data transfer can be either monologue, which means in only one direction or it can be Two-Way Alternate (TWA).

The TWA mode uses the concept of a *turn*. A turn is similar to the Presentation layer token. An application entity that sends data must have the turn. RTS describes a mechanism for exchanging the turn, just as Presentation Layers exchange tokens. The RTS uses the services of the Presentation and Session Layers. RTS has few Presentation Layer service requirements, but uses many Session layer functions.

1984 X.410 describes a special Presentation Layer entity commonly called the X.410 mode. The X.410 mode is a minimal Presentation Layer implementation. In this mode, no negotiation of abstract and transfer syntax occurs. Only one transfer syntax exists and it is described in *CCITT X.409*. This transfer syntax is commonly called Abstract Syntax Notation One (ASN.1).

RTS requires the following Session Layer functional units:

- Kernel
- Exceptions
- Minor Synchronize
- Half-Duplex
- Activity Management

During Session connection establishment the tokens and the sync point serial number take on initial values. During the data transfer phase an activity can be interrupted; a new activity can run for a period before the original activity resumes. Each Session Layer inserts sync points at intervals to facilitate recovery from an error. Exceptions can occur or in extreme situations, the connection can abort.

5.6.6   Differences between 1984 and 1988 X.400

CCITT produced an enhanced set of X.400 recommendations in 1988. ISO also produced the MOTIS specification, which is almost identical to the X.400 standard. 1988 MHS introduces the concept of a Message Store (MS). The MS allows for the condition where a recipient machine is temporarily unavailable (e.g., a powered OFF personal computer). An additional protocol P7 defines the relationship between the UA and the MS.

Another important advantage pertains to the method of describing message body parts. A body part is a type, such as ASCII text, videotext, or voice. The new 1988 standard encodes body parts in a much more flexible manner, which simplifies the definition of new body parts by standards committees.

1988 X.400 uses the normal mode of the ISO Presentation Layer instead of the X.410 mode. This makes the abstract syntax negotiation function available to the MHS.

A 1984 implementation does not interwork with a 1988 implementation, except under strictly controlled environments. Although the installed base of 1984 level products is very large, 1988-based products exist. Users with 1984 products or users planning to purchase 1984 products, must build a migration strategy to address the interworking issue as 1988 products become more generally available. The December 1989 NIST OIW Agreements contains a study describing interworking between 1984 and 1988 implementations.

5.7   TCP/IP File Transfer

The TCP/IP network family describes two file transfer functional profiles called File Transfer Protocol (FTP) and Trivial File Transfer Protocol (TFTP). Request For Comments *RFC 959* describes FTP and *RFC 783* describes TFTP.

5.7.1   File Transfer Protocol (FTP)

FTP is the more robust and functionally rich of the two TCP/IP file transfer profiles. Both application software and persons can use FTP depending on the implementation. FTP describes a Network Virtual File System (NVFS), which is similar, but much simpler than the OSI FTAM virtual filestore. Various options regarding file content, such as character set types and record formation are available, providing file definitions similar to the FTAM document type. Again, these options are much more simple than the ISO FTAM file definitions.

5.7.1.1 FTP Model

FTP describes two principal entities called the User or Client and the Server. The user is either a person or application software. The user initiates all file transfer actions. A user requests that a file transfer occurs between itself and a server or a user requests a file transfer between two remote servers.

The user and server have two sections: a Data Transfer Process and a Protocol Interpreter. Both nodes have a local file system, which may be very different in structure. So, a mapping function may need to occur during file transfer. The Data Transfer Processes (DTPs) are responsible for transmission of the file content. The Protocol Interpreters (PIs) set up control connections to manage transfer of a file. The user node has an interface, either an operator utility or an application programming interface.

If a user initiates a transfer between two servers then two control connections form instead of one. Note that in this case the user node does not participate in a data connection.

5.7.1.2 Services

The two basic file transfer operations are Retrieve and Store. Retrieve instructs a server to transfer a copy of a file in its local filestore over an existing data connection. The data connection can be to a user node or to another server node. The store function prepares a server to accept a file over the data connection. Optionally, a user can append a file by having a server add data to it.

In addition to file transfer operations, the user can request certain file management functions. A user can request that a server delete or rename a file in its database. A user can request directory functions. A server can be asked to remove a directory, make a new directory, or report a list of files that exist in a directory.

Finally, the user has various control functions available to it. The system command reports the operating system of a server. The status command reports the state of an ongoing file transfer and the abort command stops an active operation.

5.7.1.3 FTP Control Connection Protocol

FTP control connection occurs between a user PI and a server PI. The user PI initiates the control connection, which means that a server PI must be *listening* or available to accept an incoming connection request. After the control connection establishes, the server DTP initiates a data connection to the listening user DTP.

When a user wants a transfer to occur between two servers, the user PI first establishes two control connections to two listening servers. The user PI then instructs one server to listen for a data connection and the other server to initiate a data connection.

An FTP control connection uses the TCP/IP TELNET protocol, which was defined to address virtual terminal. An FTP command travels as a TELNET string. Every command results in one or more replies, which simplifies synchronization of requests and actions. Replies indicate success or failure to execute an action.

The status and abort commands can transmit over the control connection at the same time that data is moving over the data connection. However, some servers may not be able to support two simultaneous connections and FTP describes a method using the TELNET Interrupt Process signal to address such limitations.

5.7.1.4 FTP Data Connection Protocol

The server DTP initiates and (normally) terminates a data connection. A data connection closes in one of the following ways:

- The server indicates a normal close following completion of a transfer operation.

- The server closes the data connection due to detection of an unrecoverable error.

- The server indicates a close following receipt of an abort command from the user.

- The control connection is somehow lost resulting in the server closing a connection.

- If the transfer mode is such that end-of-file is implied by closing the data connection then the server or the user can close the connection, depending on the direction of data movement.

After a server DTP initiates a data connection to a listening user DTP, they must set certain parameters called *transfer parameters* before actual file data can exchange. Transfer parameters apply to structure, transfer mode, and data representation structure.

Before a user issues a service command, such as store or retrieve, it can issue one or more transfer parameter commands. These commands allow a user to specify values for the transfer parameters to the server. If the user does not issue a service command for a parameter then an FTP default applies.

5.7.1.5 File Structure Command

A user can specify one of three values for file structure:

- File-Structure (no structure)
- Record-Structure
- Page-Structure

The default (File-Structure) means that the file transmits as a continuous, flat file. No semantics apply to borders such as records. A record-structured file contains groups of sequential records. This structure allows transmission of text files. Page-structured files, also called random-access files, are contain one or more groups of data called a page. Different page types are defined:

- Last Page
- Simple Page (normal)
- Descriptor Page (informational)
- Access-Controlled Page (secured)

5.7.1.6 Transfer Mode Command

The transfer mode command selects between block, compressed, or stream transmission modes. The default is stream mode. A server sends block mode files as groups of header-data pairs. Each section of data follows a header containing a length or count field, as well as a descriptor that indicates end of block or end of file.

Compressed mode is a time-saver, especially for very large files with replications or fillers, such as spaces. Special mechanisms allow compression of a file that has areas where bytes are repeat or of a file that has areas with continuous spaces.

The stream mode indicates that the data transfers as a stream of bytes. End-of-file is indicated either explicitly with a special character or implicitly (if the file structure is of type FILE), by the sender closing the data connection.

5.7.1.7 Data Representation Command

The user specifies a data representation for the transmission of a file. Available choices include:

- ASCII
- EBCDIC
- Image
- Local

Image files are binary files. Local files apply to files that have a semantics or significance to the length of a piece of information. This solves the problem where one host, the sender, uses 36-bit words and another host, the receiver, uses 32-bit words. The receiver has to use two local, 32-bit words to store a single logical word.

5.7.2 Trivial File Transfer Protocol (TFTP)

TFTP is a compact, simple utility suitable for machines with limited processor resources (processing power and memory) and meager functional requirements. TFTP provides only the capability for the user to read or write data from/to a server. Data can be an ASCII file, a binary file or ASCII characters for terminal display. Like FTP, conversions occur on a system that does not store characters in ASCII format. Machines that display EBCDIC characters, such as many IBM computers, must convert any ASCII display streams they receive.

The protocol is surprisingly simple. A user initiates a connection by sending a read request or a write request to a server. The server responds with either a positive acknowledgement (write request) or the first data packet (read request).

After the connection establishes, file or display data transmits in 512 byte groups. The receiver acknowledges each data packet with an ACK packet. The last packet associated with the file contains less than 512 bytes. When the receiver ACKs this last packet the TFTP session terminates.

Either side can abnormally terminate a session if an error occurs, such as receipt of an improperly formed packet or a local problem such as a full disk. A node reports an error by sending an error packet, which can be lost or dropped by the network. A timeout mechanism allows detection of a lost error packet.

5.8   Upper-Layer Interface Examples

Interfaces serve as windows between the network product and user application software. You must become notably familiar with the interface before designing a driver for a network application. Part of this study includes an understanding of the underlying network technology, because the user interface often includes commands to set-up or control lower-layer functions.

Selection of a network technology includes a careful consideration of the interface in addition to the underlying layers. Obviously, the stack and datalink/physical layer characteristics affect interworking. The interface affects portability.

Portability is the ability to move software from one platform to another. If you spend months developing a network application for a personal computer and later the need arises to run that application on another platform, such as a mini-computer, then you do not want to re-write the application. Instead, you port the application in a fraction of the time it takes to re-write it.

If possible, select network products with standard interfaces. Unfortunately, most standards-based interfaces were created by companies rather than standards organizations such as ISO. However, work has begun in ISO and other standards groups to produce specifications for network interfaces. MAP/TOP also produced standards for interfaces.

The following sections describe examples of standard interfaces. The NETBIOS interface specification, IBM's SNA LU 6.2, and the MAP/TOP Application Interface Specification are important, because they represent a variety of interfaces found on network products useful throughout the enterprise.

The NETBIOS interface is an IBM creation, but many vendors produce products that include this now de-facto standard. The SNA interfaces for traditional VTAM and LU 6.2 appear primarily on IBM products. However, more and more vendors supply LU 6.2 interfaces for their third-party products. The MAP/TOP Application Interface Specification appears on products from several vendors.

5.8.1   NETBIOS Interface Specification

IBM first produced the Network Basic Input/Output System (NETBIOS) in 1984. Since then it has become an industry standard. From the perspective of IBM, NETBIOS is a way to provide portability of user applications across a wide variety of IBM network products. Now, so many NETBIOS products are available from additional vendors that portability to non-IBM platforms is possible.

Such products run on computers with the DOS, UNIX, OS/2 and other operating systems. NETBIOS can run on TCP/IP, OSI, and proprietary stacks. The underlying Datalink/Physical Layer technologies include 802.3, token ring, and proprietary technologies.

Interworking between two NETBIOS nodes is only possible if both nodes have similar stacks below the interface. Both products must also map interface commands to protocol primitives in precisely the same way. Standards exist that define how NETBIOS commands are mapped to TCP/IP and OSI primitives.

NETBIOS is simple compared to other Application Layer interfaces. In fact, NETBIOS resembles a Transport Layer interface, because the services is supplies are basic data transfer functions and a few extras. The services fall into four categories:

- Name Support
- Session Support
- Datagram Support
- General Commands

5.8.1.1 NETBIOS **Name Support**

NETBIOS provides three commands related to network address resolution. Without name resolution an application program has to refer to a peer node using a hardware address, which is not very user-friendly. This name support is a rudimentary form of directory services that allows application programs to reference logical names instead of hardware addresses.

The user issues an Add Name command to register a logical name for one node. A name is unique within the network. If some other node already has that logical name then an error message is sent to the offending node. Each node maintains a table of registered names. This table, which maps logical names to hardware addresses, frees you from having to specify a network address.

The Add Group Name performs a similar function for a group of nodes rather than a single node. This means that a NETBIOS application can send a message to several nodes by using a group name as the destination. The Delete Name command removes an entry from the name/address tables. This name is now available to another node.

5.8.1.2 NETBIOS **Session Support**

Session support allows connections to establish, allows data to exchange in both directions and allows connections to terminate gracefully. These services are very similar to the services the Transport Layer of the OSI model provides.

Session establishment commands include Call and Listen. A program uses the Call command to initiate a session while Listen is the passive form that a responder uses. A session establishes if an application issues a Call to a program that has previously issued a Listen.

After the session establishes both nodes can send and receive data. One kind of send does not require an acknowledgement (Send No-Ack), thereby providing an unconfirmed service. The confirmed mode (Send) means that the user is informed when the receiving node has receives the message. An application may issue a send to transfer data in a single buffer or can instead issue a Chain Send, which sends data from two separate buffers.

An application program issues a Receive to receive data from a node that performs a Send. If the data cannot fit into a single buffer (perhaps the sender issues a Chain Send) then two receives are necessary to obtain all of the message. A Receive can post on a single connection or a Receive-Any can post to receive data from any active connection.

5.8.1.3 NETBIOS Datagram Support

Datagram support allows an application to send data to a peer without first establishing a connection. This is similar to sending a letter instead of using a telephone. The datagram is a best-guess service, the intended recipient computer may be powered OFF and the sender would not know it. The Send Datagram command delivers a message to a single peer. The Send Broadcast Datagram sends a copy of a message to several nodes. Similarly, a node must issue a Receive Datagram or Receive Broadcast Datagram to receive such a message.

5.8.1.4 NETBIOS General Commands

The general commands allow the application to perform certain management functions. The Adapter Status command accesses the local name/hardware address table, and delivers information about network errors that occur. The application sends the Adapter Status command to the local network product or to some other node on the network. The Cancel command abort commands in progress. The Reset command returns the network product to its initial state, which means that all sessions terminate and the name/address table clears. The Find Name command determines if a single logical name is already in use by some node.

5.8.2   SNA—Logical Unit 6.2

IBM created the LU 6.2 network architecture as an answer to the demand for peer-to-peer connectivity. In traditional VTAM, a mainframe must be present in the network, because mainframe software called the SSCP controls all sessions. An LU 6.2 network does not require a mainframe.

LU 6.2 describes both a network protocol and an Application Programming Interface (API) to the network. The API is called Common Programming Interface Communications (CPIC). As a standard interface, CPIC makes it possible to write a program on one platform, such as a mainframe, and port the program to another platform that also supports CPIC, such as a personal computer.

User-written programs in the LU 6.2 environment are Transaction Programs (TPs). A TP concerns itself only with the CPIC interface and does not deal with the underlying SNA network, which can be SDLC, token ring, or X.25 links, or a combination of the three. The LU 6.2 architecture accommodates distributed processing, which means that an application runs on two or more computers.

5.8.2.1 Logical Unit 6.2 Architecture

The LU 6.2 architecture centers around an LU type 6.2. The LU executes the protocol between two CPIC nodes. The connection between two LUs is an LU-LU session, while the connection between two TPs is a conversation. The CPIC interface uses the services provided by the LU. Note that a single LU-LU session supports multiple conversations. When a TP establishes a conversation the LU first must establish an LU-LU session or use an existing session if a suitable session already exists.

An LU not only provides data communications between two TPs, it also starts and terminates TPs. A portion of the LU called Node Services provides this service. In the CPIC environment one TP initiates a conversation and the other TP receives notification of the conversation initialization. Node Services starts the initiating TP at the request of an operator. The initiating TP informs the LU of the name of the partner TP for the conversation. The LU at the receiving node, similarly, starts the TP indicated by the initiating TP. This starting and stopping of programs implies that Node Services works closely with the computer operating system of the node.

Another portion of the LU, called Side Information, is a database that contains information about the TPs, such as remote TP and LU names, as well as information regarding the mode, or options for during the supporting LU-LU sessions. Node Services uses Side Information during conversation initialization.

5.8.2.2 Common Programming Interface Communications (CPIC)

An initiating TP issues an ALLOCATE_CONVERSATION command to begin a conversation. When the remote LU receives the ALLOCATE_CONVERSATION, it starts the indicated TP. This remote TP issues an ACCEPT_CONVERSATION, which signifies that the conversation is now in place.

After the conversation is active, data transfer occurs. A TP does a SEND_DATA command to send messages to its partner. Data transfer can be confirmed or unconfirmed depending on options specified during conversation allocation. A request for a confirmation is called the CONFIRM command and the response is called the CONFIRMED command.

The LU does not always immediately send the message to the partner node. Instead, the LU will buffer messages until the TP sends a pre-specified amount of data or until the TP issues a command that causes the LU to send its buffered data, such as the FLUSH command or CONFIRM command. Data transfer is half-duplex, which means that at any given time only one TP or the other has the right to send data. The LU optionally performs manipulation on data in a manner similar to the Presentation Layer in the OSI model.

A TP requests termination of a conversation with the DEALLOCATE command. Depending on options specified during conversation allocation, DEALLOCATE also can do an automatic FLUSH or CONFIRM.

CPIC offers various commands to override conversation characteristics specified during conversation allocation. SET_DEALLOCATE_TYPE specifies whether or not an automatic FLUSH or CONFIRM occurs when a TP issues a DEALLOCATE. Other commands override conversation characteristics that Side Information defines. SET_PARTNER_LU_NAME allows the TP to override the name contained in Side Information for a single conversation. Note that Side Information does not change, any subsequent ALLOCATE_CONVERSATION commands will use the LU that Side Information specifies unless the TP re-issues a SET_PARTNER_LU_NAME.

5.8.3　MAP/TOP Application Interface Specification

The MAP/TOP user's group created an important programmatic interface standard. The MAP/TOP Application Interface Specification (AIS) was first published as part of the MAP Version 3.0 documentation and TOP Version 3.0 now references it. AIS describes interfaces to FTAM, Manufacturing Message Standard (MMS), and Private Communications (ACSE applications, such as real-time functions), as well as general functions common to these specific applications.

The goal of MAP/TOP is not necessarily to create standards. Instead, MAP/TOP compliments the activities of international standards groups such as ISO and CCITT. At the time of Version 3.0, no international API standards existed for OSI-based systems, although work was (and still is) in progress by IEEE to produce the Portable Operating System Interface (POSIX) standards. Many industry experts believe that MAP/TOP and probably GOSIP will point to the POSIX work after it stabilizes.

The MAP/TOP AIS model is quite complete in that it defines not only commands to perform data communication but also defines an Interface Service Provider (ISP) and support functions. The ISP and support functions form a foundation to support the specific data communication commands, such as FTAM and Private Communications.

The ISP is a set of functional units that support two different levels of commands called high-level and low-level commands. High-level commands provide a less complicated interface to the user and in general are easier to use than low-level commands. However, they may not offer the same level of functionality as the low-level commands. Often, a single high-level command performs a function that would require multiple low-level commands. Low-level commands map more closely to the actual protocol primitives and are useful for performing interworking tests and for fine tuning applications for performance or unique functions.

Another distinction between commands is context specific versus context free. Context specific commands require that the user have knowledge of the underlying protocol, whereas context free commands can be used without such knowledge. Low-level commands are context specific, some of the high-level commands are context specific and others are context free.

5.8.3.1 AIS Support Functions

The AIS support functions include Event Management and Connection Management. Event management describes how commands in general pass between the user application and the ISP. A command called WAIT is described that allows the user to request execution of an event, such as delivery of a message.

The AIS describes the WAIT command, but does not define a message delivery mechanism, as this varies from one operating system to another. The WAIT command allows portability of applications from one machine to another. Users may write programs using the WAIT primitive without concern for the internal message passing mechanics.

Connection management describes a set of general functions that all Application Layer entities require. As the name implies, connection management provides a mechanism for an application program to establish a connection, or association, with a peer. All Application Layer functions have the same connection management requirements and a single set of functions simplifies the AIS.

Before an application requests an association, it first must perform an Application Entity Activation command to describe to the ISP the nature of the particular functions required, such as FTAM or MMS. The application issues a CONNECT command to actively initiate a connection or issues a LISTEN command to express a willingness to accept an incoming connection request. During the life of the connection, the application can issue low-level and high-level commands. Later, an application issues a RELEASE REQUEST to close gracefully a connection or issues an ABORT to close abruptly a connection.

5.8.3.2 Low-Level FTAM Commands

To use the context-specific, low-level FTAM commands you must have considerable knowledge about the FTAM protocol. If the you issue a command at an inappropriate time, the ISP may ignore the command or terminate the association. If you attempt to transfer data during the File Open or File Select regime then a failure occurs. The low-level commands (Table 5-3) match the FTAM service primitives.

Table 5-3: Low-Level FTAM Commands

SELECT	DESELECT
OPEN	CLOSE
CREATE	DELETE
READ ATTRIBUTE	CHANGE ATTRIBUTE
READ	WRITE
ERASE	LOCATE
SEND DATA	RECEIVE DATA
DATA END	TRANSFER END
BEGIN GROUP	END GROUP
CANCEL REQUEST	CANCEL RESPONSE

5.8.3.3 High-Level FTAM Commands

High-level commands allow less sophisticated use of an FTAM product. You can do a file transfer using a single, high-level command that otherwise requires several low-level commands.

The context-free, high-level commands allows you to perform file transfers without first having to study the FTAM protocol standard. The AIS aides vendors by describing these commands in terms of the underlying low-level commands. The AIS defines the following context-free, high-level commands:

- **File Copy**—This causes duplication of a file between any two filestores.

- **File Move**—The same as a File Copy, except that the original file gets deleted.

- **File Delete**—A single file is removed from a filestore.

- **File Read Attributes**—This command delivers information about a file, such as creation date and size.

- **File Change Attributes**—Allows you to change aspects of a file, such as filename or file access control.

5.8.3.4 Context-Sensitive, High-Level FTAM Commands

High-level commands can be context-sensitive. MAP/TOP calls these commands *grouped,* because each one performs a group of low-level functions. You combine these high-level commands with other low-level commands to perform file transfers. Grouped commands simplify use of low-level commands by saving programming time. The AIS describes the following grouped commands:

- **File Open**—Performs all of the low-level commands necessary to prepare a file for actions, such as read or write.

- **File Close**—Performs the low-level commands associated with closing a file. This stops access to the file.

5.9   In Summary

This section described several upper-layer components. You must become significantly familiar with the upper-layer functions and interfaces provided by network products before you use them. ISO FTAM and TCP/IP standards-based products offer file transfer capability. CCITT X.400 offers electronic mail capability. The ISO ACSE, Presentation and Session Layers support FTAM and X.400. NETBIOS, SNA LU 6.2, and MAP/TOP AIS are three representative API standards. API standards allow you to port applications from one platform to another with minimal effort.

Chapter 6

Middle-Layer Components

6.1   Overview

The middle layers deal with accurately and efficiently passing data between end nodes. In the OSI model, the middle layers are Transport (layer 4) and Network (layer 3). These layers contain the mechanisms to ensure end-to-end data integrity, provide flow control, and establish logical connections. The middle layers also implement mechanisms to support routing and relaying.

6.2   Iso Transport Layer

In the OSI model, the Transport Layer is the highest layer that manages accurate peer-peer data delivery. The upper layers provide application and system-level services, but rely on the Transport Layer to maintain a reliable data flow.

6.2.1   Iso Transport Services

As described in *Iso 8072*, the Transport Layer provides data delivery services to its users, while hiding the exact nature of the underlying network technology. A Transport user can specify a Quality Of Service (QOS) requirement that relates to acceptable data transfer rates, error rates, and failure probability.

The Transport Layer also is responsible for the transparent delivery of raw data, without performing any data conversions (which is the upper layers' responsibility).

The industry has defined several different Transport Protocol classes. However, the services provided to the user are the same regardless of the protocol class that underlying stack supports. The Transport Layer uses several timing mechanisms, both in terms of services and protocol.

The service concept of QOS references three categories of time-sensitive parameters:

- Connection Establishment Delay
- Throughput and Transit Delay
- Connection Release Delay

A Transport Layer user can specify the minimum acceptable connection-establishment delay for a connection. If the Transport Layer is unable to establish a connection within this period, the network informs the user. You can indicate data transfer requirements and minimum connection termination delays that the Transport must provide. If the Transport Layer cannot provide the request QOS, it reports its inability to do so.

6.2.2   Iso Transport Protocol

Iso 8073 describes the protocol between two Transport providers. Table 6-1 lists the five classes of protocol.

Table 6-1: Iso Transport Classes

Class	Description
Class 0	Simple Class
Class 1	Basic Error Recovery Class
Class 2	Multiplexing Class
Class 3	Error Recovery and Multiplexing Class
Class 4	Error Detection and Recovery Class

All five classes have certain functions in common and each numerically higher protocol class provides the functionality of the lower classes plus, increasingly more capability (with a few minor exceptions). The common functions include connection establishment, data transfer, and connection termination. Each higher class has the capability of the lower classes, unless otherwise noted. Designers usually implement Class-4 Transport on top of a connectionless Network Layer, where alternatively the other classes use a connection-oriented Network Layer.

- **Class-0 Transport**—describes segmenting and reassembly in addition to the connection establishment/termination and data transfer functions. Connection termination for Class-0 is implicit, rather than explicit. This means that the Transport connection terminates at the same time that the Network Layer connection terminates. Class-0 also provides for notification of a detected protocol error, but does not have built-in error recovery.

- **Class-1 Transport**—performs the functions that Class-0 provides plus the ability to recover from Network Layer connection failures. If the Network Layer reports a connection loss, a Class-1 Transport can attempt to use an alternate Network Layer connection. Class-1 introduces sending of expedited data, which is a short, urgent message that the protocol can send out-of-turn or ahead of other queued normal data messages. Class-1 and the higher classes assign a number (similar to a serial number) to each data PDU to support flow control and sequencing.

- **Class-2 Transport**—adds the multiplexing and demultiplexing function. Class-2 Transport can use one Network Layer connection to support multiple Transport Connections. Class-2 also introduces the credit window mechanism. Using the credit window mechanism is optional. If you do not use credit windowing then the network does not use TPDU. Unlike Class-1, Class-2 does not provide for reassignment of Network Layer connections.

- **Class-3 Transport**—is basically the same as Class-2, except that the credit window mechanism is mandatory. Class-3 also supports Network Layer reassignment.

- **Class-4 Transport**—adds the capability to recover from lost, out-of-sequence, or duplicated TPDUs. To perform these functions, the layer uses several timers. Class-4 sets a timer called the local retransmission timer to represent the maximum time to wait for an acknowledgement before attempting to retransmit a TPDU. Class-4 uses another timer, the inactivity timer, to detect that the logical connection with the peer Transport has dissolved. The Class-4 Transport resets the inactivity timer each time the layer receives a TPDU from the peer. Remember that heartbeats pass between the Transport entities even when data transfer is idle.

  Unlike any other class, Class-4 not only detects out-of-sequence packets, but also has a mechanism for recovery from such errors. The lower protocol classes terminate the connection if the layer receives an out-of-sequence packet. A Class-4 Transport does not acknowledge such a packet nor does it deliver the packet to its user. Instead, it waits until it has reordered all packets before delivering the data to the user or report that an unrecoverable error has occurred.

During the connection establishment phase, the initiating Transport suggests a protocol class and the responding Transport either accepts this class or proposes a lower class. If the network suggests an alternate class, the initiating Transport can accept or reject this proposed change in protocol class.

At connection establishment time, the initiating Transport also negotiates other options such as using expedited data (within the appropriate classes). A responding node can "negotiate down" by suggesting a lower class of protocol or by proposing to delete a function (e.g., expedited data). However, a responding node cannot "negotiate up" by suggesting a higher class of protocol, nor can it suggest adding a function that the initiator did not propose.

6.2.3   Transport Layer PDUs

The Transport protocol contains PDUs for connection establishment/ termination, data transfer, and error recovery (Table 6-2). The initiator sends the CONNECT REQUEST PDU to the responder. Within this PDU is a field that indicates the calling and called Transport Service Access Point (TSAP). When the responder receives the CONNECT REQUEST, it determines if it has a local user waiting at the called TSAP. If not, the system returns a DISCONNECT REQUEST. To accept the connection, the responder sends a CONNECT CONFIRM.

The network transfers data using the Data and Expedited Data PDUs, which the receiver acknowledges with the DATA ACKNOWLEDGE and EXPEDITED DATA ACKNOWLEDGE. The DATA ACKNOWLEDGE PDU also supports flow control. The network uses the REJECT and ERROR PDUs for error recovery.

Table 6-2: Transport Layer PDUs

Description
Connect Request
Connect Confirm
Disconnect Request
Disconnect Confirm
Data
Expedited Data
Data Acknowledgement
Expedited Data Acknowledgement
Reject
Error

6.3   Iso Network Layer

The purpose of the Network Layer is to provide services to the Transport Layer and to route and relay messages in a transparent way between Transport entities.   A basic question is whether or not a connection-oriented or a connectionless Network Layer is more appropriate for a particular network. The answer primarily relies on the class of Transport Protocol that the network must support.

A Class-4 Transport performs adequately with the services that the ISO Connectionless-mode Network Services (CLNS) provides. The lower Transport protocol classes require the Connection-Oriented Network Services (CONS). Class-4 provides error detection and recovery, and does not need the connection-oriented Network Layer to perform these functions.

In the United States, Class-4 Transport has gained such popularity that many network administrators use it regardless if the underlying Network Layer is connection-oriented or connectionless; even though the connection-oriented Network Layer performs redundant functions with Class-4 Transport.

This trend is shifting in the United States—Network administrators are starting to use Class-0 Transport when the Network Layer is based on the connection-oriented X.25 standard (United States GOSIP supports this combination).

In Europe, where they have used X.25 for a longer time, they established a trend to use the lower Transport protocol classes (mostly Class-2 and Class-0). As LANs gain popularity in Europe, Transport Class-4 with a CLNS also must gain popularity.

Figure 6-1 shows important Transport/Network Layer implementation profiles. These configurations do not interwork with each other without a gateway or some other protocol conversion device. The Connectionless-mode Network is used with Class-4 Transport. MAP, TOP, United States GOSIP, and the United Kingdom GOSIP support this popular combination.

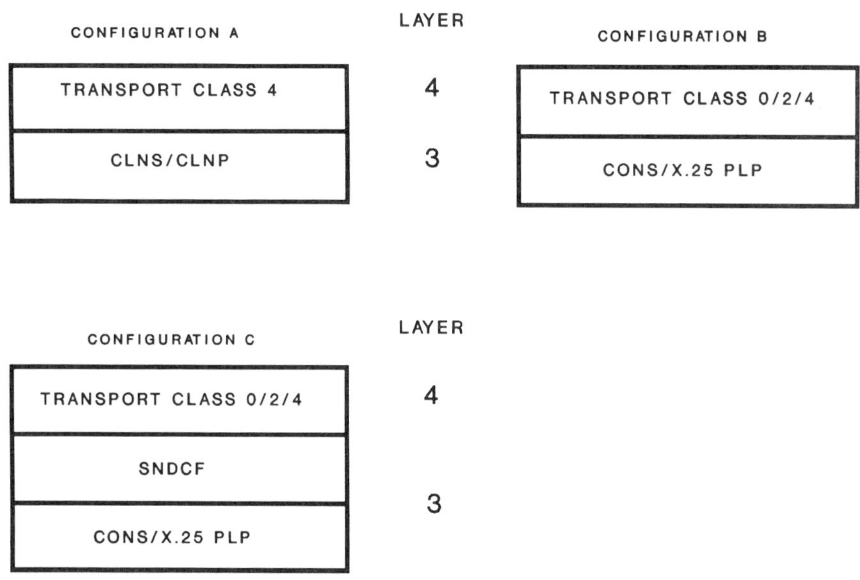

Figure 6-1: Middle-Layer Configurations

6.3.1   Iso Connectionless-Mode Services and Protocols

Iso 8473, along with its addenda, describes a set of protocols to support the Connectionless-mode Network Service (CLNS), which *Iso 8348* Addendum 1 describes.   Because this service is connectionless, there are no primitives associated with connection establishment. In fact, only two service primitives are available to the Transport Layer:

- N-UNITDATA REQUEST
- N-UNITDATA INDICATION

The CLNS provides only the capability to send and receive datagrams. The internal operations of the Network Layer are more complex. The Network Layer performs routing and relaying functions. Routing and relaying pertain to the moving of data between subnetworks. A subnetwork is a group of nodes that can reach each other directly with their datalinks. Devices called *routers* move packets between subnetworks. The layer can send an N-UNITDATA REQUEST directly to the destination end system, if the end system is reachable from the same data link as the sender.

Otherwise, the network sends the N-UNITDATA REQUEST to an intermediate system. In this case, the intermediate system forwards the packet to the end system or to yet another intermediate system. This routing function is not visible to the Transport Layer, so all end systems appear to a Transport entity to be on the same subnetwork.

The Network Layer also performs segmentation/reassembly. The Connectionless-mode Network Layer performs segmentation and reassembly if the underlying datalink packet size is smaller than the NSDU size. Again, the network hides this activity from the Transport Layer.

The Network Layer performs another function called the *lifetime* function and is to ensure that a packet does not get trapped in the network. Under certain error conditions, the network can trap a packet in an infinite loop, where the packet traverses between one intermediate system and one or more other intermediate systems. If enough packets became trapped in this manner, the entire network eventually can become sluggish and even fail.

An N-UNITDATA contains a field called *PDU lifetime*, which represents the remaining time the packet is to exist. Each intermediate system that receives the lifetime parameter, decrements it. If the intermediate systems reduce the lifetime to zero, the system discards the packet, which is preferable to the possibility of a trapped packet. An implementation must make the lifetime parameter configurable, because different values are appropriate for different network topologies.

A network with many intermediate systems can make it appropriate to set the original value of lifetime very high, because a packet may travel several "hops" before reaching its final destination. A simple network with few or no intermediate systems makes a relatively small lifetime value appropriate.

6.3.2   Iso End System-to-Intermediate System Routing

The Connectionless-mode Network Layer Protocol (CLNP) describes routing mechanisms, but does not describe how the Network Layer learns about the topology of the network. Before a Network Layer can perform routing and relaying, the protocol first must establish a topology database. *Iso 9542* describes the End System-to-Intermediate System (ES-IS) protocol that the Network Layer entities use to produce such databases and support the routing functions that *Iso 8473* describes.

The ES-IS protocol addresses the following questions:

- How do intermediate systems learn about the existence of end systems that are reachable from the local datalink?

- How do end systems learn about the existence of intermediate systems that are reachable from the local datalink?

- How do end systems learn about the existence of other end systems that are reachable from the local datalink?

You can enter statistically this information, but such a solution is difficult to manage, especially in large networks or networks with changing topologies. ES-IS mechanisms instead allow each Network Layer in the network to build dynamically tables to track the topology of the network.

6.3.2.1 Es-is Mechanisms

The ES-IS mechanisms rely on the ability to multicast packets, which means that the system can send simultaneously packets to multiple nodes on the subnetwork. The network requires two multicast addresses called All End System Entities (AESE) and All Intermediate System Entities (AISE). All end systems on the subnetwork receive a packet sent with a destination address of AESE, just as all intermediate systems on the subnetwork receive a packet sent with a destination address of AISE.

Iso does not define the binary values for these multicast addresses. Instead, registration authorities such as NIST, MAP/TOP, and GOSIP dictate the actual multicast values. These registration authorities currently express the values for these multicast addresses in hexadecimal:

- All End System Entities = 09 00 2b 00 00 04

- All Intermediate System Entities = 09 00 2b 00 00 05

Implementations must make these values configurable, because someday, some registration authority can decide to change them. These kinds of changes sometimes occur to align implementation agreements that different standards organizations define.

Example: If one country defines different values than another country, interworking between these two countries may not be possible. To correct this problem, one or both countries must migrate to new values for these multicast addresses.

6.3.2.2 Multicast Addresses

These multicast addresses make it possible for an end system to inform all intermediate systems on the subnetwork of its presence with a single transmission.

When you power ON an end system and it must engage in communication, the end system sends a message called an End System Hello (ESH) to the AISE multicast address. At this time, all intermediate systems on the subnetwork make an entry into their local databases. The system uses these entries later if the system requires routing. The end system periodically sends another ESH. When an intermediate system receives a new ESH from the same Network entity, it flushes out the old entry in the database. This process makes it possible for intermediate systems to learn about changes in the network topology. As new nodes become active or if the network administrator moves a node to a different subnetwork, the system informs the intermediate systems of this by sending and receiving ESHs.

Similarly, an intermediate system informs all end systems on the subnetwork of its presence by transmitting an Intermediate System Hello (ISH) on the AESE multicast address. Each end system that detects the ISH can make an entry into their local database. Later, when an end system must send a packet to a node that does not exist on the same subnetwork, it can forward the packet to one of the intermediate systems it learned about by listening to ISHs.

In a network that consists of a single subnetwork with no intermediate systems attached, an end system can issue a QUERY CONFIGURATION message on the AESE multicast address to locate its desired communication partner. If the desired Network entity partner is reachable and ready for communication, it responds by sending a CONFIGURATION RESPONSE directly to the node that issued the QUERY CONFIGURATION message.

6.4   CCITT X.25 Packet Layer

The CCITT X.25 recommendations describe an architecture that closely fits the OSI model. The three layers defined by X.25 map to the lowest three layers of the OSI model. The highest layer supported by X.25 corresponds closely to the ISO Network Layer. CCITT calls this layer the Packet Layer (Packet Level), which executes the Packet Layer Protocol (PLP).

6.4.1   Packet Layer Protocol (PLP)

PLP describes three phases: Call Set-Up (similar to connection establishment), Data Transfer, and Call Clearing (as in connection release). Like a Transport connection, the industry calls a PLP connection a *virtual circuit*. Unlike Transport, PLP defines two kinds of virtual circuits: permanent and switched. A Switched Virtual Circuit (SVC) corresponds to a Transport connection, because it is temporary. A Permanent Virtual Circuit (PVC) is assumed always to be present. So, if two DTEs have a PVC between them then it is as if they were always in the data transfer phase.

6.4.1.1 Logical Channel Identifier

Connections are virtual circuits, because the two peer DTEs are not concerned with the physical connections between them. As shown in Figure 6-2, DTEs communicate over logical or virtual circuits, even though the Public Switched Network (PSN) can use several different physical routes for the actual data transfer. Note that a DTE can participate simultaneously in more than one virtual circuit, so a mechanism must exist to determine with which virtual circuit a received packet associates.

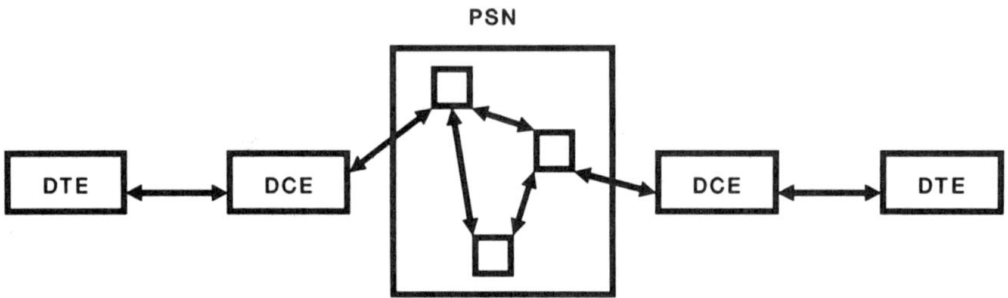

Figure 6-2: Multiple Routes through PSN

Every virtual circuit has a Logical Channel Identifier (LCI) assigned to it during Call Set-Up. Each packet sent by a DTE specifies the LCI so that the PSN knows where to send it and so that the receiving DTE knows to which virtual circuit the packet belongs. Each DTE has a separate LCI associated with a given virtual circuit. So a single virtual circuit is known to each DTE by a separate and most likely different LCI.

Because the system encodes the LCI using 12 bits, the range of possible values for an LCI is 4095 (an LCI value of zero has special meaning.) CCITT established conventions for the assignment of LCIs to virtual circuits. These conventions provide you with a method of allocating groups of LCIs to different kinds of virtual circuits.

If a DTE requires any PVCs then the network administrator assigns the group of LCIs numbered from 1-x to PVCs, where x is the maximum number of PVCs required. The industry assigns the next numerically higher group of LCIs to one-way incoming SVCs, which are virtual circuits that accept incoming calls (calls are similar to connect request primitives.)

The industry assigns the next higher LCIs to two-way SVCs, which can both call and be called. A two-way SVC can act as either initiator or responder during Call Set-Up. The user reserves the numerically highest group of LCIs for one-way outgoing SVCs, which can generate a call, but never accept a call.

Example: You can set the following LCI classes to these ranges:

- 1-99   Permanent Virtual Circuits
- 100-199   One-Way Incoming
- 200-299   Two-Way
- 300-399   Unused
- 400-499   One-Way Outgoing

The administrator of an X.25 network must specify the LCI ranges for the four kinds of virtual circuits to the network carrier when requesting subscription for carrier services. The different carriers can place additional restrictions into the LCI groupings, such as a maximum number of permanent virtual circuits that you can define.

6.4.1.2 Call Set-Up, Data Transfer, and Call Clearing

When a DTE wishes to initiate a virtual circuit, it issues a CALL REQUEST, which appears at the remote DTE as an INCOMING CALL. If the remote DTE wants to accept the call, it issues a CALL ACCEPTED packet, which appears to the initiator as a CALL CONNECTED packet.

The PSN is between both DTEs, so the PSN has an opportunity to alter the CALL REQUEST before delivering it to the responder as an Incoming Call. One such reason for altering the packet is to convert the LCI from the value that the initiator specified into a value that corresponds to the subscription profile defined for the responder. Another reason is to convert options that the initiator requests into options subscribed to by the responder. The industry refers to these options as *facilities* and they deal with flow control, reverse charging, and throughput class negotiation.

Data transfer is full-duplex and confirmed. After the network establishes the virtual circuit, both DTEs simultaneously can send data to each other. A sending DTE sends a DATA packet to transmit information and waits for an incoming RECEIVE READY packet, thereby providing the PLP flow control function. The layer allows two forms of confirmation: Local Acknowledgement and End-To-End Acknowledgement. When a DTE sends a data packet, it receives an acknowledgement as to when the local DCE receives the packet or when the remote DTE receives the packet. This all depends on how the sending DTE specifies the value of a flag called the D BIT.

All data packets have a sequence number that allow both the DTE and the DCE to detect a missing or duplicated packet. Each data packet also has a receive sequence number that represents the number of packets received, which further supports error detection.

Call Clearing occurs when either DTE wants to close the virtual circuit. The DTE that wants to close the circuit issues a CLEAR REQUEST, which the other DTE receives as a CLEAR INDICATION. The DTE that receives the CLEAR INDICATION replies with a CLEAR CONFIRMATION, which the first DTE receives and again is a CLEAR CONFIRMATION.

6.4.1.3 Other PLP Functions

The INTERRUPT packet is a special packet that requires an immediate response from the peer DTE. The layer sends the INTERRUPT during the data transfer phase, but unlike normal data packets, does not have a sequence number and is not subject to flow control rules. This is similar to the ISO Transport concept of expedited data—the layer sends the INTERRUPT packet without "waiting for its turn." The INTERRUPT packet is useful for error recovery. The layer can send a single byte of user data with an INTERRUPT packet.

DCE uses another special packet, the *DIAGNOSTIC packet*, to report an error to a DTE. If a DTE attempts to send an invalid packet, the DCE can issue a DIAGNOSTIC to the offending DTE. A DIAGNOSTIC packet contains a diagnostic code field that the DCE uses to inform the DTE of the error's nature and a diagnostic explanation field that contains the header of the offending packet.

6.4.2 Mapping X.25 to Iso Connection-Oriented Network Service

The X.25 services do not exactly match the CONS services that *ISO 8348* describes. Many Transport implementations expect to use CONS. Like Transport, CONS has connection establishment/termination services, unlike the *ISO 8348* Addendum 1 CLNS. So to satisfy the expectations of these Transports, certain mappings must be performed to run on top of X.25. *ISO 8878* defines a mapping mechanism for these similar entities. Table 6-3 illustrates how the CONS services map well to PLP services.

CONS also has two primitives called N-DATA-ACKNOWLEDGE REQUEST and N-DATA ACKNOWLEDGE INDICATION, which are more awkward to map. These primitives are represented by a special field within the PLP DATA, RECEIVE READY, and other special purpose PLP packets.

Table 6-3: Mapping CONS Services to PLP Services

CONS	PLP
N-CONNECT REQUEST	CALL REQUEST
N-CONNECT INDICATION	INCOMING CALL
N-CONNECT RESPONSE	CALL ACCEPTED
N-CONNECT CONFIRM	CALL CONNECTED
N-DATA REQUEST	DATA
N-DATA INDICATION	DATA
N-EXPEDITED DATA REQUEST	INTERRUPT
N-EXPEDITED DATA INDICATION	INTERRUPT
N-DISCONNECT REQUEST	CLEAR REQUEST
N-DISCONNECT INDICATION	CLEAR INDICATION

6.4.3   Using X.25 with Iso Class-4 Transport

The industry implemented ISO Class-4 Transport on a large scale, particularly in the United States. Most early United States implementations used a Connectionless-mode Network Layer. When MAP/TOP and GOSIP began to produce profiles for X.25 implementations, a large installed base of TP-4 implementations existed. These implementations assumed the Network Layer services were CLNS and would not function over packet switched networks, which were connection-oriented. The industry could not ignore or easily modify this large installed base, so instead they created a standard to run Transport Class 4 over the connection-oriented X.25

Implementors used the *Iso 8473* Addendum 1 as the framework for an architecture that smoothly allowed existing Class-4 Transport implementations to function over X.25 with without modifying the Transport Layer. This was desirable, because many network product vendors had already produced mature Class-4 Transport products.

This framework describes a Subnetwork Dependant Convergence Function (SNDCF) that makes the connection-oriented X.25 network appear to provide the same services that CLNS provides. The SNDCF function is simple. When Transport issues a send to the Network Layer, SNDCF establishes an X.25 connection with the destination node. If a suitable X.25 connection already exists between the two nodes then the Transport layer could use it.

All subsequent sends are over the X.25 connection until it exceeds a certain time threshold between sends. When the system exceeds this time threshold (determined by the network administrator), SNDCF assumes that Transport has terminated its connection. An SNDCF can choose to use multiple X.25 connections between itself and a peer SNDCF (e.g., if you desire a high throughput rate).

6.5 TCP/IP

Three middle-layer protocols support the File Transfer Protocol, TELNET (virtual terminal), and other upper-layer functions. These protocols are:

- Internet Protocol (IP)

- Transmission Control Protocol (TCP)

- User Datagram Protocol (UDP)

TCP and UDP use the services of IP. TCP provides a reliable, connection-oriented service, where UDP provides connectionless unreliable service. The industry refers to an implementation with IP and TCP and/or UDP as a TCP/IP implementation.

6.5.1   Internet Protocol

RFC 760 and *RFC 791* describe the Internet Protocol (IP). IP corresponds closely to the ISO Connectionless Network Layer and the industry often calls it: Connectionless Datagram Delivery.

IP provides an unreliable delivery service. Like a letter, an IP packet is not guaranteed to reach its destination. Instead, the service is "best guess" and the IP service user (i.e., TCP or UDP) must provide error detection and recovery. An IP packet can be lost, corrupted, or duplicated and the IP layer itself would not be aware of this.

All IP packets (datagrams) have the same format. The header portion has a fixed part and a variable part. The fixed part always is present and contains fields for source and destination address, segmentation/reassembly functions, Time-To-Live (TTL), checksums, and a *proto* field that the IP uses to identify the IP service user (i.e., TCP or UDP).

IP uses the TTL parameter to prevent a lost packet from forever traveling between intermediate systems in the Internet. Each node that receives a datagram, checks this field to determine if the datagram's TTL has expired. If so, IP discards the lost packet. TTL is analogous to the lifetime function that the ISO Network Layer provides.

The options portion of the IP header is optional. If present, the options portion is variable length and provides functions useful for network problem resolution and source routing. Source routing means that the sender of the datagram can specify the exact route the packet must take to reach its destination. If IP does not use source routing, the Internet itself dynamically produces a route for a packet. Following the datagram header is the actual data that the IP sends between nodes. This data can be TCP or UDP information.

6.5.2   Transmission Control Protocol

Numerous RFCs (including *RFC 793, 761*, and *675*) describe the Transmission Control Protocol (TCP). TCP corresponds closely to the ISO Class-4 Transport Layer, which designers developed to be similar to TCP in both functionality and characteristics. Perhaps the biggest difference between TCP and ISO Transport is that TCP uses only one message format. The industry calls a TCP message a *segment* and is analogous to the ISO term PDU. ISO defined different PDUs for connection establishment, data transfer, and connection termination; TCP uses the same segment to perform all such functions. A segment header, like a datagram header, has a fixed part and an options part, which is a variable length.

The fixed portion of a segment contains fields called source and destination ports. A TCP uses a TCP port to identify the upper-layer user of the TCP service. Such a service can be FTP or TELNET. Table 6-4 shows some of the currently defined reserved TCP ports. You can use the unassigned port values for general application to application functions.

Table 6-4: Sample TCP Port Assignments

TCP Service	Port
FTP DATA	20
FTP CONTROL	21
TELNET	23
TFTP	69

A TCP segment header contains fields for packet sequencing, acknowledgements, checksums, and windowing. TCP uses these fields for flow control, segmentation/reassembly, error detection, and error recovery. The TCP segment header functions perform in a similar manner to those that ISO Class 4-Transport performs. One difference between TCP and ISO Transport is that a single TCP segment can contain outbound data and an acknowledgement of received data. This task requires two separate PDUs in the ISO Transport protocol.

Following the fixed segment header, is an options field that you can use to specify the maximum segment size that a node accepts. Following the options field, is a section for actual user data.

A TCP segment header has an urgent pointer, which TCP uses to identify a portion of user data that it must deliver to the application program before the remaining user data. This is again similar to the ISO Transport concept of expedited data.

6.5.3   User Datagram Protocol

The *RFC 768* describes the User Datagram Protocol (UDP). UDP supports Trivial File Transfer Protocol and exists as a streamlined, connectionless alternative to TCP. Like TCP, UDP uses the services that the IP provides.

UDP serves merely as a multiplexer between multiple application programs and the IP layer. Just as the IP, the industry also calls a UDP message a datagram. A UDP datagram header contains only four fields:

- Source Port
- Destination Port
- Length
- UDP Checksum

UDP uses the source and destination port fields to identify the applications involved in data communications (e.g., Trivial File Transfer Protocol). The length field indicates the length of the UDP datagram, including both header and user data. UDP uses the checksum for more than checking data integrity, UDP also uses the checksum field to verify that the proper destination node and protocol port within that node is reached.

UDP is an unreliable datagram service. UDP uses the services of IP and does not provide additional protocol to support connections and error recovery. So, a UDP user (i.e., TFTP) must provide these functions.

6.6   In Summary

Middle layers move messages from a source end node to a destination end node. In the process, the system can route packets between several intermediate systems. Middle layers also are responsible for detecting and correcting transmission errors. The middle layers provide these services in a manner that is transparent to the upper layers. The industry internationally implements ISO Transport. ISO Transport continually gains more widespread support. MAP, TOP, and GOSIP networks use the ISO Connectionless Network Layer Protocol for LANs and CCITT X.25 networks for WANs. TCP/IP is a group of middle-layer protocols that the industry widely implements throughout the United States. TCP/IP also facilitated the development of other protocols, including ISO Class-4 Transport.

7.1   Overview

The industry sometimes calls the OSI Datalink and Physical Layers the *Lower Layers*. The lower layers describe links between systems in terms of physical connections, such as connectors, cable, and other media. The lower layers also address electrical signaling characteristics such as:

- Voltage
- Frequency
- Modulation/Demodulation

In some implementations, the lower layers perform logical functions such as connection establishment and flow control. This is particularly common when the middle layers' implementation includes a Class-0 or Class-2 Transport Layer.

The middle layers provide end-to-end connectivity. This means that intermediate stations (routers) can exist between the source node and the ultimate destination. The lower layers concern themselves only with connectivity between adjoining nodes. Figure 7-1 describes the distinction between Transport, Network, and lower-layer duties. Station A connects to Station B via lower-layer Link 1. Station B connects to Station C via Link 2. The middle layers ensure that a message sent by Station A arrives at destination Station C. The lower layers ensure that data moves between Stations A and B, and between Stations B and C. It is possible that Link 1 and Link 2 use entirely different datalink/physical technologies. Station B represents a router or other connecting device.

A given lower-layer implementation has an associated physical topology or layout. CCITT X.25 implementations use the point-to-point topology. Another example, called a bus topology, allows you to add nodes without much concern for the existing layout. A third example, called a ring topology, dictates that new nodes "enter the ring." This means that the new node must have a backward connection to an existing node and a forward connection to a different node. This chapter describes two implementations that use the bus topology and another implementation that uses the point-to-point topology.

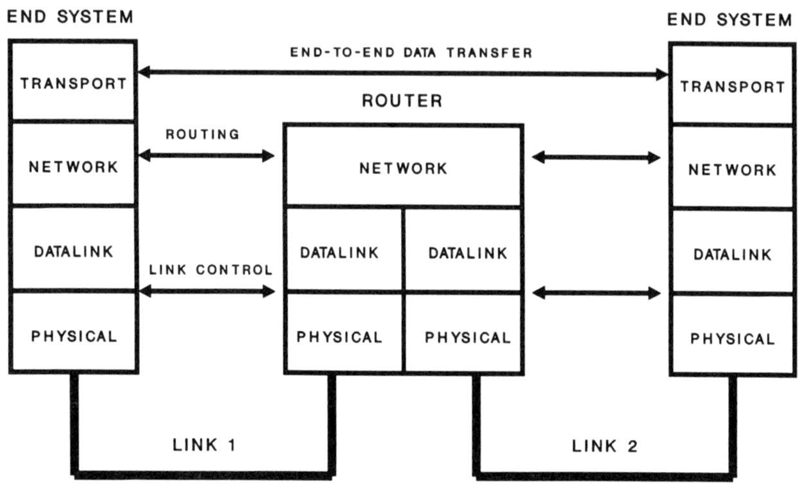

Figure 7-1: Lower-Layer Manage Links

Note that the physical topology does not force restrictions on logical connections supported by the middle and upper layers. Logical connections can exist regardless of the physical layout of the network.

The Institute of Electrical and Electronics Engineers (IEEE) and CCITT have produced widely implemented lower-layer standards. ISO has produced alignment documents, which means these standards dominate lower-layer implementations. The IEEE standards are the basis for the majority of LAN implementations, while the CCITT X.25 standards form the basis for many WAN implementations worldwide.

7.2   IEEE Lower Layers

IEEE describes a set of lower-layer implementations based on the ISO Datalink and Physical Layers. The IEEE Datalink Layer comprises of two sublayers called Logical Link Control (LLC) and Medium Access Control (MAC). LLC (upper sublayer) provides services to the next higher layer: the Network Layer (Figure

7-2). Some IEEE implementations do not have an OSI Network Layer (e.g., TCP/IP products). Some other entity would be the LLC service user. Throughout the following discussions of the LLC sublayer, the phrases "Network Layer" and "LLC service user" are interchangeable.

MAC (sublayer below LLC) uses the services of the Physical Layer. IEEE defines several types of MAC implementations. Each has an associated Physical Layer definition.

LLC accompanies a MAC/Physical pair. This convention makes the boundary between the Datalink Layer and the Physical Layer rather vague, because the MAC sublayer implementation relates directly to a given Physical Layer implementation. This causes some experts to view the MAC sublayer as part of the Physical Layer instead of as a sublayer of the Datalink Layer.

Note that LLC (IEEE standard 802.2) is present in each configuration and provides the same services to the Network Layer regardless of the underlying MAC/Physical technologies.

The IEEE standards group two common MAC and Physical definitions into specifications 802.3 and 802.4. Industry commonly calls the 802.3 standard *Carrier Sense, Multiple Access with Collision Detect* (CSMA/CD) and refers to 802.4 as *token bus*.

The Network Layer has no visibility to the underlying MAC/Physical implementation. The Network Layer always uses the services provided by LLC. The LLC uses the services provided by the MAC/Physical implementation.

7.3   IEEE Logical Link Control

IEEE defines two types of LLC: Type-1 and Type-2. LLC Type-1 provides a simple connectionless datagram service. LLC Type-2 provides a connection-oriented service with error detection/recovery and flow control. A profile specifies use of Type-1 if one of the higher layers performs error detection/recovery and flow control. If none of the higher layers perform these functions then LLC Type-2 is appropriate.

LAYER

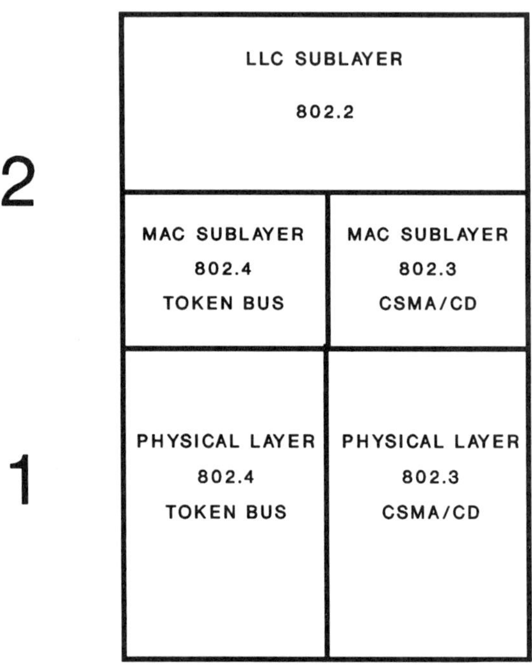

Figure 7-2: Lower-Layer Configurations

The MAP, TOP, and US GOSIP profiles use LLC Type-1 for LAN implementations, because they use the Class-4 Transport protocol. Class-4 Transport performs error detection and recovery and it is not necessary to duplicate these functions in the Datalink Layer. UK GOSIP describes configurations that use LLC Type-2 along with Transport Class-0 or Class-2. These Transports do not perform error detection and recovery functions.

An LLC implementation that supports only Type-1 operation is a Class-1 LLC. An LLC implementation that supports both Type-1 and Type-2 LLC is a Class-2 LLC (Figure 7-3). A Class-1 LLC always provides connectionless Type-1 LLC service. A Class-2 LLC can provide the connectionless Type-1 LLC service in some cases and provide the connection-oriented Type-2 service in other cases. Such an implementation can be useful in a node that is capable of using either Class-4 or Class-0/2 Transport. This node can communicate with peers that support either category of Transport.

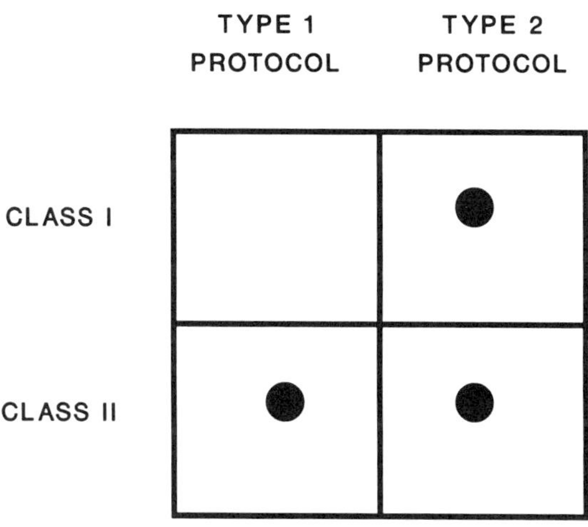

Figure 7-3: LLC **Classes**

Example: Suppose Node A, with a Class-2 LLC, interworks with Node B, which has Transport Class-4. Node A also interworks with Node C, which uses Transport Class-0. The Class-4 Transport connection between Node A and Node B does not require Type-2 LLC. The Class-0 Transport connection between Node A and Node C requires a Type-2 LLC, because Transport Class-0 does not perform error detection and recovery.

7.3.1   LLC PDU Structure and Formats

All LLC Type-1 and Type-2 PDUs have the general structure shown in Figure
7-4. The Destination Service Access Point (DSAP) field identifies the LLC service
user on the receiving node that is to receive an incoming PDU. The Source
Service Access Point (SSAP) identifies the LLC service user on the sending node.
For two communicating Network Layers, the SSAP identifies the Network Layer
that sent the message and the DSAP represents the recipient Network Layer.

Figure 7-4: LLC PDU Structure

The next field after the two address fields is the Control Field. This field
identifies the format or category of the PDU. The Control Field also contains
various protocol-related information.

Every LLC PDU is either an information transfer (I-format), a supervisory
(S-format), or an unnumbered (U-format) PDU. One important distinction
between PDU formats is whether or not the sequence number field is present. A
sequence number field is useful to flow control and error detection/recovery
functions.

- An I-format PDU contains a sequence number field. These PDUs carry
  upper-layer information in the connection-oriented LLC Type-2 mode.
  Like S-format PDUs, I-format PDUs contain a sequence number field.

- S-format PDUs support flow control and error detection/recovery
  functions.

- The U-format PDUs do not contain a sequence number field. These
  PDUs support upper-layer data exchange in the connectionless LLC Type-
  1 mode. U-format contains other specific functions besides data
  exchange.

The last field in an LLC PDU is the Information Field. The information field contains an integral number of octets (this field is sometimes not present). For example, the information field can contain higher layer PCI and user data. The three LLC PDU formats have associated commands and responses (Figure 7-5).

7.3.2   Type-1 LLC Services and Protocol

Services are the functions that a layer makes available to its user, such as the next higher layer. Protocol involves the exchange of PDUs between one service provider (layer) and another service provider. IEEE network standards, like OSI network standards, describe service primitives as well as protocol data units. These service primitives describe function calls and parameters. The parameters pass between the service user and the stack. Vendors implement this process any way they choose. They even hard-code values for parameters, which makes them fixed. There is no way to test conformance of service primitives. The important conformance issue is that the stack properly supports the protocol. You can test protocol conformance by using protocol analyzers. The standards documents provide descriptions of service primitives to help product vendors and other implementors understand how to build conformant equipment.

7.3.2.1 LLC Type-1 Service

The Type-1 LLC provides only data transfer services. No connections establish and no error detection/recovery functions occur. The Network Layer has two primitives available:

- L_DATA.request
- L_DATA.indication

An LLC Type-1 user issues an L_DATA.request to send data to a peer. IEEE does not define the actual mechanism the Network Layer uses to issue this primitive. This function is implementation-dependent (defined by the product vendor). For example, the Network Layer can use a software interrupt to signal delivery of an L_DATA.request to the LLC sublayer. The LLC sublayer presents an L_DATA.indication to the user when data arrives.

COMMANDS	RESPONSES
I-FORMAT	
I-Information	I-Information
F-FORMAT	
RR-Receive Ready	RR-Receive Ready
RNR-Receive Not Ready	RNR-Receive Not Ready
REJ-Reject	REJ-Reject
U-FORMAT	
UI-Unnumbered Information	UA-Unnumbered Acknowledgement
DISC-Disconnect.	DM- Disconnected Mode
SABME-Set Asynchronous	FRMR-Frame Reject
Balanced Mode Extended	
XID-Exchange Identification	XID-Exchange Information
TEST-Test	TEST-Test

Figure 7-5: LLC PDUs

7.3.2.2 Type-1 LLC Protocol

Type-1 LLC operations use the following PDUs:

- Unnumbered Information (UI) Command
- Exchange Identification (XID) Command
- Exchange Identification (XID) Response
- TEST Command
- TEST Response

Three of the PDUs are command PDUs and the other two are response PDUs. The XID and TEST response PDUs associate with command PDUs—the UI PDU does not have a response PDU. All LLC Type-1 PDUs are U-format commands and responses.

The first PDU (Unnumbered Information UI) provides a datagram function. This unconfirmed function does not have a response PDU. This datagram function carries upper-layer information between two Network Layers. This information includes PCI and user data. When the Network Layer issues an L_DATA.request the Type-1 LLC sublayer sends a UI PDU. An incoming UI PDU causes the receiving LLC to issue an L_DATA.indication to its user. Packets can arrive out of order, they can duplicate themselves or become lost, and neither LLC sublayer can detect this. Higher layers must provide mechanisms to detect and correct these error conditions.

An LLC sends the Exchange Identification (XID) PDU to provide information about its characteristics to a remote LLC. The XID specifies the type of service it supports (Type-1, Type-2, or both). The node that receives the XID command PDU returns an XID response PDU with information about its own characteristics. In this way, both LLCs learn each other's capabilities.

The TEST PDU tests the transmission link between two LLCs. One LLC sends a TEST command PDU to another node and waits for that node to return a TEST response PDU. If the response arrives within a reasonable amount of time, LLC assumes the link is operational. The user determines what is "a reasonable amount of time." (A reasonable amount of time generally is less than ten milliseconds.) A TEST command also can contain additional data that the LLC sublayer must echo in the TEST response PDU. The data can be a test pattern.

The UI PDU carries data between two peer Datalink Layer users. The UI differs from the XID and Test commands, because it represents a direct response to a service request from the Network Layer. The LLC sublayer sends the XID and TEST command PDUs for some other reasons:

- The node recently activated (you powered-ON the system) and an internal mechanism requested the action.

- An operator requested the function, perhaps as part of an effort to resolve a network problem.

- An automated network management function requested the action.

According to IEEE, an LLC implementation must be able to send an XID or
TEST response PDU, but the capability to generate an XID or TEST command PDU
is optional. A conformant implementation must act as responder, initiator is
optional.

7.3.3   Type-2 LLC Services and Protocol

Type-2 LLC operation is somewhat more complex than Type-1 LLC, because
it requires additional mechanisms to provide the following functions:

- Establish connections
- Perform flow control
- Recover from errors

LLC Type-2 operation is almost identical to X.25 LAPB. The CCITT LAPB
standard represents Layer 2 in the X.25 model. The LAPB standard derives from
the LLC Type-2 definition. The LLC Type-2 Service primitives divide into the
following functional categories:

- Connection Establishment and Termination
- Data Transfer
- Reset
- Flow Control Between LLC and the Network Layer

LLC Type-1 defines two service primitives: L_DATA.request and
L_DATA.indication. LLC Type-2 uses this two-phase operation for one category
of services. For the other categories, it uses a three-phase operation (Figure 7-6).

A three-phase interaction starts when an LLC Type-2 user issues a request.
This results in an indication to the user at the receiving end. A confirmation
returns to the initiating user of the interaction, but the confirmation does not
come directly from the responding user. Instead, the LLC service provider
(sublayer) issues the confirmation. The local LLC sublayer can direct the
confirmation (Figure 7-7) or the remote LLC can indirectly cause the confirmation
(Figure 7-6). As with the OSI upper layers, an LLC user issues requests and
receives confirmations. Unlike the OSI upper-layer 4-phase operations, an LLC
user never issues responses.

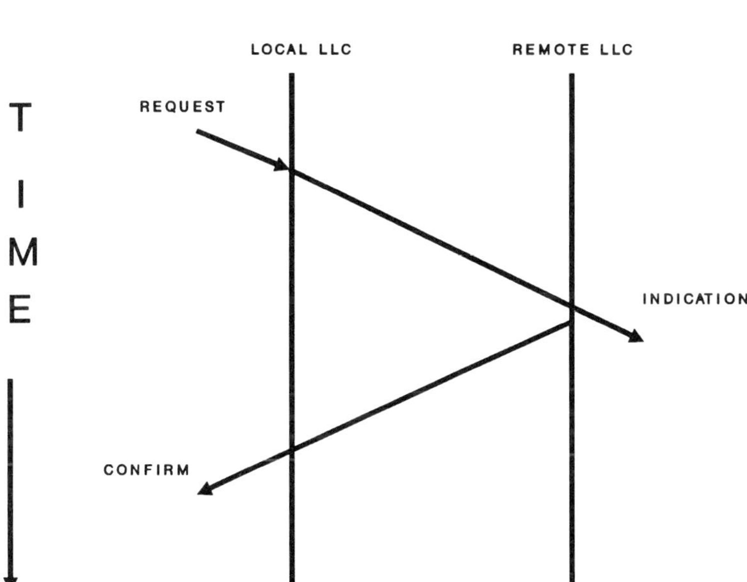

Figure 7-6: Three-Phase Service

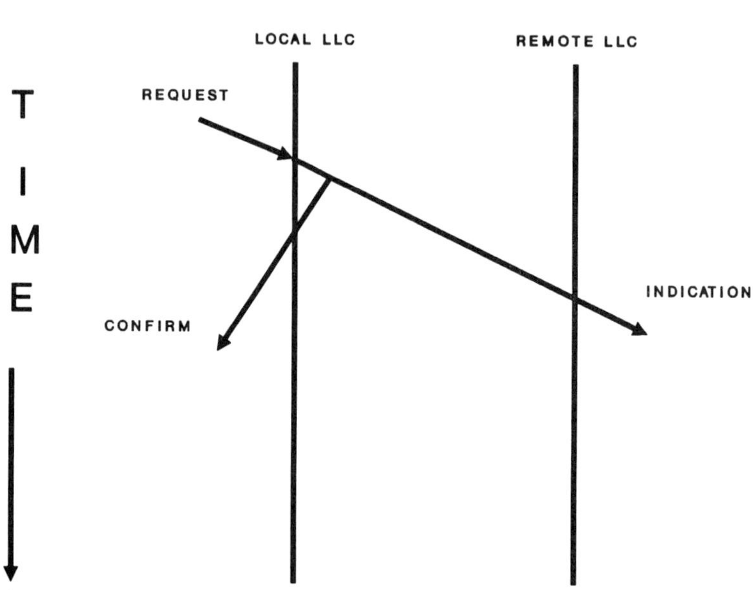

Figure 7-7: Three-Phase Service Alternate

7.3.3.1 Establishing/Terminating LLC Type-2 Connections

LLC Type-2 connections have three phases just as OSI connections have three
phases:

- Connection establishment
- Data transfer
- Connection termination

Before two peer LLC Type-2 users can send data, they must establish a logical
connection. After both sides complete their data exchange or if an unrecoverable
error occurs, the connection termination phase begins. At this time neither LLC
can send data.

The connection establishment operation involves the following service primitives:

- L_CONNECT.request
- L_CONNECT.indication
- L_CONNECT.confirm

The LLC sublayer sends/receives the following PDUs to support those services:

- Set Asynchronous Balanced Mode Extended (SABME) command
- Unnumbered Acknowledgement (UA) response

An LLC Type-2 user issues an L_CONNECT.request to start the connection-establishment phase. This causes the LLC sublayer to send a SABME command PDU to the remote LLC. This is functionally equivalent to the Transport Layer T_CONNECT PDU. IEEE calls this PDU SABME, either side can send data during an LLC Type-2 connection without permission from the other side.

After the connection forms, either side can send data with equal authority. An unbalanced connection dictates that one side is master and that the other side is slave. In an unbalanced connection, a slave requires permission to send data.

SABME implies extended sequence numbers, which means seven bits long. In the basic mode, sequence numbers are three bits long. Some of the LLC Type-2 PDUs contain sequence numbers to provide error detection and recovery.

When the remote LLC receives the SABME PDU, it knows that a peer is attempting to establish a connection. In response, the remote LLC delivers an L_CONNECT.indication to its user.

The remote LLC must inform the initiating LLC that it acknowledges the connection. It sends an Unnumbered Acknowledgement response (UA) PDU to the initiating LLC. When the initiating LLC receives the UA, it delivers an L_CONNECT.confirmation to the user that started the connection-establishment process. At this time the two peer LLC users have a connection and can send data to each other. Eventually one LLC user elects to close the connection for one of the following reasons:

- The LLC user finishes sending data.

- An internal error occurs. The node runs out of memory or an operator requests shutdown.

The connection-termination process is similar to the connection establishment process and involves the following service primitives:

- L_DISCONNECT.request
- L_DISCONNECT.indication
- L_DISCONNECT.confirm

To provide these services, the LLC sublayer uses the following PDUs:

- Disconnect (DISC) command
- Unnumbered Acknowledgement (UA) response

The Network Layer that terminates the connection issues an L_DISCONNECT.request. This causes the local LLC sublayer to send a DISC command PDU to the remote LLC sublayer. Receipt of the DISC PDU causes the remote LLC sublayer to present an L_DISCONNECT.indication to the termination responder. The termination responder considers the connection closed.

After the remote LLC sublayer issues the L_DISCONNECT.indication to its service user, it sends a UA response PDU to the local LLC sublayer. This is an acknowledgement of connection termination. As a final step, the local LLC sublayer delivers an L_DISCONNECT.confirm to the termination initiator.

7.3.3.2 LLC Type-2 Data Transfer

Data transfer for LLC Type-2 operation occurs after a connection establishes. This confirmed service provides the following primitives to the Network Layer:

- L_DATA_CONNECT.request
- L_DATA_CONNECT.indication
- L_DATA_CONNECT.confirm

The names of these data transfer service primitives contain the word CONNECT to differentiate them from the L_DATA primitives. L_DATA_CONNECT primitives apply to the connection-oriented mode, while L_DATA primitives apply to the connectionless mode.

LLC uses the following PDUs to provide this data transfer service:

- Information (I) command
- Information (I) response
- Receive Ready (RR)
- Receive Not Ready (RNR)
- Reject (REJ)
- Frame Reject (FRMR)

The Information command and response PDUs are I-format PDUs, while the other four are S-format PDUs. Information command and response PDUs contain two sequence number fields. The first, called the *send sequence number* N(S), represents the number associated with the packet an LLC sends. The other field, called the *receive sequence number* N(R), represents an acknowledgement to a packet sent by the remote LLC. The S-format PDUs contain an N(R) field, but do not have an N(S) field. The N(S) and N(R) sequence number fields within a single Information PDU serve two purposes:

- It puts a tag or serial number on an outbound data packet.
- It provides acknowledgement of receipt of data in the opposite direction.

An LLC sublayer that receives an Information PDU examines the value of N(S) and constructs a new PDU with N(R) set to N(S) + 1.

Example: Assume an LLC sends an Information PDU with N(S) equal to 50. The LLC does not receive an acknowledgement (a subsequent Information PDU with N(R) equal to 51) within a certain time. LLC considers the packet lost and the sender must retransmit the packet.

7.3.3.3 Information Command and Response PDUs

The distinction between an I-command PDU and an I-response PDU is somewhat confusing. Both transfer data between LLC users. An I-command PDU requires an I-response PDU. The I-command forces the remote LLC to send an immediate acknowledgement to a data transmission. The alternative to using an I-command PDU is to send data using an I-response PDU. The remote LLC does not have to acknowledge an I-response. A data transfer session between two LLCs can occur using only the I-response PDU.

An LLC sublayer user issues an L_DATA_CONNECT.request to initiate data transfer. This causes the local LLC to send an Information PDU to the remote LLC. The Information PDU contains the information that the local user wants to send to the remote user. After it receives the Information PDU, the remote LLC delivers an L_DATA_CONNECT.indication to its user. The L_DATA_CONNECT contains the data sent by the other node.

The remote LLC sends a response to acknowledge the Information PDU. Several responses are possible. When the local LLC sublayer receives this response it issues an L_DATA_CONNECT.confirm to the initiating user. An LLC that receives an Information PDU can do one of the following:

- **Case 1**—If it has an outbound Information PDU ready for transmission, it can send this Information PDU. This serves two purposes: it acknowledges receipt of data in one direction and it sends data in the other direction.

- **Case 2**—If it does not have information to send, it sends either a Receive Ready (RR) response PDU or a Receive Not Ready response (RNR) PDU.

In both cases, the remote LLC constructs a new packet to acknowledge receipt of the Information PDU. This new packet is an Information, RR, or RNR PDU. The remote LLC sets the N(R) field of this new packet to the value of N(S) + 1 in the received Information PDU. In Case 2, the receiver constructs and sends an RR if it is immediately ready for another Information PDU. If the receiver needs more time, it uses the RNR, perhaps because of a temporary memory shortage.

7.3.3.4 LLC Type-2 Flow Control

RR and RNR provide a flow control mechanism. This flow control mechanism occurs between two peer LLC sublayers. Another form of flow control occurs between a single LLC sublayer and its service user.

If an LLC sublayer receives an RNR PDU, it cannot send more data until the other side is ready. When the other side is ready for more data, LLC sends one of the following PDUs:

- An Information PDU

- A Receive Ready PDU
- A Reject (REJ) response PDU

7.3.3.5 LLC Type-2 Error Detection/Recovery

LLC sends the REJ PDU as a response to a certain error condition: reception of an Information PDU with an incorrect N(S) value. An incorrect N(S) value indicates that LLC received an out-of-sequence packet. The N(R) field of a REJ PDU contains the value that the receiver expects in the N(S) field of the next Information PDU. When a sender receives a REJ PDU the sender must examine the N(R) field and try to retransmit the Information PDU associated with that field.

LLC handles a slightly more severe error in a different way. If an Information PDU arrives with an invalid R(S) value, the receiving LLC sends a Frame Reject (FRMR) response PDU instead of the REJ response PDU. An invalid R(S), as opposed to an incorrect R(S), is one that is out of the legal range of R(S). An invalid R(S) value indicates a protocol violation. An incorrect R(S) represents an out of sequence packet and LLC responds with the REJ response PDU.

LLC sends the FRMR if an Information PDU arrives with an invalid (too much) amount of data. After a FRMR is sent, the LLC peers must restart or reset the datalink connection. This means that the LLC peers must repeat the connection-establishment procedure involving SABME and UA. This resetting procedure sometimes results in the loss of data. LLC can retransmit the data later, after the new connection forms.

7.3.3.6 How LLC Handles Invalid PDUs

One other error detection/recovery mechanism is worth mentioning: invalid LLC PDUs. Invalid PDUs can occur during a glitch or temporary period of electronic noise. The LLC sublayer checks each incoming PDU and ensures that it contains valid values for the following:

- SSAP
- DSAP
- Control field
- An information field (optional)

LLC also ensures that each PDU contains an integral number of octets.

Example: A PDU must not be five and a half bytes long.

In each of these situations, the error recovery function is to discard the packet. LLC acts as if it did not receive the packet. Meanwhile, the sender waits for an acknowledgement that never arrives. Eventually, the sender retransmits the packet. A sending LLC retransmits an unacknowledged Information PDU several times. Some products allow you to determine the number of times to retransmit an unacknowledged Information PDU. Other less-flexible products hard code the value.

7.3.3.7 LLC Type-2 Reset Service

The LLC sublayer user or LLC itself can start the connection reset function. LLC starts this procedure if a protocol error occurs. If the LLC sublayer user is the Network Layer, the Network Layer can explicitly reset the LLC connection. Perhaps an unrecoverable internal error occurred.

The reset procedure returns the stack to a known state. From this known state the Network Layer can perform recovery functions. Two peer LLC sublayers can attempt to recover directly from an error state. Direct recovery requires a more sophisticated state machine than restarting from a known state. The reset service uses the following service primitives:

- L_RESET.request
- L_RESET.indication
- L_RESET.confirmation

The PDUs exchanged during the reset operation are:

- Set Asynchronous Balanced Mode Extended (SABME) command
- Unnumbered Acknowledgement (UA) response
- Optionally, Frame Reject response FRMR

The Network Layer presents an L_RESET.request to the LLC sublayer to initiate the reset operation. This causes LLC to send a SABME command to the remote LLC. The remote LLC can either:

- Return a UA response PDU to the initiator, indicating that the connection resets.

- Return a Disconnect Mode (DM) response PDU, indicating that the connection closes instead of resets.

If the connection resets, both LLC sublayers set their sequence number counters to zero. The next value of R(S) in an Information PDU applies for data flow in both directions. The initiating LLC delivers an L_RESET.confirm to the Network Layer, while the remote LLC delivers an L_RESET.indication to its service user. Both Network Layers know that the connection resets.

If the connection closes, both LLC sublayers issue an L_DISCONNECT.indication to their users. The connection-establishment procedure repeats if the two users want to send more data to each other.

7.3.3.8 Flow Control between LLC Type-2 and the Network Layer

Two peer LLC sublayers perform flow control at the protocol level, using the Receive Ready and Receive Not Ready PDUs. LLC Type-2 service defines another kind of flow control between the LLC sublayer and its service user. This flow control function involves the following service primitives:

- L_CONNECTION_FLOWCONTROL.request
- L_CONNECTION_FLOWCONTROL.response

There are no PDUs associated with this service, because the operation is between a service provider and a service user instead of between two sets of peer service user/provider pairs. An vendor can choose to develop a product that associates these flow control service primitives with the flow control PDUs described. An LLC user sends an L_CONNECTION_FLOWCONTROL.request to indicate the amount of data it can accept.

Example: The Network Layer can use L_CONNECTION_FLOWCONTROL.request to inform the LLC sublayer that it can hold 10 kilobytes of incoming data. The LLC sublayer delivers only 10 kilobytes worth of data unless it receives another L_CONNECTION_FLOWCONTROL.request from the Network Layer. If more than 10 kilobytes of data arrives from the remote node, the local LLC must buffer the data and wait until the Network Layer reports readiness to receive more data.

An implementation can use RNR to throttle or slow down the remote LLC. The local LLC prevents the remote LLC from sending more data than the local Network layer can process.

L_CONNECTION_FLOWCONTROL.indication applies to flow control in the opposite direction. The LLC sublayer sends the primitive to the Network Layer to describe its data buffering capacity. If the Network Layer exceeds this limit, there is no guarantee that the LLC sublayer can buffer all of the data. In this overflow condition, LLC can drop or discard some of the data.

7.3.4   LLC Service Requirements from the MAC Sublayer

LLC Type-1 and LLC Type-2 have simple service requirements. Both types require the ability to send and receive packets, without the need for connection establishment or error recovery. Both types of LLC use the following service primitives, which the underlying MAC sublayer provides:

- MA_DATA.request
- MA_DATA.indication
- MA_DATA.confirm

MA_DATA stands for Medium Access Control (MAC) data. All three names start with MA_DATA, because the MAC sublayer provides all of these services. An LLC issues a MA_DATA.request to the MAC to request the transmission of a packet. The remote MAC delivers an MA_DATA.indication to LLC after it receives an incoming packet. The sending MAC passes a MA_DATA.confirm to the local LLC to report status of the transmission.

If an error occurs during the data transmission, MAC reports the error in the MA_DATA.indication. The kinds of errors that can occur depend on the MAC implementation.

7.4   IEEE 802.4—Token Bus

The Manufacturing Automation Protocol (MAP) profile has adopted the IEEE 802.4 token bus technology. Industry recognizes MAP as an important lower-layer solution to factory automation. IEEE 802.4 describes two kinds of MAC sublayer/Physical Layer combinations:

- Broadband
- Carrierband

7.4.1   Token Bus Features

The token bus standard appeals especially to factory network implementors, because it addresses several specific factory network requirements. Ideally, an automated factory network has the following characteristics:

- It simultaneously transmits data, video, and voice on the same cable (or other medium).

- It functions well in an electrically noisy environment.

- It provides a deterministic data transmission service. Real-time application programmers must understand the worst-case period of time for a packet to reach a destination.

Token bus implementations address these requirements better than other MAC/Physical configurations. Broadband technology allows multiple signals at various frequency ranges to share the same cable. This means that a single broadband cable system can carry data, video, and voice information at the same time. Many factory network implementors must provide all three kinds of information exchange to their users. Data communication provides a mechanism to coordinate computing devices, while video and voice transmission supply valuable communication tools for people.

While less expensive than broadband, carrierband only supports data communication and does not provide this multi-purpose transmission capability. Both broadband and carrierband have noise resistance and are deterministic. Broadband and carrierband technologies provide a suitable immunity to the kinds of electrical and electro-magnetic noise found in automated factories. Factory equipment (turbines, motors, and engines) emit signals at frequencies that disturb some lower-layer technologies. Properly installed and maintained broadband and carrierband networks survive in the harsh factory environment.

Broadband and carrierband both provide deterministic data delivery. Both implementations use the MAC protocol responsible for the deterministic quality. This protocol involves a logical token. An implementor must understand that even though an 802.4 MAC/Physical network provides deterministic data transfer, activities within the higher layers may not be so deterministic. Real-time application developers must consider the non-deterministic quality of the higher layers.

Two other aspects of token bus appeal to factory network implementors:

- The protocol is efficient under heavy loads.

- The access mechanism is fair, which means that each station in the network has an equal share of the network bandwidth.

The efficiency of the protocol under heavy loads is because access is synchronous. The MAC logical token management provides the fairness quality.

7.4.2   IEEE 802.4 MAC Sublayer

As the name implies, token bus networks use the concept of a logical token. This token passes from one node to the next in a logical ring. According to the rules of token bus, a node can transmit only when it holds the token. The 802.4 standard describes a protocol that manages possession of the token, including:

- How a node enters the logical ring.

- How a node recognizes that it has the token.

- How a node knows where to pass the token to when it finishes transmission.

Like other bus technologies, 802.4 describes a flexible topology that allows you to add new nodes to the network without having to maintain a physical ring. A bus topology allows you to add new nodes and cable sections as if the new nodes were new branches of tree. Even though a token passes among nodes in a circular direction, you need not connect the nodes into a physical ring. The concept of a ring is entirely logical; the physical location of a node has no impact on its position in the logical ring.

802.4 and other IEEE MACs provide connectionless data transmission services to the LLC sublayer. The 802.4 procedure to provide these services is quite simple. When LLC has data to send, MAC constructs a frame, waits until it has the token, and transmits the frame. The complex part of 802.4 MAC is station management. Station management describes the procedures and protocol to manage the logical ring.

7.4.2.1 Station Management

All MAC entities in the network cooperate to provide management of the logical ring. Each 802.4 MAC sublayer in the network performs a complex station management function. Each station has an internal state machine called the Access Control Machine (ACM). The ACM on one node works with the other ACMs in the network to provide the following functions:

- Logical ring establishment
- Ring member addition/deletion
- Error recovery

The discussion of these functions is a simplified version of the actual processes, but demonstrates the concepts of logical ring management.

7.4.2.2 Slot Time

For these functions to operate properly, every station must have accurate timers, many of which relate to a reference timer called *slot time*. Slot time can range from a few micro-seconds to a few milliseconds. A network implementor must ensure that every 802.4 node uses the same value for slot time. Otherwise, the algorithms that support the logical ring fail, resulting in network failure. Products that support 802.4 must give the network implementor a method of setting slot time. This usually is a software parameter that gets passed to the ACM of the product.

7.4.2.3 Logical Ring Establishment

A logical ring requires at least two active stations, because you consider the ring established when two or more nodes are passing the token. The ring establishment procedure starts when the first node in the network attempts to participate in the token passing process. A node performs the following tasks to enter the logical ring:

1. It listens passively, trying to detect whether or not the ring has already established.

2. If after a pre-determined number of slot times, it does not detect activity, the node assumes that the ring:

   a. Does not exist.

   b. Has been lost due to a network error and that the ring needs to re-initialize.

3. In either case, the ACM enters into a state known as claim token. In this state, the node sends a number of frames called claim_token frames, and listens for other transmissions. One of the following things happens:

   a. No other transmissions are heard. The node assumes possession of the token.

   b. Two or more other nodes simultaneously attempt to claim the initial token. A back-off procedure begins. Each node waits a period of time (based on slot time) before it attempts to obtain the token.

After a node claims the token, the ACM enters into the use-token state, which means the node can send data frames. The node remains in the use-token state until one of the following happens:

- Its token holding timer expires.

- It has no more data to transmit.

The token holding timer runs for a fixed amount of time. The network administrator determines the value for the token holding time. Each node in the network uses the same value for its own internal token holding timer. This is how 802.4 offers a fair share of the network capacity to each node in the ring. Each node has the opportunity to possess the token for the same amount of time. If a node does not require the token for the entire holding timer period, it can surrender the token early. This helps to allow the maximum network traffic.

7.4.2.4 Ring Member Addition/Deletion

When a node is ready to leave the use-token state, it enters into the token passing state. A node that enters into the token passing state does one of the following:

- **Case 1**—If it knows which node is next to receive the token, it passes the token to that node. Such a node is known as the successor to the token holding node.

- **Case 2**—Optionally, even though the successor is known, the node can offer the opportunity for new stations to enter the ring.

- **Case 3**—If the node does not know the identity of its successor the node can offer the opportunity for new nodes to enter the ring. A node may not know its successors identity, because the ring is initializing or because a ring recovery procedure is underway.

The first two cases apply to normal network operation, while the third case applies to ring establishment. Under normal operation, a time-based algorithm occurs within each ACM to determine whether the node must send the token to its successor (Case 1) or offer an opportunity for new nodes to enter the ring (Case 2).

A token holding station sends a frame called solicit successor to offer ring entry to a new node (Case 2). The token holding station now enters into a state called *await response*. A station in the await response state listens for one slot time. During this period new stations can send a response to the solicit successor frame. This response represents a request to enter the logical ring. Two things can happen:

- A single station issues a response. This station becomes a member of the ring and becomes eligible to receive the token.

- More than one station simultaneously attempts to enter the ring. This results in a short period of confusion on the wire. Invalid signals appear on the medium, because two or more stations simultaneously attempt to issue a response to the solicit successor frame. These stations enter into a back-off condition; each station waits a variable amount of time before it tries to enter the ring.

In the ring establishment mode (Case 3), the token passing node always issues a solicit successor frame. The token passing node does not know the identity of its successor. Just as with normal operation, the ACM enters into the await response state and listens for valid responses to the solicit successor frame it sent. When the token passing node hears a valid response, a new station becomes a member of the ring. This new ring member participates in the token passing operation.

7.4.2.5 Error Recovery

During normal operation, a node performs the following series of actions:

1. Waits for the token.
2. Optionally sends data while in possession of the token.
3. Enters into the token passing state.

If the token passing procedure fails, the logical ring breaks. The token passing node initiates a series of error recovery procedures. The error recovery operation involves an attempt to re-establish the logical ring.

Initially, the token passing station assumes that the error is transient and that recovery is possible with the least amount of impact to network throughput. The first attempt to re-establish the ring is to re-send the token to its successor. If this fails, the token passing station assumes that its successor has failed and tries to assign another node as its new successor. This involves sending a frame called who_follows and waiting for a response to this frame. Two things can happen:

- **Case 1**—The token passing station hears a valid response to the who_follows frame. The token passing station now has a valid successor.

- **Case 2**—The token passing station does not hear a valid response to the who_follows frame. The station assumes that the network is inoperable or that its own receiver circuitry has failed. The station stops trying to re-establish the ring. The node listens for activity on the medium. If valid frames are heard, the node can attempt to establish the ring.

7.4.2.6 Synchronous Data Transmission Value

The token bus data transmission procedures illustrate the synchronous nature of 802.4. Each member of the logical ring sends data only when it has the token. This means that during normal operation, nodes do not simultaneously send data packets. Because no contention can occur during data transfer, 802.4 performs well under heavy network traffic. Other MAC technologies, such as IEEE 802.3, support an asynchronous data transmission. IEEE 802.3 allows any node to send data at any time. A sending node takes the chance that another node attempts to send data at the same time. This results in a contention or collision. A collision requires a back-off procedure, which results in a loss of aggregate network throughput. The chances of a collision are higher under heavy network loads.

Maintenance of synchronous data transmission involves overhead associated with token management frames. Under heavy network loads this overhead amounts to less waste than that encountered with asynchronous data transmission. Under heavy loads the collisions happen so often that the waste associated with collisions exceeds the overhead associated with token management frames.

7.4.3   IEEE 802.4 Broadband Implementation

The broadband token bus implementation allows simultaneous transmission of data, video, and voice. Broadband uses coaxial cable medium. The value of broadband to the automated factory is that one cable system supports all three functions and eliminates the need for three separate physical medias.

Token bus cable resembles the medium that cable television companies use bring video signals to our homes. The primary difference is that token bus uses much higher quality wire, shielding, and connectors.

Broadband systems use an active medium. A device called a head-end remodulator amplifies signals on the wire. Industry calls head-end remodulators *headends*. An 802.4 station transmits low-power signals onto the wire and the headend amplifies these signals. Other 802.4 stations listen to the amplified signals produced by the headend. Vendors design the receiver circuitry of a station to receive the amplified signals generated by a headend. This circuitry is less expensive than circuitry capable of directly receiving the low-power signals generated by 802.4 stations.

Signals that stations transmit to the headend travel on the reverse channel, while signals transmitted from the headend to the stations move on the forward channel. All of the stations transmit on the reverse channel and a single transmitter (the headend) transmits on the forward channel.

A channel is associated with a frequency range. With broadband technology it is possible to define several frequency ranges and allocate several reverse-forward channels to these pre-defined frequency ranges. This makes it possible to have multiple logical data transmission paths available on a single-cable system. This is what MAP has done: they defined three separate reverse-forward channel pairs. This makes it possible for a cable system to support three times the throughput of a single data transmission path. This capacity for high throughput makes broadband technology appropriate for network backbones. Applications found in large, automated factories also benefit from high-throughput networks.

7.4.3.1 Jabber Inhibit

802.4 and other technologies provide an error recovery function called *jabber inhibit*. Jabber inhibit prevents a single, faulty station from crashing the entire network. Typically implemented as a watchdog internal to each station, jabber inhibit circuitry starts a timer when the transmitting circuitry begins to put signals onto the wire. If the transmitter continues to send signals beyond a pre-determined time threshold, the jabber inhibit circuitry automatically disables the transmitter circuitry. This way, a node is not allowed to jabber or speak nonsense, which can cause other stations on the network to fail.

7.4.4　IEEE 802.4 Carrierband Implementations

Carrierband networks offer a single data transmission channel and do not allow simultaneous data, voice, and video transmission. In spite of this, carrierband networks are useful in factories, particularly in automated workcells with about 30 or fewer stations.

Carrierband networks use a passive medium, as opposed to the active broadband medium. Carrierband networks do not require headends. Carrierband stations receive the same signals generated by other stations; there is no concept of reverse and forward channels.

Because carrierband networks use passive medium, the distance between stations and the overall length of the cable system are usually less than that allowed with broadband systems. Carrierband networks can use repeaters to extended the length of the medium. Repeaters receive signals on one section of cable and amplify the signals before forwarding to another section of cable.

Although carrierband does not offer the same level of services that broadband does, it is desirable for the following reasons:

- Its lower cost makes it appropriate for applications that do not require the high-bandwidth of broadband. A single carrierband node often sells for less than half the cost of a single broadband node.

- Carrierband networks do not require headends. This saves money and means one less piece of equipment to maintain.

Although carrierband networks are smaller than broadband networks, vendors must implement the jabber-inhibit function in carrierband stations. Often, carrierband networks support communication between robots and other motion control devices. Jabber-inhibit indirectly supports the safety of factory personnel. Jabber inhibit can conceivably prevent a faulty station from crashing a network and prevent the failure of an important safety device (such as a robot work area intrusion detection device).

7.5   IEEE 802.3 CSMA/CD

IEEE 802.3 is a very common lower-layer LAN technology. These networks exist in virtually every large organization and serve the needs of offices and factories alike. Many common network families operate over IEEE 802.3, including OSI Profiles such as MAP, TOP, and GOSIP, as well as TCP/IP. Because this technology has become so popular, the market and manufacturing processes for IEEE 802.3-based products have matured. This means that prices are competitive and high quality is common.

IEEE 802.3 describes a bus topology and as with 802.4, you can add new nodes to an existing network in a flexible manner without concern for the existing topology of the network. CSMA/CD must provide rules that define how and when a station accesses the network, because the physical layout alone does not dictate an access method.

IEEE 802.4 defines a logical token access method; a station must possess the token before it can send data. IEEE 802.3 defines a very different access method. IEEE 802.3 is known best for its access method, called *Carrier Sense, Multiple Access with Collision Detect* (CSMA/CD). CSMA/CD allows stations to transmit asynchronously data, unlike the token passing technologies such as token bus.

7.5.1   Carrier Sense, Multiple Access with Collision Detect

With CSMA/CD, network access is asynchronous. The possibility exists that two or more nodes can try simultaneously to send data. This results in a collision. A collision is easy to detect, because if two stations attempt to send data at the same time, the signals on the wire are temporarily invalid. The receiver circuitry assumes that a collision has occurred if it detects this period of invalid signals.

CSMA/CD provides a mechanism for recovery from a collision. Collisions are part of normal operation, and are not errors, unless the frequency of collisions per second exceeds some acceptable number. CSMA/CD describes a mechanism to reduce the collision probability. A station must listen to the network for a period of time before attempting to transmit. If the station detects activity, the station is said to have sensed or detected a carrier.

If the station senses carrier, the station must wait until the wire becomes quiet before it begins its own transmission. A station must not interrupt a transmitting station. A collision should occur only if two or more nodes are both waiting for the currently transmitting station to finish.

If two stations detect a collision, both nodes responsible for the collision back off. Both stations wait a variable amount of time before attempting to retransmit. Each station that enters into the back off state waits a random amount of time before attempting retransmission. This reduces the probability of a repeat collision.

The acronym CSMA/CD has the following meaning:

- Carrier Sense (CS) means that a station must be able to detect activity on the network.

- Multiple Access (MA) means that more than one station can attempt to transmit a frame at the same time.

- Collision Detect (CD) means that a station knows when a transmission has resulted in a collision.

7.5.2   IEEE 802.3 MAC/Physical Layer Implementations

Usually, the 802.3 MAC sublayer exists in silicon, in the form of a self-contained chip. Often, this chip is part of a network board. You can purchase these products and add them to a computer in an empty slot. Sometimes vendors integrate this chip into the base computer. This chip normally represents the MAC sublayer and provides logic to manage access to the network.

An IEEE 802.3 station attaches to the network via a drop cable. The drop cable connects the station to a separate unit that represents the Physical Layer. This unit is called an *Attachment Unit* (AU) or transceiver. The AU provides the proper voltages, frequencies, and support for the medium of a specific Physical Layer implementation. For example, one common CSMA/CD AU implementation operates at one mega-bit per second over twisted-pair (similar to telephone wire).

Another common AU implementation operates at 10 mega-bits per second over coaxial cable. The AU architecture allows a single MAC implementation and a single product to function over a variety of applications. You must not modify this product for each application. The concept of an AU benefits the network implementor as well as product vendors. Network implementors can switch to a different AU and use existing network boards (and software) if their Physical Layer implementation changes. Network product vendors can sell such a single product in multiple markets.

7.6   CCITT X.25 Lower Layers

CCITT X.25 has become an important Wide Area Network (WAN) standard for enterprise network applications. The X.25 Packet Layer Protocol relates to the OSI Network Layer. This sections describes X.25 at Level 2 and Level 1, which relate to the OSI Datalink and Physical Layers, respectively.

The need to connect various kinds of computers from multiple vendors has encouraged the development of data communication standards for LANs and also has encouraged implementors to use WANs based on the X.25 standard for the same reasons. The X.25 standard allows implementors to connect their LANs to other LANs, between buildings, and even between countries, using standard protocols.

As mentioned previously, X.25 defines the interface between Data Terminal Equipment (DTE) and Data Circuit-terminating Equipment (DCE). A DTE belongs to the network user, while the DCE belongs to the network carrier, such as public and private packet switched service providers. A DTE interfaces to a DCE over a single, dedicated cable, which comprises a point-to-point connection. The topology of the network defined by X.25 is simple with only two nodes: the DTE and the DCE. However, the purpose of X.25 is to allow a DTE to communicate with another DTE. The complete topology to support DTE to DTE communication involves two point-to-point networks with a public switched network (PSN) between them.

The X.25 Level 2, called *Link Access Protocol, Balanced* (LAPB), describes the logical connection between a DTE and DCE. Vendors today rarely implement an earlier standard, known as Link Access Procedure (LAP), which describes an unbalanced relationship between nodes.

The DTE is not concerned with how the PSN gets data to the other DTE. The PSN is assumed to be reliable, and that all data delivered between the sending DTE arrives at the receiving DTE, unless the PSN reports a network failure.

The X.25 Level 1, called the *Physical Level*, defines the connectors, cable, and electrical/electronic technology to move packets between the DTE and the DCE. Several Physical Level standards exist that define a wide range of performance and media types.

7.6.1　X.25 Level-2 LAPB

The X.25 Level 2, commonly called LAPB, is based on the IEEE Type-2 LLC standard. In fact, LAPB procedure is so similar to Type-2 LLC that it would be redundant to give an exhaustive description of LAPB. Instead, the differences between LAPB and LLC Type-2 described are here, along with additional information regarding subscription parameters that must be understood by an X.25 network implementor.

7.6.1.1　Similarities and Differences between LAPB and IEEE LLC

LAPB must perform the same function that LLC Type-2 performs—manage logical connections, move information between two directly connected nodes, and recover from various errors. LAPB defines the same procedures for connection establishment, sequenced information transfer, and error recovery via the reset function, as used by LLC Type-2.

The PDUs or frames LAPB uses are a subset of the PDUs that IEEE LLC uses minus the TEST and XID commands and responses. The XID function provides a mechanism for one LLC to determine the characteristics of another LLC, such as connectionless mode Type-1 or connection mode Type-2 capability. This function does not apply to LAPB, which does not have the connectionless mode option and does not require XID. LAPB does not require the TEST function, because the network is point-to-point, and failure of one node would become immediately obvious to the other node.

Another minor difference relates to the sequence number field for supervisory and information PDUs. For LLC Type-2 operation, a logical connection begins when one node sends a Set Asynchronous Balanced Mode Extended (SABME)

PDU, which means that the sequence number field for the connection is extended or seven bits long. For LAPB, the connection initiator has the option of instead sending a Set Asynchronous Balanced Mode (SABM) packet without the extended, which implies use of the basic-mode sequence number field, which is three bits long.

Another important difference between the IEEE Datalink Layer and X.25 Level 2 relates to the IEEE MAC sublayer. IEEE MAC sublayers, such as 802.4 and 802.3, provide access mechanisms for networks with two or more nodes. These access mechanisms are not necessary on the point-to-point X.25 topology and there is no concept of a MAC sublayer in X.25. The X.25 Physical Level must manage bi-directional information transfer between the DTE and the DCE, but this task is much simpler than that performed by 802.3 or 802.4, again due to the more simple topology of X.25.

7.6.1.2 X.25 Level-2 Subscription Parameters

When a network implementor contacts a PSN provider and places an order for a connection, the PSN provider asks the subscriber several questions regarding options that relate to the service. Two questions asked by the network carrier relate to the X.25 Level 2. The PSN provider asks you to select values for the T1 timer and parameter N1.

You must choose a value for T1 and N1 and careful selection can result in superior network performance. The T1 parameter establishes a time period that the DTE or DCE waits for an acknowledgement to an information packet before initiating a retransmission. This retransmission is identical to the LLC Type-2 process. Parameter N2 specifies how many times a node retransmits a packet before assuming that the logical connection has failed. If a node retransmits a packet N2 number of times, the connection reset procedure begins.

If the user provides too large a value for T1 or N2, network performance decreases because error detection and recovery take too long. However, if you set the value for T1 or N2 too low, many unnecessary retransmissions or reset procedures can occur and again, network performance can suffer.

Sometimes, the PSN carrier offers suggestions for setting T1 and N2. The best thing to do is to take the advice of the carrier. Over time, as you gain experience, you can monitor retransmission and connection reset activity of the network and you can change these values to tune the network for optimum performance. The PSN carrier charges you a one time fee to change the subscription parameters, which makes it undesirable to change these values very often.

7.6.2   X.25 Physical Level

X.25 Level 1 defines the physical connection between the DTE and the DCE. At the time CCITT produced the X.25 recommendations, standards already existed for connectors, cables, and modems for point-to-point connections. CCITT adopted these existing standards and developed new standards in anticipation of new technology. CCITT recommendation X.21 and a companion standard, X.21 bis, document the X.25 Level 1 standard. However, it is common to refer to these recommendations as part of the X.25 standard.

X.21 bis is partly based on the RS-232-C standard, which already existed at the time CCITT developed X.25. The RS-232-C standard has been widely implemented and understood for many years. X.21 also refers to another standard, called V.35, which describes a 35-pin connector instead of the 25-pin connector used by RS-232-C. For lines with transmission speeds of 48 kilo-bytes per second and above, you can use CCITT V.35. For slower speeds, you can use the RS-232-C standard.

Implementations based on X.21 bis can use voice grade modems, which means that you can use packet-switched networks based on mature telephone technology. In addition to the X.21 bis standard, CCITT developed X.21 to address future implementations, specifically use of completely digital connections, which many expect to become more common in the future. The X.21 standard does not allow the use of voice grade modems, and are not as common as X.21 bis. As digital circuit switching technology becomes more common, X.21 may be more commonly implemented.

7.7   In Summary

The lower layers provide information exchange between directly connected nodes. This function varies in complexity, depending on the functions supplied by higher layers and depending on the underlying network topology. In implementations with higher layers that perform flow control and error detection/recovery, the lower layers must not perform those functions. In other implementations, the lower-layers perform these functions. The X.25 LAPB, which is based on the IEEE LLC sublayer, performs these functions for WAN applications. LANs based on IEEE 802.4 require a sophisticated MAC sublayer, because the network topology supports two or more nodes, while the X.25 topology is point-to-point and does not require a robust MAC function.

Chapter 8

Connecting Devices

8.1   Overview

Computer network systems often connect hundreds or thousands of devices and span buildings, campuses, even countries. Enterprise network builders require a method to separate these large networks into small subnetworks for several reasons:

- Different lower-layer technologies apply best to different applications.

- A single, huge network is to complex to manage/administer.

- Separation prevents a single fault from disturbing the entire enterprise network.

- If all devices within an organization share the same network, the lower layers flood with too much traffic and performance suffers.

Network architects use connecting devices to subdivide the enterprise network into smaller, manageable segments. These devices include:

- Bridges
- Routers
- Brouters
- Gateways

A fifth device called a *repeater*, also connects one subnetwork to another. These Physical Layer devices physically extend the length of a subnet and do not provide any isolation. A repeater resembles an electrical extension cord. While they are useful in enterprise networks, their function is simple.

Some connecting devices connect more that two subnetworks. This device is a box with three or more network attachments. Each attachment provides connectivity to a different subnetwork. The industry often calls these devices *multi-segment connecting devices*.

8.2   Forwarding and Encapsulation

Connecting devices perform forwarding, encapsulation, or both depending on product design and user selection. Some devices perform only one or the other by design, others allow the you to configure one or both functions.

Forwarding means packets move from one subnetwork, through the connecting device, and arrive at a node on the other subnetwork, as shown by the path Client A uses (Figure 8-1).

Sometimes a packet traverses several connecting devices and subnetworks as shown by the path Client B uses. The industry calls each passage through a connecting device a *hop*. Forwarding requires only one connecting device, but enterprises usually have dozens or hundreds of connecting devices depending on the size of the network system.

Encapsulation involves two connecting devices (Figure 8-2). A packet arrives at the source boundary connecting device. The connecting device wraps or encapsulates the arriving packet inside a new packet. The device sends the new packet to the other border connecting device, which strips off the wrapper and delivers the original packet to the destination device. The middle network, called the enterprise *internet*, is the backbone of the enterprise network.

Encapsulation allows packets to cross transparently an internet with a different middle-layer implementation. Some lower-layer technologies, such as token ring, are difficult to forward; encapsulation provides an alternative.

8.3   Differences between Connecting Devices

Connecting devices differ according to which layer they comprehend. Higher layer connecting devices provide more functionality and are more complex to build than lower-layer devices.

- Bridges implement Layer 2—Datalink Layer.

- Routers implement Layer 3—Network Layer.

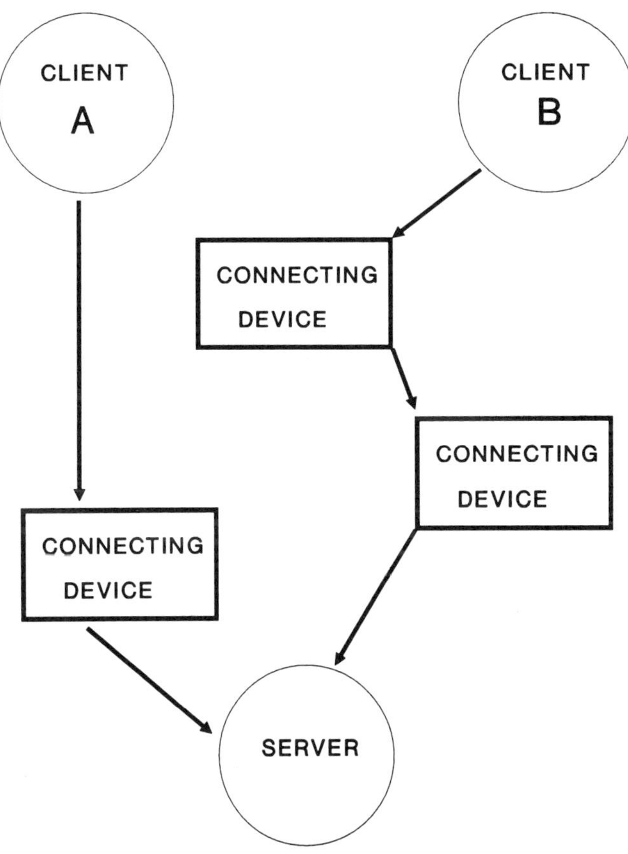

Figure 8-1: Forwarding

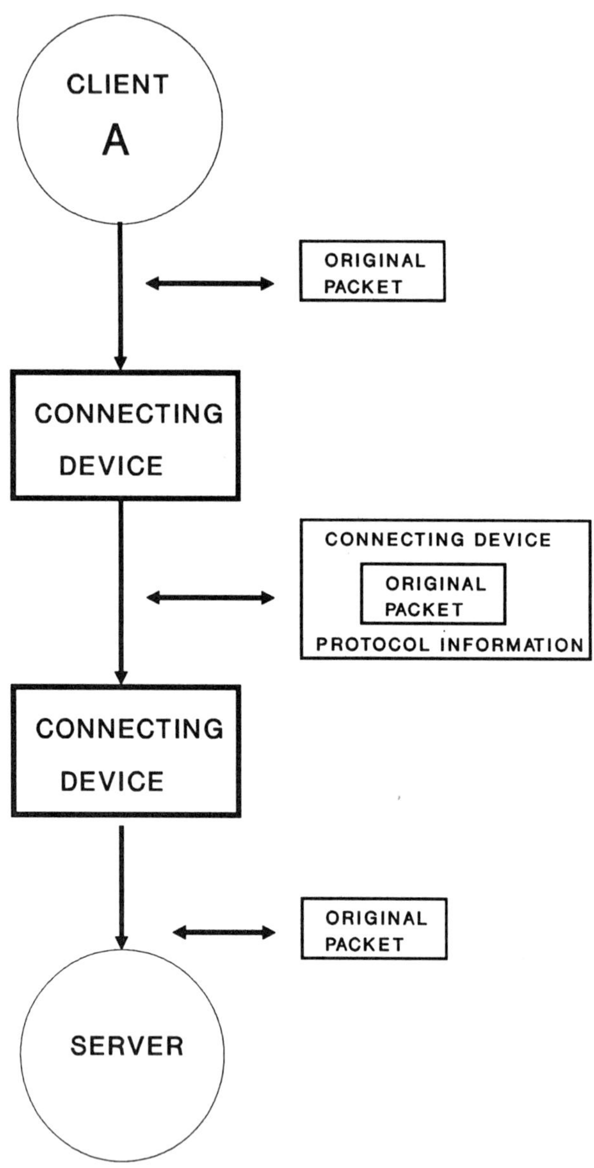

Figure 8-2: Encapsulation

- Brouters are super-sets of both devices. They simultaneously work at Layer 2 and Layer 3.

- Gateways implement Layer 4 or higher.

Note: that the OSI community uses these terms, other communities use different terms. The TCP/IP community refers to a Layer 3 connecting device as a *gateway*.

8.4   Bridges

As lower-layer devices, bridges appear invisible to end systems. The sending and receiving end systems do not know the bridge exists in the network system topology.

8.4.1   Bridge Functions

Bridges convert one lower technology into another or they attach two subnetworks with identical lower layers. The bridge function in the first case is obviously to allow packets to move from one end system to another end system with a different lower technology. Without the bridge, these end systems would be unable to communicate. In the second case, when both end systems have identical lower-layer technologies, the function of a bridge is more complex. These bridge applications provide isolation between subnetworks by filtering the flow of packets.

Bridges have internal databases or tables that allow them to decide when to forward packets. Bridges automatically construct these forwarding tables and people like network administrators, add information into them. Because bridges are Datalink Layer devices, the forwarding tables contain information about MAC addresses and do not have any middle- or upper-layer information.

Example: The bridge in Figure 8-3 starts listening passively to traffic on both subnets A and B. The bridge builds a forwarding table based on source MAC addresses of each packet it detects. In this way, the bridges knows that Stations 1 and 2 are on subnet A and that Stations 3 and 4 are on subnet B.

When Station 1 sends a packet with a destination MAC address of Station 4 it forwards the packet to subnet B. Note that end system 1 attempts to send the packet directly to Station 4. The bridge "pretends" that it is Station 4 and acts on the packet even though the destination address is not its own. The bridge does not forward packets sent by Station 1 with a destination MAC address of Station 2. The bridge alternatively filters or drops these packets.

In the multi-segment configuration, forwarding and filtering function behaves the same, except that the bridge passes a packet to one of several destination subnets. If subnet C exists, the bridge builds a table for it just as it does for subnets A and B. It forwards packets to subnet C to either subnet A or B based on its forwarding tables.

8.4.2   Bridge Configuration

Most bridges allow you to add manually rules into the forwarding tables. You may want certain nodes to remain unreachable from other subnetworks for security reasons or you may want to prevent multicast or broadcast packets from crossing a subnetwork boundary for performance reasons.

Example: Assume subnet A contains file servers and print servers. You may want to allow end systems on subnet B to access the printers on subnet A, but not allow them to access the file servers. A manual entry allows the bridge to filter packets based on individual MAC addresses.

8.5   Routers

As middle-layer devices, routers are visible to end systems. If you put routers into your network, the end systems must be able to communicate with them.

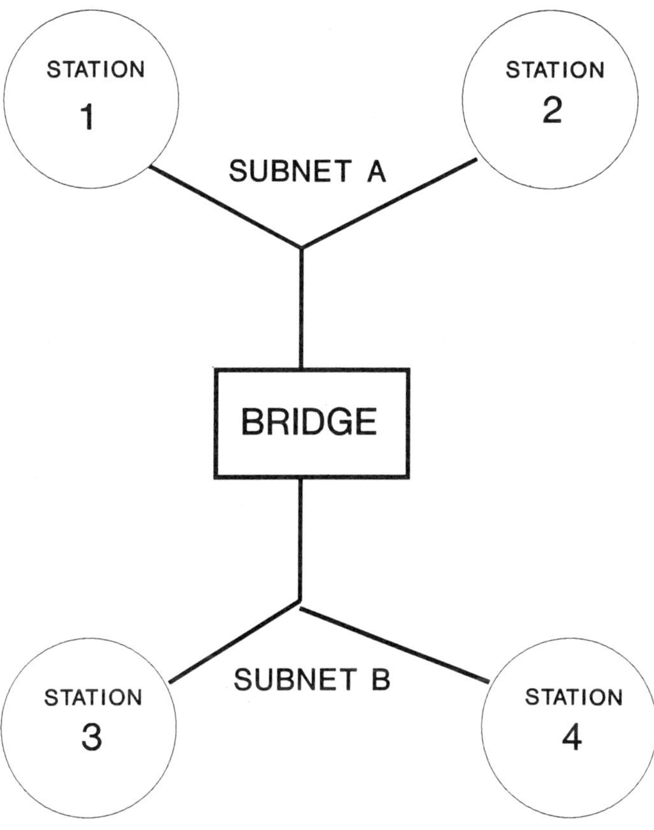

Figure 8-3: Bridge

8.5.1   Router Functions

Like bridges, routers can connect subnetworks with different lower-layer implementations. Both subnetworks must use the same middle-layer protocol. In the encapsulation mode, two routers can relay packets between two subnetworks with identical middle layers even if the internet between them uses a different middle-layer protocol.

Routers use internal databases called *routing tables.* Some of the information for the routing tables comes from the router itself, while you can manually enter other information. These tables are similar to bridge forwarding tables except that they include Network Layer information.

Routers build entries into their routing tables in various ways depending on the protocol family they support. OSI routers listen to ES-IS HELLOs, which end systems periodically multicast. The router makes an entry that associates a MAC address with a Network Layer address for each end system on the subnetwork.

An end system that wants to route a packet to a remote subnetwork, sends this packet directly to the MAC address of the router (or to a router multicast address) instead of the MAC address of the remote end system. The sending station indicates the destination Network Layer address, which the router uses for the routing table reference.

Example: Station 1 in Figure 8-4 sends a packet destined for Station 4 by indicating a destination MAC address of All Intermediate Systems to which a broadcast that all OSI routers listens. The Network Layer address matches that of Station 4. The router accepts the packet, changes the destination MAC address to match Station 4, and moves the packet to Station 4. The router knows the MAC address for Station 4, because it had earlier built a routing table entry based on an ES-IS HELLO that Station 4 sent.

In the multi-segment configuration, the router behaves the same except that it has router entries for three or more subnetworks. Multi-segment routers move packets to the subnetwork that contains the end system with the proper Network Layer address.

Most routers built today are multi-protocol, which means that they simultaneously route OSI, TCP/IP, and other protocols. If subnets A and B contain both OSI and TCP/IP nodes, a multi-protocol router performs OSI routing when appropriate and TCP/IP routing for TCP/IP connections.

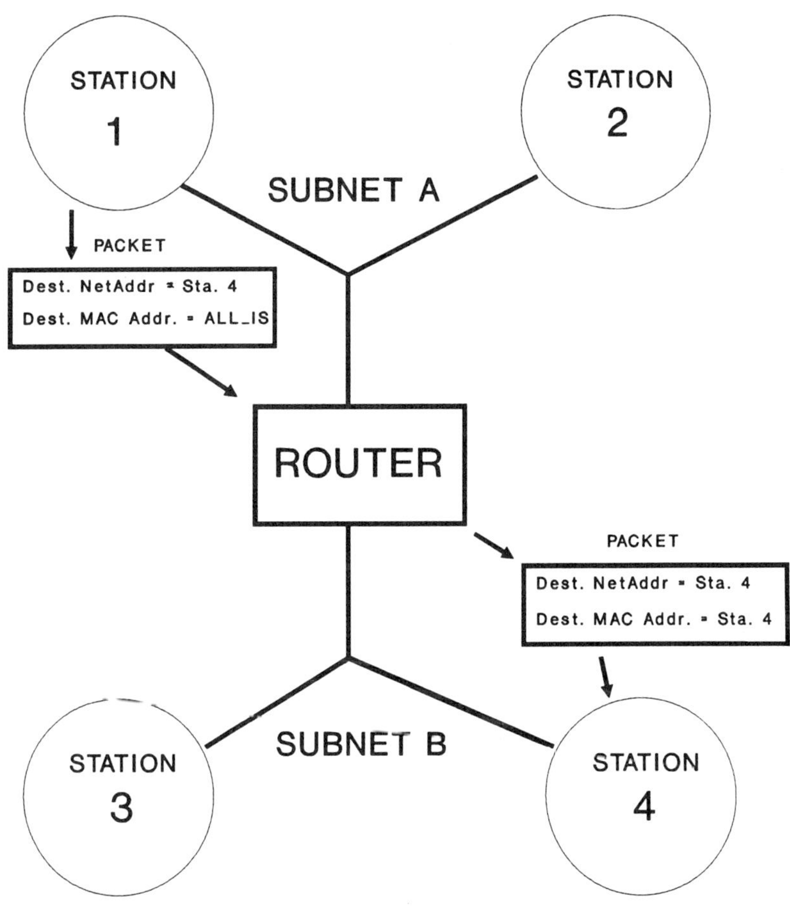

Figure 8-4: Router

8.5.2 Router Configuration

You can enter directly static or fixed information into a router. You do this, because some end systems in your network may not support the ES-IS HELLO function. Your router does not make an entry into its routing table, because it does not know how. Some products implement a Network Layer that does not send these multicasts. You must type entries that map the MAC addresses of these devices to their Network Layer addresses.

You must make manual entries if the router behaves in the encapsulation mode. Encapsulation takes a packet from one subnet, wraps it within a packet of a different protocol, and sends it to another router. This operation involves two different protocols and often you do not want cross-protocol translation of routing tables between routers.

Example: A common encapsulation implementation involves an internet based on X.25. The X.25 WAN serves as the backbone between several LANs. You do not want periodic routing table multicasts to traverse between routers over the X.25 network, because your service provider bills you for X.25 usage by the packet. It is less expensive to make the one-time manual configuration.

8.6   Brouters

Most connecting devices built today are brouters, which are combinations of bridges and routers. A brouter is two in one: it can bridge and it can route. A brouter routes packets if possible and bridges them otherwise.

Brouters build both forwarding and routing tables. In the multi-segment configuration, you can configure these flexible devices to bridge to some subnets and route to others.

You configure a brouter as if it were a router, then you perform additional configuration as if it were a bridge. Some protocols are not routeable, so you configure bridging between end systems with these protocols.

8.7   Gateways

Gateways implement Layers 4 or higher of two or more different protocols. This makes them the most complex and difficult to manage of all connecting devices. There are very few standards for gateways and each gateway product varies in some way from every other. Some gateway implementations are transparent to end systems and others are not. It is possible to make very general statements only about gateways:

- Gateways appear as two end systems rather than as two intermediate systems.

- Gateways involve a manual configuration more complex and inflexible than other connecting devices.

- Gateways usually disappoint network users, because functions of one protocol do not always map one-to-one to functions of other protocols.

8.8   Choosing Connecting Devices

Many enterprise networks follow the technology offered by vendors. Single-segment bridges were available first and as soon as they offered adequate performance, many organizations put them into their networks. Single-protocol routers were implemented somewhat later than bridges, partially because users did not understand them and partially because routing protocols had to be developed.

Multi-segment bridges and routers appeared next, followed by multi-protocol routers and finally multi-segment, multi-protocol brouters. Gateways have been available since the industry first interconnected networks.

This means that existing enterprise networks contain a variety of existing connecting devices, which must be one of your top considerations when you architect new connecting devices into your enterprise network system. You cannot ignore the investment your organization has put into the existing network infrastructure, nor can you be over-conservative and dogmatically add more of the existing technology. You must balance the cost of making existing devices obsolete against the benefits achieved by migrating to new equipment.

The best functionality for your money is multi-segment, multi-protocol brouters, which are the newest of all connecting devices. They are the most flexible and most manageable of all enterprise connecting devices. In fact, most connecting devices sold by bridge and router vendors have purchase options to make them a brouter.

Routers filter more efficiently than bridges. A bridge forwards a multicast or broadcast, while a router only forwards packets with Network Layer addresses associated with remote subnetworks.

Bridges have less software processing to perform than routers and are faster. A bridge can forward more packets per second than a router. However, the hardware platforms and micro-processors used by product vendors makes this performance difference insignificant in many implementations. In fact, a robust brouter often performs sufficiently and offers all of the benefits of both a bridge and a router. Use bridges for special-purpose, high-speed connections between two subnets with heavy traffic between them.

Some enterprises that build large, bridged networks are now migrating to routed networks. Routed networks make more efficient use of lower-layer bandwidth and you can manage routes from a central location, in real-time, using network management tools. Routers offer a more sophisticated form of isolation.

Use gateways only when absolutely necessary. You spend more time configuring gateways and answering user's questions with these devices than you do with any other. Use a gateway when protocol conversion is critical and no other method of application mapping is possible.

8.9   Summary

Network system architects use connecting devices to sub-divide physically and logically the enterprise network system. Connecting devices vary according to the protocol layer at which they operate. Bridges functions at Layer 2, routers function at Layer 3, and Gateways functions are at Layers 4 and greater. Brouters, a combination bridge/router, operate at both Layer 2 and Layer 3. Connecting devices use tables to forward or route packets between subnetworks. Selection of connecting devices involves tradeoffs between existing equipment, performance, cost, and manageability. Many organizations today prefer the brouter over the other connecting devices, because of flexibility and manageability.

9.1   Overview

Management of modern enterprise networks offers a firm challenge to architects and administrators. You must administer, monitor, and repair your network as needed or you compromise the value of your network. Enterprise networks include multiple network families and protocols, which create problems that do not exist in a homogenous network, such as an SNA domain or a public telephone system. You must possess expertise in each protocol family. These protocols share the same physical media, but have different characteristics important to network managers.

9.2   Network Management Functions

The term *network management* covers a broad area relating to the behavior of your network. The goal of network management is to keep your network performing satisfactorily, allow for reconfiguration, tally usage for billing purposes, and provide security against unauthorized usage of resources. ISO formally divides these functions into the following categories:

- Fault Management
- Configuration Management
- Performance Management
- Accounting Management
- Security Management

9.2.1   Fault Management

You want your network to function properly. You do not want a file server to be available only occasionally. You want to maintain the integrity of your network's data communication and you want resources to be available when you require them.

Fault management includes three phases:

- Fault Detection
- Fault Isolation
- Fault Resolution

You must detect faults as quickly as possible and resolve them before they impact network operation. Faults are not always immediately obvious. Sometimes a fault remains hidden, growing more damaging until it becomes more severe and visible to users or network maintenance personnel.

Example: A client workstation connected to your network contains a faulty board that starts jabbering as the temperature of the board increases. When the user powers ON the workstation, the board begins to heat. At first, the problem is undetectable, but as the temperature increases inside the workstation, the board gets hotter and the jabbering increases. Ultimately, he user notices poor response time due to the garbage packets that the jabbering board transmits. The jabbering engulfs network bandwidth and competes with other users' applications.

After you detect a fault, you must take the extra step to isolate the problem. You may become aware that some node in the network jabbers, but you do not know which node is guilty.

Fault resolution follows fault isolation. You may determine which workstation jabbers, but the solution may require further study. You also may determine that the workstation jabbers with greater intensity after it powers ON, but you do not know that heat produces the problem. The corrective measure may be to replace the board or the solution may be to replace the faulty cooling fan in the workstation.

9.2.2 Configuration Management

Your network topology changes: new nodes become active, workstations and servers change location, and people obtain new network cards for their personal computers. Configuration management means allowing for these changes with little or no impact on network functionality. You want changes in configuration to be simple and have little or no repercussions on your network users. As a network administrator, you must be aware of changes, which often happen outside of your control. Enterprise networks sometimes grow so rapidly that configuration tasks become unmanageable. You want to know when changes occur, because changes in configuration often result in changes in network application behavior.

Configuration management also includes monitoring and management of path selection for virtual circuits. You must control the connecting devices that route and relay packets between nodes. You may want certain clients to have access to the high-speed routes and have other clients use the less-expensive, low-speed routes.

9.2.3 Performance Management

Users have expectations for response time and throughput: when they press [Enter], they do not expect to wait several seconds for a response from the network. They also do not expect a simple file transfer to take an hour. Performance management means analysis of network activity and ensuring that the system operates efficiently.

Sometimes a poorly performing network involves a fault, such as in the previous example. Other times, the network has enlarged and its application bandwidth exceeds the capacity of the products or technology on which you built the network. Poor configuration can cause substandard performance. You must periodically monitor performance and plan strategies that resolve performance problems.

9.2.4 Accounting Management

Telephone companies send their customers a bill each month. These bills detail the telephone system usage for each customer and include a total fee for system usage. Some corporations offer enterprise networks to users at a cost-based on resource usage.

In the past, corporations internally charged a department for each physical connection to a network. As network complexity and costs continue to rise, network support organizations want to bill their users according to actual usage instead of by the cable connection. This allows the cost of the network to associate itself more adequately with business reasons for changes, such as performance and connectivity enhancement.

9.2.5   Security Management

In dissimilar enterprise networks, security management means more than ensuring that each user has access to an administered set of data. With multiple network families/protocols and dramatic network expansion, security management means allowing users to access the data they require, instead of security mechanisms blocking access to data. Sometimes security management means closing the gaps created by differences in how two different network technologies support security.

> **Example:** A gateway connects two network families, but one network family supports passwords for file access and the other does not. You must solve this problem or the users of one product family do not have access to the files in the other system.

As the administrator, you must monitor who accesses what data and you must prevent or correct unauthorized access. You also must allow all users to access whatever data they are entitled to access without security system roadblocks.

9.3   Management System Architectures

Network management systems have three primary components:

- A manager,
- An agent, and
- A Management Information Base (MIB).

A manager builds a MIB with information it collects from agents (Figure 9-1). A user interfaces to the management system through the manager. The interface can be menu-driven software, which means the manager component is a console. The administrator monitors and controls network behavior from a central location.

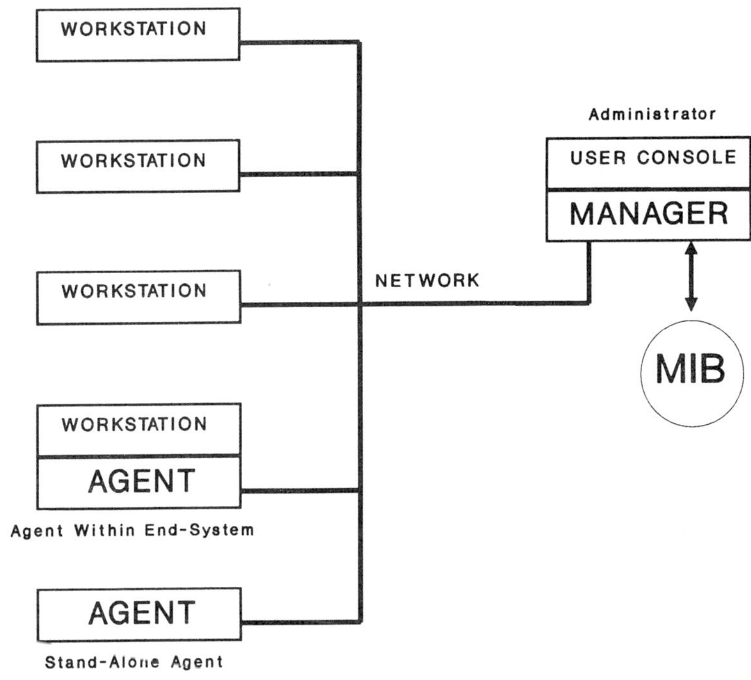

Figure 9-1: Management Information Base (MIB)

The agent component continually gathers information about the network and periodically sends this information to a manager component. The manager component stores this information as *objects* within the MIB, which is the depository for management information. An *object* is a single piece of information or a set of information. Sometimes the manager component processes the objects before storing them. Often the manager compacts the data or combines information from several agents to form more complex and useful objects. An agent receives network information via an attachment to the network. These agents can be stand-alone nodes in the network or can be an integrated part of a workstation or server. Agents gathers statistics, such as the:

- Number and size of packets transmitted (on a per-node basis).
- Number or frequency of corrupt packets.
- Network usage sorted by protocol, workstation, or department.
- Conversations (which workstations communicate with which servers).

The agent component gathers this information, stores it locally, then *flushes* or forwards the information to the manager component. At flush time, the agent can erase the current statistics and start gathering new values for objects. An agent can transmit objects to a manager over the same network that it monitors or it can send the data over a dedicated path such as a remote line. The remote line is invaluable when the network itself malfunctions.

The MIB can reside completely on a single manager component or you can distribute the MIB over several manager agents. Architecturally, the MIB can be a single file system or several files shared by several file systems. From a manager console, you can observe activity relating to several segments of your network. Each network segment has an agent that flushes data to your console, which displays it on a screen and/or saves it on a hard disk. You can further process the data using a word processor or publishing package, so that the information is in the most appropriate format. Agents perform another function called *events*. An event is a predefined activity that an agent performs in response to a particular occurrence.

> **Example:** A manager instructs an agent to send a message when network activity exceeds a threshold. The manager becomes aware of heavy activity and can take action (i.e., route management) to accommodate the network load.

9.4 TCP/IP Simple Network Management Protocol

The industry has widely implemented the TCP/IP Simple Network Management Protocol (SNMP). Defined by the TCP/IP community, SNMP provides tools useful for managers of TCP/IP and other product families.

RFC 1098 describes the protocol between managers and agents. *RFC 1065* defines a standard MIB called MIB-I by industry participants. *RFC 1158*, a new MIB called MIB-II is in draft form. Products today implement both MIB-I and MIB-II.

9.4.1   Communication between SNMP Managers and Agents

Managers communicate with agents over either the User Datagram Protocol (UDP) or over a Datalink Layer connection. This means that communication is connectionless, because both UDP and the TCP/IP Datalink definition are connectionless.

You must use UDP if an agent is on a remote segment on the other side of a router, because the Datalink interface cannot traverse a router. UDP uses the services of the Internet Protocol (IP), which allows passage through routers. The messages include:

- GetRequest
- GetNextRequest
- GetResponse
- SetRequest

The agent sends an object to the manager at the manager's request. An SNMP manager sends a GetRequest or GetNextRequest PDU to an agent, which causes the agent to send a GetResponse. UDP or the Datalink carries these commands as Application Layer data. A manager sends a SetRequest PDU to an agent to assign a value to a variable.

Example: A manager uses the SetRequest command to set a value for a router's internal routing tables.

SNMP agents gather and set internally statistics defined by MIB-I or MIB-II and forward this information to managers when requested to do so. Agents perform events called *traps*, which means they send unsolicited messages under certain conditions, such as:

- A node(s) becomes active/inactive.

- Security violations.

- Node or gateway failure.

All of the SNMP commands are unconfirmed, which means that the agent does not know if the manager successfully received the object. For SetRequest, the manager does not know if the agent receives the PDU, nor does it know if the agent successfully sets the object to the assigned value.

9.4.2   Iso Common Management Information Protocol/Service

In the ISO community, manager and agent components provide the Common Management Information Service (CMIS) and communicate with each other using the Common Management Information Protocol. *Iso 9595* and *iso 9596* respectively detail CMIS and CMIP. Additionally, ISO defines the five management functions in the following documents:

- Fault Management (*Iso 2687*)
- Configuration Management (*Iso 2686*)
- Performance Management (*Iso 2673*)
- Accounting Management (*Iso 2689*)
- Security Management (*Iso 2698*)

These ISO papers and several others related to network management are in various stages of completion. Several are years away from final approval.

The importance of the ISO network management standard relates to global network management systems. The SNMP standard, although more mature, is not adequate for large enterprise networks, especially international networks. The MIBs defined by SNMP were produced within the TCP/IP community without input from international bodies.

The ISO community includes all nations and includes input necessary to produce global network management systems. NIST OSI Implementors' Workshop, along with European, Asian, and Australian partners, work together to produce MIBs appropriate for international networks. Iso network management allows creation of much more complex objects than SNMP. An ISO object can have attributes, states, and relationships, in addition to values. Iso objects can link to other objects. These functions are awkward to implement using SNMP. These complex objects allow more powerful operations, but require more processing than SNMP actions.

9.4.3　Communication between Iso Managers and Agents

Unlike SNMP, CMIP uses the upper layers for communication between agents and managers. A logical connection forms, complete with data integrity, dialogue management, and format conversion, which the upper-layers perform. Some CMIS services, unlike SNMP services, are optionally confirmed:

- M-EVENT-REPORT (confirmed/unconfirmed)
- M-GET (confirmed only)
- M-SET (confirmed/unconfirmed)
- M-ACTION (confirmed/unconfirmed)
- M-CREATE (confirmed only)
- M-DELETE (confirmed only)

A confirmed service requires a response from the entity performing the service. ISO describes services between peer Common Management Information Service Elements (CMISE), rather than in explicit manager/agent contexts. This model, more flexible than the SNMP model, allows two nodes to act as manager/agent when appropriate.

A CMISE uses the M-EVENT-REPORT service to report an event. The M-SET and M-GET services allow a CMISE to assign a value to an object maintained by another CMISE. M-ACTION instructs a CMISE to perform a function. M-CREATE and M-DELETE respectively allow formation and removal of objects.

9.5　Network Management Implementations

Network management implementations for enterprise networks are still new and not yet perfected. Networks based on IBMs SNA are very manageable, as are other proprietary and homogeneous networks. Enterprise networks with several concurrent active protocols require a more general network management system than a single-protocol network.

The strategy in the 1990s for enterprise networks involves using a set of protocols and services, such as SNMP and/or CMIP/CMIS. Some confusion exists in industry about SNMP and CMIP/CMIS; these are just tools, not network management solutions. Some people hear that a product implements SNMP and they think that this product acts like other SNMP products about which they have read. SNMP, which is both services and protocols, is a vehicle only on which you can build a network management system for your network. The same applies to CMIP/CMIS, the standards do not tell vendors how to build a product.

Vendors have built different network management tools using primarily SNMP, with plans for CMIP/CMIS during the mid-to-late 1990s. Although they all use the same SNMP protocols and services, their functions are different, as are their human interfaces.

Architecturally, SNMP and CMIP/CMIS are interchangeable. A system consists of agents and managers that communicate according to the rules of one or the other. Agents and managers maintain MIBs as defined by standards groups or as a system maintains a custom MIB defined by the vendor itself. Network management functions are so broad that vendors create custom objects to provide functions marketable enough to provide sales. Often, a vendor devises a very useful function that they cannot implement using a standard MIB, so they invent their own.

9.5.1 Using SNMP to Create a Distributed Analysis System

Network support groups within enterprises usually have protocol analyzers, which are nodes that collect and display information about network activity for an administrator. These devices are software that runs on a personal computer along with a Network Interface Card (NIC). They collect information about activity, such as packet transmission, faulty packets, conversations between nodes. As a single stand-alone device, this product allows you to monitor activity on a single segment. Enterprise networks contain multiple segments, which means you need multiple analyzers. Even worse, you must be physically in front of the analyzer to use it. This may mean that you must walk to another building to use the analyzer to study a remote segment.

You can access groups of analyzers from your office if the analyzers support SNMP. Your workstation on your desk functions as the manager component, the remote analyzers function as agents. Your workstation issues GetRequest commands to each analyzer and displays information about each of the segments at a single central location. The MIB required for this function may be beyond MIB-I or MIB-II, so you would have to define your own objects.

Example: You build a protocol analyzer that tracks virtual circuits, including time connection establishment initiates. MIB-I and MIB-II do not have suitable objects to allow communication of virtual circuit data, so you must build your own pre-defined object.

9.5.2 Using SNMP in Connecting Devices and End Systems

Another way to implement network managers and agents is to put agent capability into routers, bridges, repeaters, and end systems. An SNMP agent built into a router can report route information to a manager and allow the manager to change routes for certain virtual circuits. A bridge or repeater with an agent can report faults or activity thresholds to your central manager. End systems themselves can periodically report information to managers.

This last implementation offers the powerful function of reporting activities internal to the node itself, such as hardware and operating system configuration, memory usage and CPU usage. Such a system allows you to calculate the entire cost or efficiency of a network application, in terms of backbone usage and memory/CPU usage within the nodes. This makes it possible to view your entire network and computers as a single logical machine. Eventually, vendors will probably implement managers and agents within the network interface hardware circuitry itself in the form of silicon logic.

9.6 Summary

Managing enterprise networks is more difficult than managing homogeneous networks. Each network family has different mechanisms for similar functions, which means that network management strategies must be broad enough to encompass various protocols technologies. ISO divides network management functions: fault, configuration, performance, accounting, and security management. Enterprises have implemented the first network management systems using SNMP. Future systems will use ISO CMIP/CMIS. The ISO model is much more complex and robust than SNMP and satisfies requirements for global, international network management systems. SNMP and CMIP/CMIS are tools, not solutions. Products and systems use SNMP as a delivery mechanism for distributed applications. SNMP can reside within analyzers or within connecting devices and end systems.

10.1   Overview—A Case Study

Many corporations and government agencies have an internal support group responsible for implementing networks, keeping these networks productive, and evaluating new network products. In these enterprises, a network support group performs a service to information system planners by providing data communications between the various computing devices used for daily operations. The following describes an imaginary network support group and their activities within a hypothetical company called ABC *Manufacturing.*

Although the ABC corporation does not exist, the activities in this chapter represent real experiences. This discussion of ABC and its network support group is valuable to network implementors and product vendors, because it illustrates the goals, requirements, and problems relative to the typical enterprise network.

ABC builds the mythical *widgets* using a combination of techniques including computerized factory automation. Throughout the factory, efforts are in progress to increase the productivity and quality of widgets by carefully planning the implementation of computer-controlled processes. These new processes cause an increase in the demand for computer networking.

ABC formed the Network Support Group (NSG) to satisfy the increasing demand for connectivity among a growing number of computing devices. This increase in demand involves not only new computing devices, but also involves a growing number of diverse computer systems. The trend within ABC is to use a larger variety of computers, which makes networking solutions more challenging.

10.2   Factory and Corporate Networks

The ABC enterprise network includes a complex factory network. Similar to other factory networks, this network has an 802.4 broadband backbone and several small subnetworks, many of them 802.4 carrierband-based. Other subnetworks use 802.3 technology as the lower-layer technology; the remaining layers are non-standard proprietary technologies. Throughout the rest of the corporation, 802.3 is common along with SNA and other proprietary technologies.

A large variety of middle-layer and upper-layer protocols exist throughout the company, in products based on OSI, CCITT, TCP/IP, and SNA. For WAN connectivity, CCITT X.25 serves a major role. This diversity of technologies and protocols has evolved over the years and has grown to a point that the cost of providing network support services has become visible to upper management.

Consider that the NSG group must have the skills and equipment to install and maintain several kinds of network technologies. Because it is rare to find a single person skilled in many network technologies, the NSG group must retain several high-paid network specialists, which represents a significant cost to the organization. Because the group supports many network technologies, they also must possess several different kinds of analytical equipment for the purpose of resolving network problems, for network performance tuning, and for evaluating new products.

Many of the subnetworks within ABC do not connect to the remaining networks, either because they do not require connectivity to the other networks or because the cost to provide connectivity does not justify the effort. In other situations, it is desirable to interconnect subnetworks that have different lower-layer technologies. ABC accomplishes this with bridges, routers, and in some instances, the less-desirable: gateway.

These connecting devices provide different levels of connectivity between dissimilar networks. When ABC uses bridges and routers to expand the range or performance of a network or to provide security, ABC considers this a worthwhile expense. However, when ABC requires gateways solely for the purpose of interconnecting two dissimilar networks, ABC considers the expense wasteful and continue to seek alternatives to these devices.

The general strategy of ABC management is to reduce networking support costs by encouraging network architects to implement new networks using standard network family products. Whenever possible, existing networks also must migrate to standard technologies. In particular, the NSG group has the charter to implement networks based on the compatible MAP, TOP, and GOSIP profiles.

By migrating to a compatible set of internationally standard technologies and protocols, upper management believes that network support costs decline, because the corporate network becomes less complicated. The benefits of a standards-based network include:

- Decreases the number of network specialists required,
- Simplifies internal education programs,
- Reduces the quantity of various network analytical equipment, and
- Eliminates the extravagance of gateways.

10.3   Network Support Group Responsibilities

The NSG groups operates as a company within a company; it has a service to offer and it has a customer base. NSG must be sensitive to the requirements of its customer: the enterprise network users. A primary strategic responsibility of the NSG group is to listen to the network users, because management measures the success of the group in terms of customer satisfaction.

In addition to customer satisfaction, upper management directs the NSG to find ways to migrate to OSI standards and to implement new networks with these standards, as long as OSI technologies can satisfy the customer. NSG builds non-OSI networks if using proprietary technologies is the only means to meet their network users' requirements.

The NSG group achieves these high-level goals by performing the following activities:

- New Product Evaluation
- Network Implementation
- Problem Resolution

Each of these activities places the NSG group into the role of network consultant. The users rely on the support group to help them from the time they identify a network requirement and to continue to help when the network enters production. To perform these functions, the NSG group must be experts in a variety of network product families, including standards-based product families.

NSG personnel attend seminars, participate in standards organizations, and constantly increase their network knowledge by reading product and standards documentation. Network support personnel often perform an active role in standards organization by helping to develop new standards, profiles, and implementors' agreements.

10.3.1 New Product Evaluation

The computer network industry is young compared to some technical industries, which means that new products frequently emerge that cause their predecessors to become obsolete. New product evaluation is a continual function of the NSG group. The quicker they evaluate and understand a new product, the sooner this new product is available to the network users. New products can make the enterprise more productive.

When the NSG group evaluates a new product, they look for the following qualities. Does the product:

- Perform a function useful to the ABC network users.

- Interwork properly with other products in the same network product family.

- Have sufficient built-in administrative and debugging facilities.

- Provide adequate performance in terms of throughput and reliability, to make it useful in a production network.

- Provide sufficient documentation so that users can understand it and the NSG group can support it.

After the NSG proves the new product satisfies these qualities, the NSG group places the product on the list of available technologies for network implementations. When network users have a requirement for a new data communication application, they refer to this list to see if the NSG has evaluated any applicable products that solve their problem. If there are no products available that meet their needs, they can ask the support group to help them find a new product and evaluate it as a possible solution to their needs.

New product evaluation often involves a joint effort between the NSG group and the product manufacturer. The product vendor often commits technical personnel to the product evaluation effort, forming a partnership between the NSG group and the product vendor.

10.3.2 Enterprise Network Implementation

The NSG group participates in the implementation of new networks throughout the enterprise. This process begins with a request by a department for a new network or to improve an existing network.

An improvement may be to expand a network, to make the network faster, or to migrate from a proprietary technology to a standards-based technology.

A network implementation progresses through the following phases:

1.   **Analysis Phase**—Detailed analysis of the new network requirements.

2.   **Identification/Selection Phase**—Identification and selection of available products to satisfy the requirements.

3.   **Pilot Program Phase**—A pilot program to prove viability of the product selections.

4.   **Production Placement Phase**—Placement of the new products into the production environment.

These phases occur serially and it occasionally is necessary to return to an earlier phase if you encounter an unanticipated problem.

Example: You identify a set of interesting products, but during the Pilot Program, one or more products proves to be too unreliable. The implementation effort then returns to the Identification/Selection Phase.

10.3.3 Problem Resolution

The responsibilities of the NSG group do not end when they implement a network. After a network enters production, you most assuredly will encounter problems. Problems can appear immediately after installation or may not surface until certain circumstances transpire (e.g., you add one more node to the network). Example problems include the following:

*   Most of the time, network operation is satisfactory, but sometimes the network experiences a significant drop in performance.

*   Some of the nodes are unable to send data to certain other nodes.

*   A particular node fails only when you perform a certain function.

In these situations, the NSG group assumes a troubleshooting role and uses various methods to resolve the problem. Sometimes these errors occur in production, but do not occur in the laboratory. A resolution of these problems must occur in the production environment, during third shift or during relatively idle periods, so that you do not disturb business activities.

10.4   Support Group Tools

The NSG group uses equipment, documentation, and special software to perform their daily tasks. Consider the most important and expensive tool of all: network expertise.

You cannot gain expertise in computer networks merely through schooling and reading. This expertise requires a type of intuition that you only can acquire through years of experience. Part of the complexity revolves around the fact that knowing whether or not a product conforms to a standard means understanding the standard itself, which is a serious undertaking.

A network expert must have an understanding of the abstract concepts the standards present and must possess the practical experience gained by implementing networks based on standards. This is why network experts cost so much and is one of the reasons why ABC management has set a priority to reduce the number of network technologies within the corporation.

10.4.1 Protocol Analyzers

Protocol analyzers provide a window into the network, allowing the support group to monitor activity at several layers. Earlier protocol analyzers allowed the operator to observe activity of only the lower layers, but modern analyzers provide middle- and upper-layer information and represent a powerful troubleshooting tool. Some analyzers parse an entire packet based on such complex protocols as FTAM and X.400 and display the contents of every field of every layer along with diagnostic information, such as protocol violations.

A protocol analyzer commonly takes the form of a personal computer with a Network Interface Card (NIC) and accompanying software. The personal computer becomes a member of the network, constantly listening and displaying network activity. Most analyzers also can transmit to the network for the purpose of simulating a faulty node or for the purpose of introducing a specific circumstance that is difficult to produce using actual network nodes. You can use protocol analyzers for product evaluation, network troubleshooting, and many other purposes.

10.4.2 Documentation

The NSG group has a large library of documentation related to product information and standards. The standards documentation provides a point of reference for building products and for determining conformance to the standards. Standards documentation classifies into three categories:

- Base standards (i.e., ISO specifications, IEEE specifications, and CCITT recommendations).

- Profile definitions (i.e., MAP, TOP, and GOSIP).

- Implementors' agreements (i.e., NIST and OIW Agreements).

Understanding the interworking relationship between standards-based products requires that the support group have an understanding of all three categories of documentation. The NSG group uses all of these documents to perform product evaluation and to troubleshoot problems.

10.4.3 Test Software

The NSG group uses special test software to perform its network support activities. This software runs network nodes and provides the capability to simulate specific network situations, such as the establishment of a logical connection and the subsequent transmission of data. This test software normally uses an Application Programming Interface (API) that the network product provides. Sometimes the product manufacturer provides this software as part of the product package. Other times, the support group must produce this software.

10.5 Example New Product Evaluation

Before NSG allows a new product onto the ABC enterprise network, they first must formally evaluate the product. If the product satisfies the NSG requirements, the product becomes available for implementation within the production network.

The following illustrates a new product evaluation cycle. The NSG customer is the manufacturing department, which uses a complex network for automation and other purposes.

The product for evaluation is a File Transfer Machine (FTM) and allows file transfer between a mainframe computer and other OSI FTAM-based file transfer stations. Because the ABC factory network users have mainframes and use OSI FTAM in the factory, the FTM satisfies the first criterion for acceptance:

1. *The product performs a function useful to the ABC factory network users.*

10.5.1 Product Factory Requirements

The FTM product interests the NSG group, because the factory network users have a requirement for a mainframe file transfer product that interworks with their mini-computer workcell controllers, which already support FTAM.

The application involves a CAD/CAE process that begins on the mainframe. Process engineers use CAD/CAE software on the mainframe to produce robot programs. After they develop robot programs, they transfer the programs to the robot workcell controllers, which are mini-computers. The FTM must interwork with the mini-computers to be useful for this application.

10.5.2 Starting Evaluation

The NSG group contacts the FTM vendor and requests a unit for evaluation and the vendor responds by providing a unit. The vendor also indicates that they support the evaluation process by providing technical assistance if problems arise with the new equipment.

The NSG team installs the FTM in their interoperability lab along with a mini-computer running FTAM, consequently simulating the potential production application for the new product. This test lab environment allows the NSG group to determine if the FTM satisfies the second requirement for acceptance:

2.　*The product properly interworks with other products in the same network product family.*

The NSG plan to evaluate interworking between the mini-computer and the FTM is to define a group of test scenarios that exercise the FTAM capabilities of both machines. Both of the products can function in all four FTAM roles and so the plan is to test the FTM as the:

- Initiator Receiver
- Initiator Sender
- Responder Receiver
- Responder Sender

The team creates a sample test file with data that simulates an actual production function. The file contains a robot program representative of what the mainframe sends to the mini-computer. The NSG engineers intend to send the file from the FTM to the mini-computer and back again to verify that the data does not change during the process. They first perform this function using the FTM as the FTAM initiator and then repeat the steps using the mini-computer as the initiator. This procedure is important, because sometimes two products interwork when one side is the initiator, but do not interwork when the other side is the initiator.

10.5.3 Lower-Layer Interoperability

The first physical experience of the NSG group is to connect the cabling between the FTM and the mini-computer. The lower-layer technology is 802.4, which means that they require a headend remodulator for the laboratory testing.

According to the documentation of both products, the 802.4 MAC sublayers attempt to establish the logical ring and start passing the token after you power ON the computer. An LED illuminates on the FTM product when the token passes between itself and another node. However, when the NSG engineers power ON the FTM and the mini-computer, this light does not illuminate, which indicates that the token is not active.

The NSG engineers try to resolve this first problem by checking the cabling connections and by checking the screens of the computers, looking for any helpful diagnostic information that the monitor may display. The cabling connections prove to be reliable and no diagnostic information displays on the monitor, so the engineers use their experience to determine the next step.

The engineers know that the 802.4 parameter slot-time can affect interworking between two or more nodes. After they study the FTM documentation, they discover that the default value for slot-time is different from that of the mini-computer.

After examining the IEEE standards, the MAP profile documentation, and the NIST OIW agreements, the engineers learn that there is no standard value for slot-time. Both nodes conform to standards, even though they do not interwork without reconfiguring one or the other. The standards organizations do not standardize slot-time, because slot-time must be user-configurable, usually according to the number of nodes in the network, which vary from one network to the next.

The FTM manuals include instructions on how to change the factory setting of the slot-time. When you power ON the computer, the FTM product reads a configuration file. This file contains user-selectable settings for slot-time and other critical parameters. After the NSG engineers change the value to match the mini-computer, the logical ring establishes, as indicated by the LED on the FTM hardware.

10.5.4 Middle- and Upper-Layer Connections

Now that the logical ring establishes, the next step is to establish connections at the middle and upper layers. The NSG engineers must configure both the FTM and the mini-computer to connect to each other. This configuration includes the parameters listed in Table 10-1.

Table 10-1: Configuration Parameters

Layer	Parameter
Network Layer	Network Address
Transport Layer	Transport Selector
Session Layer	Session Selector
Presentation Layer	Presentation Selector
FTAM Sub-Layer	Initiator Identifier Password

Both the FTM and the mini-computer have local values for each of these parameters, but before an FTAM regime can establish, the FTAM initiator must know the values with which the responder associates. Both the FTM and the mini-computer products use the Connectionless Network Layer Protocol (CNLP) implementation and the Network Address parameter identifies the destination for every packet that passes between the two machines.

The two products use the Class-4 Transport Layer implementation, which means that they use Transport Selector only during connection establishment. Similarly, the upper layers of both products are connection-oriented, so they use the remaining parameters only during connection establishment. The initiator attempts to establish a connection at Transport, Session, Presentation, ASCE, and FTAM by sending connection establishment messages to the responder.

The connection establishment messages contain values for the destination selectors, as well as the FTAM initiator identifier and password parameters. When the responder receives these messages, it checks the values for these parameters; if any parameter does not match the local configuration of the responder, the FTAM regime does not establish.

The first configuration step is to make two charts: one for the FTM and one for the mini-computer. Each chart describes the values for the local parameters. The ABC NSG team selects carefully the local parameters to ensure that each value conforms to the ISO, MAP/TOP, and NIST OIW agreements.

The ISO standard is very lenient in this category, because they design base standards to be applicable to a wide range of implementations. The ISO standards describe broad ranges for these parameters. The profiles and implementors' agreements often describe more restrictive ranges for parameter values, which makes it easier to build products that interwork with other vendors' products.

Regarding parameter ranges, you always must consult the MAP/TOP profiles and the NIST OIW agreements to see if a standard exists for a more restrictive range for that parameter. In this example case, the NSG engineers discover a discrepancy: the NIST OIW dictates that a Transport selector be 32 octets or less in length, while the MAP/TOP standard dictates a length of two octets or less.

The safest action in this situation is to adhere to the more restrictive standard, in this case, the MAP/TOP standard of two octets. By staying within the range of the stricter standard, you maximize the probability of interworking with other data communication products, because some products may conform to NIST OIW, while other products conform to the MAP/TOP specifications. Figure 8-1 shows the NIST OIW agreements for the configuration parameters.

In the example situation, the NSG selects a PSAP value for the FTM with a length of six bytes. They inadvertently select a value outside of the range NIST OIW specifications. This error later creates a problem for the NSG team.

After the ABC NSG team configures both machines for local parameters, the next step is to configure the remote information into both nodes. They configure the FTM with the mini-computer information, which appears as a remote node, and they make a similar remote definition on the mini-computer.

Table 10-2: NIST Agreements' Selector Limits

Parameter	Length
Transport Layer Selector (TSAP)	Up to 32 Octets
Session Layer Selector (SSAP)	Up to 16 Octets
Presentation Layer Selector (PSAP)	Up to 4 Octets

10.5.5 Protocol Analysis

The NSG team decides to use the following three tools for protocol analysis:

- A protocol analyzer,

- Debug tools built into the FTM, and

- Debug tools built into the mini-computer.

The protocol analyzer attaches to the network. It captures packets sent between the computers and provides debugging information.

In addition to the protocol analyzer, the FTM and the mini-computer have debugging capability in the form of traces, which means that they display messages describing their internal activity during operation. This debugging function normally remains disabled, because data communication is slower due to the processor cycles necessary to capture and display these traces. However, during the test and evaluation process, performance is not important, while debugging information is critical. The ABC NSG team enables debugging on both machines.

The NSG engineers are ready to attempt a file transfer. First, they use the FTM as the FTAM initiator and the mini-computer as the responder. They create a very small test file on the FTM for test purposes. A small file provides fewer potential problems than a large file and during these early test phases the goal is to keep the variables as simple as possible.

The NSG engineers send the small file as an FTAM Type-1 file, which means that the computers treat the file as text data instead of binary data. The mainframe represents text data in the EBCDIC character set while the mini-computer represents data in the ASCII character set.

By using FTAM document Type-1, the NSG engineers test the capability of the FTM and mini-computer to translate correctly between the two different character sets. On the FTM mainframe, the file contains five lines of text and displays as follows:

```
HELLO WORLD
HELLO WORLD
HELLO WORLD
HELLO WORLD
HELLO WORLD
```

If the test succeeds after the file transfer, the file must look the same on the mini-computer as it displays on the mainframe.

10.5.6 File Transfer

The first attempt to send the small file from the FTM to the mini-computer fails and the engineers attempt to resolve the failure by looking at the information provided by the protocol analyzer and by looking at the traces that the computers display. The protocol analyzer contains a substantial amount of information, because the test network is very busy.

Several other groups within the ABC company are performing tests on the network at the same time as the FTM to mini-computer testing. The analyzer displays all of the test network activity, which makes it difficult to distinguish the FTM/mini-computer information from that of the other tests. The NSG engineers configure the analyzer to filter out the FTM and mini-computer messages from the rest of the traffic on the test network.

Most analyzers include utilities to capture packets that associate with particular nodes and display packets that associate with a single operation. After the ABC NSG team configures the analyzer to filter out the FTM and mini-computer packets, they repeat the test and again the failure occurs.

10.5.7 Middle-Layer Analysis

The analyzer shows an attempt by the FTM to establish a Transport connection with the mini-computer. A total of eight connect request PDUs display on the analyzer, but the mini-computer does not respond with a connect acknowledge. The FTM apparently retransmits connect request PDUs, because it is not receiving an acknowledgement.

The engineers check the Transport Layer configuration of the FTM and find that the vendor configured it for eight retransmissions, which agrees with the information the protocol analyzer displays. The question becomes "why doesn't the mini-computer accept the Transport connection that the FTM initiates?"

The next step is to examine any debug information that the two computers display. The FTM displays trace information that agrees with the analyzer: the FTM makes eight unsuccessful attempts to establish a Transport connection, but does not receive a connect acknowledge. The mini-computer does not display any helpful information.

After further study of the information that the protocol analyzer displays, the ABC NSG teams discovers the answer: the destination or called Network Address that the FTM sends does not match the mini-computer local Network Address configuration. The NSG engineers accidently defined the mini-computer Network Address as: 47.0004.0039.0003.090000010112.01 instead of 47.0004.0039.0003.090000010222.01.

This subtle configuration error is sufficient to prevent the two machines from interworking. The FTM sent connect requests with an incorrect value for the destination Network Address and the mini-computer ignored the incoming connect requests. The solution to this problem is to reconfigure the remote definition for destination Network Address.

10.5.8 Upper-Layer Connection Analysis

After they reconfigure the FTM, the engineers repeat the test; this time with better results. The analyzer displays a single Transport connect request and a single connect acknowledgement by the mini-computer. However, the file transfer fails, apparently due to an upper-layer problem.

According to ISO standards, the upper layers establish their connections after the Transport Layer connection establishes. The Transport Layer normal data flow carries the upper-layer connect request messages. The NSG engineers see that the Transport connection establishes and that the upper-layer connection establishment messages are present in the first FTM Transport T-Data PDU and that the mini-computer sends an upper-layer connection rejection in its first Transport T-Data PDU.

This time the protocol analyzer displays a NIST OIW violation—the Presentation selector that the FTM sends is outside of the valid range NIST OIW specifications. The NSG engineers refer to the NIST OIW documentation and find that a Presentation selector must be a maximum of four octets or bytes. The FTM sends a value of 5555555555 for the source or "calling" Presentation selector and the analyzer recognizes this error. This value is five octets long, which is too long for a NIST OIW conformant-configuration.

However, because a parameter is outside of the NIST OIW conformant range, it is not automatically outside of the range for a particular product. Many products accept parameters beyond the range of standards—the important design issue is to ensure that a product supports at least the minimum range that the standards allow.

In this case, the mini-computer stack supports the precise NIST OIW range and fails due to an out-of-range parameter. To correct this problem, the NSG engineers reconfigure both machines. The local Presentation selector for the FTM becomes 5555 and the mini-computer definition for remote Presentation selector also becomes 5555.

The ABC NSG team repeats the test and this time the small test file successfully transfers from the FTM to the mini-computer. After examining the file at the receiving mini-computer, the data in the file appears to be identical to the file on the sending mainframe. The data displays as five lines of "HELLO

WORLD," but the size of the file is different. This is not an error. The size of the file changes, because of the differences in the ways the two operating systems store text files.

The mainframe operating system does not provide the concept of a new line or carriage-return line-feed, while the mini-computer uses a one-byte character for those purposes. The mainframe keeps a record of the length of each line in the file and does not insert a special character into the file itself. The mini-computer inserts a new-line character into the file data, which means that the length of the file increases by five bytes when it transfers from the mainframe to the mini-computer.

10.5.9 Large File Transfer Analysis

At this point, the NSG team decides that the small file transfer test was a success and proceeds to the next test, which involves a large file. This test places the mini-computer into the initiator-sender role, which means that the FTM serves as responder-receiver. After the file transfer starts, the FTM computer enters a lock-up state, which means that it fails to operate. The transfer of the large file causes the mainframe to discontinue FTAM processing, which means that a severe error occurs on the FTM.

The protocol analyzer displays information proving connections establish at all of the layers and show some of the large file data going from the mini-computer to the FTM. The debug information on the mini-computer indicates that a file transfer begins and that after some of the data transfers, the FTM Transport Layer stops sending acknowledgements. The mini-computer assumes that the FTM node fails or that a severe network error occurs (e.g., a broken cable). The mini-computer issues a disconnect and displays the diagnostic message:

```
Transfer aborted due to lost communication link
```

The NSG engineers study the screen on the FTM, which indicates that an FTAM regime establishes, but there are no file data transfer messages. Apparently, the FTM fails when it receives the incoming file data. The NSG team decides to print out a copy of the protocol analyzer traces and FAX them to the FTM manufacturer. They also contact the FTM factory and provide an account of the test to the support engineers.

In the mean time, the ABC NSG team proceeds with other tests while they wait for information from the FTM engineers. They discover that the FTM can send large files, but always terminates when it tries to receive large files.

After they study the protocol traces, the FTM factory engineers discover the problem and provide the ABC NSG engineers with a solution to their problem. The FTM product has a user-selectable parameter for FTAM Layer PDU size, which defaults to a relatively small value. This parameter is not in the product documentation and the NSG engineers could not have known about this limitation.

After examining the NIST OIW implementors' agreements, they determine that an FTAM product must support an FTAM PDU size of seven kilobytes. The FTM product defaults to a maximum FTAM PDU size of three kilobytes, which is less than what the standard specifies. The mini-computer sends FTAM PDUs seven kilobytes in length, which is within the range of the implementors' agreements and the FTM fails, because it can handle only three kilobytes. This means that the FTM is not conformant and is the cause of the problem.

After they understand the problem and the ABC NSG reconfigure the FTM according to instructions from the factory, large files transfer successfully in both directions. This is an example of an error that relates to product documentation, as well as to the product itself. For a product to be useful, the documentation must be equally high in quality as the product. Before the NSG group allows the FTM product to go into production, the FTM vendor or the ABC NSG group must update the documentation to include the F-PDU feature. Another more preferable solution is that the FTM vendor corrects the problem by changing the default F-PDU size to align with the NIST OIW agreements (seven kilobytes). This improves the quality of the product and prevents other customers from encountering the same problem.

10.5.10   Performance Analysis

Now that large file transfers work, the next step is to test performance of the product. For this test, the team disables the debugging function on the FTM and the mini-computer to ensure that the computers dedicate the maximum amount of computer cycles to the file transfer. What the NSG engineers discover is that file transfer performance is rather poor and they attempt to analyze the cause.

They learn that a relatively long time exists between each file data PDU. The protocol analyzer displays a time-stamp for each message it collects. The time-stamps show that the Transport and upper-layer connections establish quite quickly, but that delays occur between each file data PDU. This test is with FTAM document Type-1, which means that the mainframe performs character set translations for the file data.

When they repeat the test using FTAM document Type-3, which is binary file transfer, the gap between the file data PDUs dramatically reduces. The NSG team determines that the FTM is inefficient at translating between the EBCDIC and ASCII character sets and that the translation causes the poor performance with FTAM document Type-1. The ABC NSG recommendation to the factory network users is to use FTAM document Type-3. However, this creates a problem for the factory network users, because their application requires transfer of robot programs in text mode rather than binary mode.

The NSG support team decides to consider another solution. They write test software for the mini-computer to perform translation from binary to text. The mini-computer software translates all files it receives from binary to text. This translation program requires a certain time to execute, but this time may be less than the delays that accompany FTAM document Type-1 transfer.

Another issue that supports this plan is computer usage—the mainframe computer frequently supports multiple users, including CAD/CAE engineers, which means that they already over-burden the mainframe. However, the mini-computers have relatively small loads and may be more efficient at binary to text translation. In this example case, the effective performance is higher when the mini-computer performs the translation and the ABC NSG recommends to the factory production group to use binary file transfer and allow the mini-computers to perform the translation.

10.5.11   Pilot Program

Before the NSG support allows the FTM product to enter production, they establish a pilot program to determine reliability of the product. A pilot program is an extended test of a network system to ensure that the products are reliable over a prescribed time.

The support group develops test software on the FTM to repeatedly send files to the mini-computer. The test program uses the API of the FTM. The test software uses a group of test files; each file tests a different production scenario, such as different file sizes and different data content combinations. The support group also writes software on the mini-computer to test the integrity of the files. Like the FTM test software, this program uses the API that the mini-computer provides.

If the system detects an error, the system displays and logs the errors in a status file. The tests run for days or weeks and the support group determines the Mean Time Between Failure (MTBF). If the MTBF meets the standards that the NSG group defines, the product can enter production. Otherwise, they must resolve the reliability issue, either by compelling the product vendor to correct the problem or by resolving the problem themselves.

10.6   In Summary

Many users of large factory networks have a support group that evaluates new products and helps place these products in production environments. These groups comprise network analysts with expertise in different network product families. These groups use several tools including protocol analyzers, debug software, and standards documentation. The group evaluates new products for interoperability, functionality, documentation, performance, and reliability. Understanding the evaluation cycle benefits network users and product vendors, because this cycle demonstrates the implementation of network products into the factory network.

Chapter 11

Enterprise Network Migration

11.1 Overview

Enterprise networks found in the largest corporations, government agencies, and universities comprise various network families. This results in high maintenance and educational costs, complex gateways, and it requires numerous network experts to maintain the network. Many organizations struggle with the issue of network migration—most organizations know what they want to accomplish, but do not know how to attain their networking goals.

Upper-level management personnel understand the value of data communication standards and have set the goal to migrate enterprise networks away from their present state. In most cases, the present network state is a multiple network architecture. Their goal is to migrate toward a single, standards-based enterprise network (most notably OSI and its alignment partners CCITT, SPAG, ANSI, and IEEE).

When evaluating a migration strategy, you must separately consider each network technology or you may compromise a critical network application, but you also must consider the network as a whole. This creates a dilemma—how can your enterprise network become completely standards-based and still provide your network users with the functions on which they have become dependent?

Enterprise networks have become almost unmanageable, because of the many network families that they embrace. Each network product family offers a different combination of functionality, performance, and connectivity. These products help your users to remain productive and competitive.

During the 1980's, a few large corporations tried to force an immediate migration from their existing networks to a standards-based network, but their network users refused to forfeit the technologies that allowed them to execute their day-to-day activities. The rapid migration strategy failed, because it did not receive the network users' support. A successful migration strategy must allow your users to continue their operations—you cannot abruptly discard the existing functionality and replace it with new capabilities that the OSI standards offer.

11.2   Migration Strategy

Some organizations have produced a strategy that moves the enterprise network toward OSI standards and also allows your users to continue the same practices they use with the old architecture. Many vendors support this strategy. The appearance of products designed to work with this strategy verifies the existence of vendor support. The details of this strategy varies from one organization to the next, but the concept is constant:

1.   *Define the enterprise backbone in terms of the OSI model middle layers.*

2.   *Develop new applications using OSI standards as appropriate products become available.*

11.2.1 Define Network Backbone as Middle Layer

The traditional view of the enterprise backbone was from the lower layers.

Example: You determine that your network's backbone is IEEE 802.3 or IEEE 802.4 broadband (lower-layer based). To begin migrating your network, you now define your network backbone as ISO Class-4 Transport (TP-4) on top of a Connectionless Network Layer Protocol (CLNP), and allow options for the lower-layer and upper-layer implementations.

If you begin migrating your system as illustrated in the example, you have simplified the problem of end-to-end connectivity. You can send messages from one end-system to another without going through a gateway. You have not restricted lower-layer and upper-layer implementations. Your users can choose their own media types and can continue to use the upper-layer functions with which they are familiar. You have reduced the complexity of the backbone by specifying a single, middle-layer implementation, which means you require only enough expertise to maintain an OSI backbone instead of multiple, middle-layer technologies.

This strategy provides an intermediate phase for enterprise network migration. It does not provide your organization with instant standards from top to bottom, but it does provide significant cost savings and a reduction in network complexity.

11.2.2 Develop New Applications Using OSI Standards

The second part of this strategy brings your network to a standards-based state. The reason that your users resist change is because their existing applications already work. The thought of relinquishing a system that satisfies their needs is not appealing. You must make your users realize that as the industry develops new applications, you users forfeit nothing by building those applications on new products.

This strategy does not provide an organization with an immediate OSI enterprise network, but gradually introduces new applications that are based on OSI products. The enterprise network steadily becomes homogeneous. More importantly, your users support this strategy, because you do not require them to surrender their current functionality.

11.3   SML-Based Backbone

Today's enterprise networks incorporate numerous network product families, some of which have connectivity to other kinds of products via gateways (Figure 11-1). These backbones require experts in each of the network families. If you attach a protocol analyzer to your network's backbone, it captures packets associated with TCP/IP, OSI, and various proprietary middle-layer implementations. If an application fails, you require a specific support expert to resolve the problem: whom you call depends on which middle-layer implementation failed.

Figure 11-2 shows an improved backbone with a single, Standard Middle Layer (SML) implementation. Support for the SML-based backbone requires experts in only one discipline. Note that existing upper-layer functions are still available to your users. The upper layers of a product are to what your users' applications interface and define the network functions. With the SML implementation, your users are not exposed directly to the fact that the backbone has migrated towards a standard.

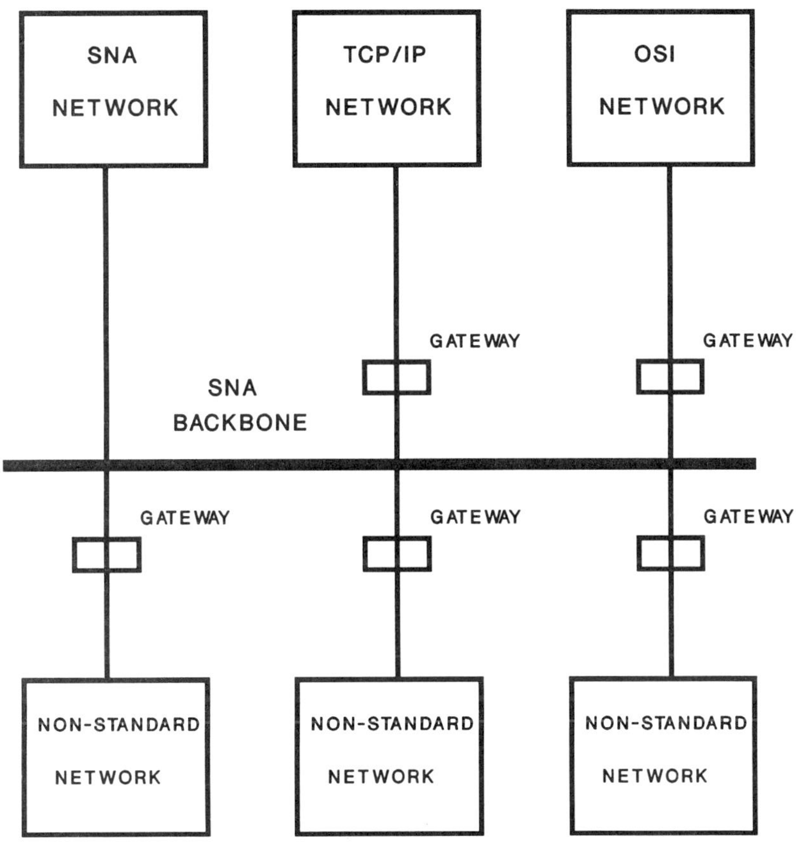

Figure 11-1: Network Families Connect via Gateways

The exact specification for the SML varies from one organization to the next. TCP/IP is an obvious choice (especially in the US), because of the large installed base. ISO TP-4 on top of CLNP is prudent, because of the numerous products that are based on these standards and because there is a growing support for this middle-layer combination. Other implementations include ISO TP-0 or TP-2 with Connection-Oriented Network Service, which fits neatly with adjoining CCITT X.25 WANs. At least one organization has chosen CCITT X.25 alone as the SML for their migration strategy.

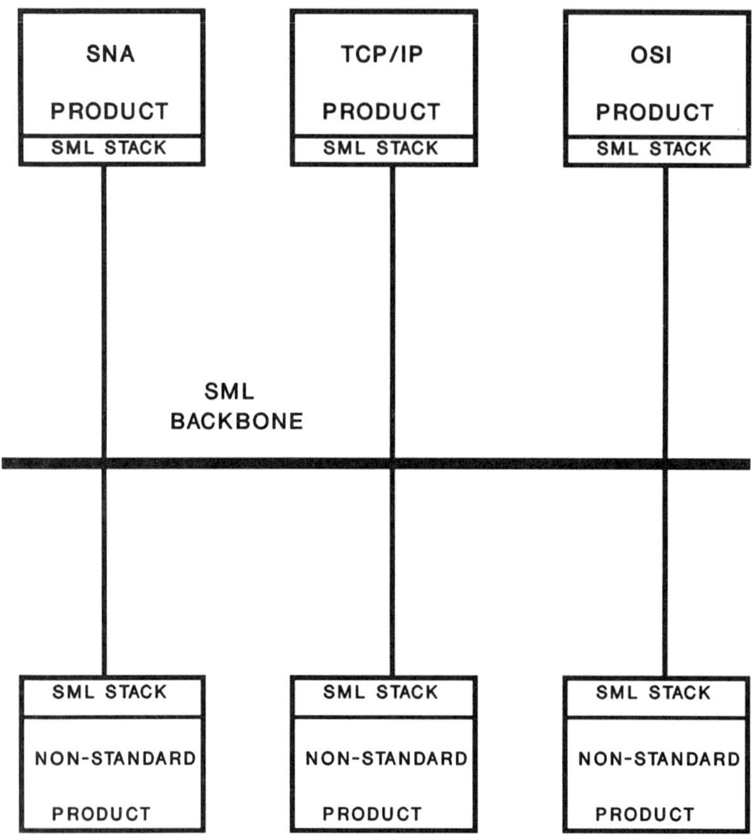

Figure 11-2:　SML Backbone

11.4　SML-Product Implementations

The SML migration strategy can be successful only if your vendors cooperate with your users to build products that support your architecture. Many important vendors already have produced such products and others have supporting products under development. The architecture for a typical SML product is shown in Figure 11-3. The middle layers align with the enterprise backbone SML, while options are available at the lower and upper layers. This product still exposes

your users to the same functionality they had with the old product, because you
have not changed the upper-layers.

<table>
<tr><td>PROPRIETARY

UPPER

LAYERS</td><td>PROPRIETARY

UPPER

LAYERS</td><td>PROPRIETARY

UPPER

LAYERS</td></tr>
<tr><td colspan="3" align="center">STANDARD

MIDDLE

LAYERS</td></tr>
<tr><td>LOWER

LAYERS</td><td>LOWER

LAYERS</td><td>LOWER

LAYERS</td></tr>
</table>

Figure 11-3: SML Typical Architecture

Most SML products look more like Figure 11-4. These products operate over
the old, non-standard middle layers and also can operate over the SML. This
often proves useful during the initial migration period, when some machines are
not yet equipped with SML products. This product interworks with other SML
machines and also interworks with the machines waiting to be equipped with SML
products.

A few product vendors have built implementations shown in Figure 11-5.
These products best fit the SML and total migration strategy, because they offer
the ability to produce new applications using a full OSI stack. Recall that the
second step to the migration strategy calls for new applications to be developed
using OSI at all layers. The author's recommendation is to encourage you to
procure and use these products and to urge vendors to build such products.

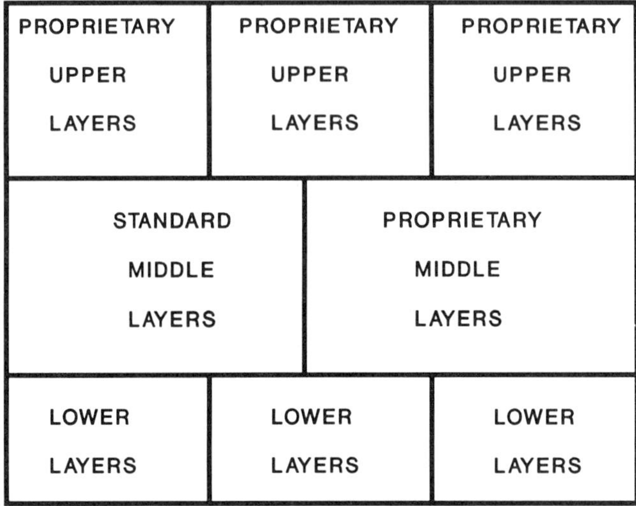

Figure 11-4: Older SML Products

Figure 11-5: Newer SML Products

11.5   In Summary

Because of the many network product families they include, today's enterprise networks have become complex and expensive to manage. A strategy to migrate to standards must have your network users' support, which means that your users must retain their current functionality during the transition.

The SML strategy moves the enterprise network toward OSI migration and allows your users to continue to use their existing applications. The first phase for the SML strategy is to view the backbone from the OSI model middle-layers. Complete migration to OSI must be gradual.

The second phase allows new applications to be built on OSI products as appropriate products become available. The long-term goal is to have a homogeneous standards-based network. You can best accomplish this with products that allow your users to employ their existing proprietary applications and also allows them to build new applications using standard protocols and services.

Glossary

ACK

Acknowledgement. Confirmation of receipt of data.

ACSE

Association Control Service Element. Sub-layer of OSI Application Layer. Responsible for establishment/termination of associations between application entities.

ANSI

American National Standards Institute. United States standards organization. Member of ISO.

API

Application Programming Interface. Routines that a programmer calls to send and receive data over a network.

Application Entity

Portion of Application Layer, such as FTAM or Directory Services that performs services to Application Processes.

Application Layer

Layer seven of OSI model. Provides interface to Application Process.

Application Process

Software that uses services of a network, such as a database management application. Resides outside of the protocol stack, in the host computer environment.

ASCII

Character encoding scheme common in personal computers.

Backbone

Cable or other medium that connects department networks.

Base Standard

Protocol specifications produced by large organizations such as ISO, CCITT, and IEEE.

Bridge

Connecting device that implements the Datalink Layer.

Broadcast

To send a message to all reachable destinations, as opposed to a single destination.

Brouter

A combination bridge and router. Routes if possible, bridges otherwise.

CCITT

Consultive Committee for International Telephone and Telegraph. Standards organization that often aligns with ISO.

Checksum

Error detection mechanism between computers.

CLNS

Connectionless Network Service. The OSI term for a Network layer that sends datagrams and does not establish connections.

CMIP

Common Management Information Protocol. The OSI standard protocol for communication between network management stations and network management agents.

CMIS

Common Management Information Service. Services that CMIP provides to network management applications.

CONS

Connection-Oriented Network Service. The OSI term for a Network layer that establishes connections.

CRC

Cyclical Redundancy Check. Error detection mechanism between computers.

CSMA/CD

Carrier Sense Multiple Access with Collision Detect. Name for IEEE 802.3 standard for Datalink layer.

Datagram

Message sent that does not expect an acknowledgement.

Datalink Layer

Layer two of OSI model. Sends data between two directly connected nodes.

DCE

Data Circuit-terminating Equipment. The X.25 device that connects to the packet-switched network.

DIB

Directory Information Base. Collection of addressing information for OSI networks.

DTE

Data Terminal Equipment. The X.25 device that attaches a computer to a DCE.

EBCDIC

Character encoding scheme common in IBM computers.

ES

End System. The OSI term for a node that provides an interface to a network application.

ES-IS

End System to Intermediate System. The OSI family protocol that allows routers to learn about existence of end systems.

Ethernet

Datalink and Physical layer standard similar to IEEE 802.3.

Filtering

A bridge filters packets, which means it moves packets from one segment to another only if destination resides on other segment.

Flow Control

Protocol mechanism to ensure that a sending node does not send data too quickly to another node and mechanism to ensure that a program does not send data too quickly to a stack.

FTAM

File Transfer Access and Management. The OSI family standard for exchange of files between computers.

FTP

File Transfer Protocol. The TCP/IP family standard for exchange of files between computers.

Gateway

Connecting device that implements all layers of OSI model. Connects two completely dissimilar networks. The TCP/IP community uses the term *gateway* to mean *router*.

GOSIP

Government OSI Profile. Term for an OSI profile that a government implements. Several governments, including the United States and the United Kingdom have GOSIP profiles.

IEEE

Institute of Electrical and Electronics Engineers. Standards organization that describes Datalink layer and network management implementations.

Implementors' Agreements

Restrictions and clarifications to base standards that make it practical to implement standards based networks. The NIST OIW is an example.

IS

Intermediate system. The OSI term for a router.

IS-IS

Intermediate System to Intermediate System. The OSI family protocol that routers use to exchange information.

ISO

International Organization for Standardization. Known as ISO, because of its French name.

LAN

Local Area Network. Network that covers relatively small area, between offices or buildings.

LAPB

Link Access Procedure Balanced. Datalink layer of X.25.

LLC

Logical Link Control. The IEEE standard for upper-sublayer of Datalink layer.

MAC

Medium Access Control. The IEEE standard for lower-sublayer of Datalink layer.

MAP

Manufacturing Automation Protocol. Standards profile for factory networks.

MIB

Management Information Base. Database of statistics that a network management system accumulates.

Multicast

To send a message to a group of destinations, as opposed to a single destination.

Network Layer

Layer three of OSI model. Routes information between end systems.

Network Management

Process to manage fault, configuration, accounting, security, and performance of a network.

NIC

Network Interface Card. A card that fits into a slot of your computer and provides a MAC interface to a network.

NIST OIW

National Institute of Standards and Technology, OSI Implementors' Workshop. Standards group that develops specific rules for implementing OSI protocols.

OSI

Open Systems Interconnect. Data communications model on which many protocols families are based.

PCI

Protocol Control Information. The part of a PDU that contains control information as opposed to user data.

PDU

Protocol Data Unit. A single message that two peer layers exchange.

Physical Layer

Layer one of OSI model. Prepares packets for transmission over cable or other medium.

PLP

Packet Layer Protocol. The X.25 standard for the Network Layer.

Presentation Layer

Layer six of OSI model. Performs conversion between dissimilar operating systems.

Profile

A collection of base standards and implementors agreements that describe interworking in a computer network environment. Examples include MAP, TOP, and GOSIP.

Protocol

Set of rules that computers use for transfer of information.

RFC

Request For Comments. The TCP/IP community term for network protocol standard.

Router

Connecting device that implements Network Layer of ISO model.

SDU

Service Data Unit. Information that layer (N) transmits for layer (N+1).

Session Layer

Layer five of OSI model. Manages activities and dialogue control between nodes.

SMTP

Simple Mail Transfer Protocol. The TCP/IP family standard for electronic mail transfer.

SNA

Systems Network Architecture. Protocol family that IBM developed for communication between computers.

SNMP

Simple Network Management Protocol. The TCP/IP standard protocol for communication between network management stations and network management agents.

SSCP

System Services Control Point. The SNA Physical Unit Type 5. Manages communication between SNA devices.

TCP/IP

Transmission Control Protocol and Internet Protocol. Popular Layer four and three protocols that the Department of Defense, the university community, and businesses implement.

TELNET

The TCP/IP family standard for virtual terminal.

TOP

Technical and Office Protocols. Standards profile for implementation of OSI protocols in the office and engineering environments.

Transport Layer

Layer four of OSI model. Provides reliable data exchange between end systems.

UDP

User Datagram Protocol. The TCP/IP family Transport layer datagram standard.

Virtual Terminal

Network function that allows you to access a remote computer as if you connect directly to that computer.

WAN

Wide Area Network. Data network that covers large areas between cities or even countries.

X.25

The CCITT standard for packet switching over WANs.

X.400

The CCITT standard for electronic mail exchange.

X.500

The CCITT standard for directory services.

802.2

The IEEE standard for Logical Link Control sublayer.

802.3

The IEEE standard for CSMA/CD MAC sublayer.

802.4

The IEEE standard for token bus MAC sublayer.

802.5

The IEEE standard for token ring MAC sublayer.